C000162314

Urban Movements and Their Impact on Spatial Transformation

Studies in Critical Social Sciences Book Series

Haymarket Books is proud to be working with Brill Academic Publishers (www.brill.nl) to republish the *Studies in Critical Social Sciences* book series in paperback editions. This peer-reviewed book series offers insights into our current reality by exploring the content and consequences of power relationships under capitalism, and by considering the spaces of opposition and resistance to these changes that have been defining our new age. Our full catalog of *SCSS* volumes can be viewed at https://www.haymarketbooks .org/series_collections/4-studies-in-critical-social-sciences.

Series Editor
David Fasenfest (York University)

New Scholarship in Political Economy Book Series

Series Editors
David Fasenfest (York University)
Alfredo Saad- Filho (King's College London)

Editorial Board
Kevin B. Anderson (University of California, Santa Barbara)
Tom Brass (formerly of sps, University of Cambridge)
Raju Das (York University)
Ben Fine ((emeritus) soas University of London)
Jayati Ghosh (Jawaharlal Nehru University)
Elizabeth Hill (University of Sydney)
Dan Krier (Iowa State University)
Lauren Langman (Loyola University Chicago)
Valentine Moghadam (Northeastern University)
David N. Smith (University of Kansas)
Susanne Soederberg (Queen's University)
Aylin Topal (Middle East Technical University)
Fiona Tregenna (University of Johannesburg)
Matt Vidal (Loughborough University London)
Michelle Williams (University of the Witwatersrand)

Urban Movements and Their Impact on Spatial Transformation

Cumhur Olcar

Haymarket Books
Chicago, IL

First published in 2023 by Brill Academic Publishers, The Netherlands
© 2023 Koninklijke Brill NV, Leiden, The Netherlands

Published in paperback in 2024 by
Haymarket Books
P.O. Box 180165
Chicago, IL 60618
773-583-7884
www.haymarketbooks.org

ISBN: 979-8-888-90223-3

Distributed to the trade in the US through Consortium Book Sales and
Distribution (www.cbsd.com) and internationally through Ingram Publisher
Services International (www.ingramcontent.com).

This book was published with the generous support of Lannan Foundation,
Wallace Action Fund, and the Marguerite Casey Foundation.

Special discounts are available for bulk purchases by organizations and
institutions. Please call 773-583-7884 or email info@haymarketbooks.org for more
information.

Cover design by Jamie Kerry and Ragina Johnson.

Printed in the United States.

Library of Congress Cataloging-in-Publication data is available.

Segui il tuo corso, e lascia dir le genti
DANTE ALIGHIERI, *Divina Commedia*

• • •

To my grandfather
"Yörük Yiğit Emmi"

∵

Contents

Introduction

1   Focus and Context

Disciplines that band together to carry out urban studies will be able to understand urban movements in the forthcoming years better and implement resilience plans with appropriate policies, strategies, and models. However, new urban studies should recognise that the rate of urbanisation occurring in developing regions is higher than the speed of urbanisation in developed regions and that it is happening profoundly. The urbanisation process of today takes place in a more intertwined manner and is connected with the global world compared to its history (Davis, 2011). Furthermore, this urbanisation pattern is the driving force behind rapid cultural, economic, environmental, financial, physical, political, social, and technological changes that directly affect urban geography (Brenner and Keil, 2006). Around these changes taking place at the global and local level, urban movements are a concept and reality that has a series of direct effects on the city and its flexibility (Wheeler and Beatley, 2009). Considering protests that have been arising increasingly after entering the millennium, urban movements are the main reason and the trailblazers of the expected changes in the city, specifically in developing countries. Urban movements are developments that structurally trigger the process of major, enormous, and rapid changes to reach from one level to another stable level (Leitman, 1999; Scott, 2002). However, a new paradigm was born in the *Age of Cities*, the era we live. Based on this paradigm, migration is no longer a movement from the rural to the urban as was it used to be the case but rather from city to city or from the city to the metropolis in this now-urbanised world. This development explains why urban movements arise from the development of cities and are gradually increasing. The history of urbanisation reveals approaches and ideologies that discovered this connection way before. For instance, *commune* means city. It represents the city's administrative power and living spaces. For this reason, the founders of the *communist* ideology, as well as the research conducted by scientists later have focused on this cause-and-effect relationship. However, the studies in the following years, as well as this study, would try to explain why urban movements represent the bulk of a series of urban rights that concerns cities' own values and that aim to liberate and develop in every respect the vital character of urbanisation.

The property (real estate)-based advancing developments that occur today cause an increase in urban movements as the main force that changes and shapes urban functions, land uses, changes in central and historical areas, and development plans. Although an increase in urban movement stimulates urban participation, it cannot contribute much to social flexibility. In the absence of opportunities for a more participatory city administration, urban protests limit the impact of urban movement and create spaces for new movements. While the urban community seeks to have their voices heard and needs met, urban movements can focus on a new construction process by organising internal flexibility or response to be established against change. As a matter of fact, not-for-profit foundations, local actors, and citizen associations can encourage local communities, activities and events by getting involved with them to eliminate disadvantages that are deep-rooted by spreading the flexibility that the city needs and they can also shape their events (Zagorin, 1982; Herrschel, 2013; Tilly and Wood, 2013).

In this day and age that witnesses the peak in globalisation, the revised centre of the city and its surroundings are undoubtedly new geography in terms of urbanisation. This new protected area diversifies and differentiates in size, density, and connections. This development is a product of increasingly localised, meticulously commissioned and specifically tailored globalisation (Swyngedouw et al., 2003: p. 3). With the new urban region becoming more evident, cities are reaching and penetrating regions farther away from their own spaces with different populations, a mixed commercial economy, aggregated and expanded industry, specialised services, advanced technology and dense transportation opportunities, ingrained social, cultural, and political institutions, and creative centres. This said process can be labelled as an urban consolidation within the global urban region for cities in the transformation process. This new development may lead to more regulations, increased costs, and widening equality gaps by bringing about new conflicts or advantages (Fainstein, 1995; p. 9; Hall, 1977: pp. 72–4).

When considering the cities undergoing transition, the new urban geography can be seen as a space fused with resources, production and consumption. This new order may be regarded as the urban economy transforming to improve economic growth against emerging global competition. However, this new environment of space and competition can also be considered a development that sparks debates on socio-cultural identity and citizenship, creates privilege in the urban area, and that increases environmental concerns. The increasing inequality in the provision of urban services towards the city's peripheries from the city centre raises the question of why urban transformation is realised for the minority instead of the majority. This defiance emerges as a dilemma and creates a transformation syndrome (Fainstein, 1995; Lloyd-Evans and Potter, 1998; Scott, 2002; Wallerstein, 2004; Clark, 2005).

Urban administration of cities that are in the process of transforming unfortunately remains weak in responding to urban concerns of today. Administrations deprived of infrastructure, revenue, and specialised personnel cannot successfully undertake such issues as real estate costs, affordable housing, homelessness, investment, unemployment, environmental degradation, traffic, pollution, clean water, waste management, energy efficiency, and transportation. In fact, to respond to such needs and concerns, establishing a transparent administration and forming fruitful collaborations are essential for transforming cities. Unless such cooperation and participation are achieved, the areas that remain open will unfortunately be filled by unwanted groups, and the reaction of urbanites will result in a series of violent actions that shall harm the city. However, urban movements can be shaped by both the governing and the governed for a more beneficial development effort and participatory action (Satterthwaite, 1999: pp. 13–4; Friedmann, 2002b: pp. 127–8; Tallon, 2010: p. 9).

When considering the destruction of urban habitat, the growing economic gap among citizens, the inconsistency in the constructed urban environment and services, increasing pollution in the urban environment, and rising inequality regardless of age, gender, and ethnicity suggest that the sustainability crisis valid for cities is not only due to environmental reasons but also to the product of the new global and regional inter-city network that are in the process of being established and reformatted. In the light of this new formation, these newly developed connections within and between cities will form the core of research on why urban movements occur or increase (Lloyd-Evans and Potter, 1998; Amin et al., 2000; Sassen, 2001; Sassen, 2002; Friedmann, 2002a; Moulaertet et al., 2003; Sassen, 2006).

Every visible or not evidently perceivable movement in the city will be dissected and evaluated in this study. There is a need to define the sustainable urban agenda directly related to urban characteristics to better analyse urban movements. However, during an assessment of urban movements, it must be borne in mind that each city has its own characteristics and that it has its own transformation style for sustainability surrounding these characteristics. Such awareness will also enable the 21st-century city administration to understand the causes and effects behind urban movements as the core of the strategic components to be established within the new cultural, economic, environmental, political, and social visions (Lefebvre, 2014 Leitman, 1999; Satterthwaite, 1999; Larice and Macdonald, 2007; Wheeler and Beatley, 2009; Lees et al., 2010).

Cities should transform and develop themselves to be able to provide the same quality and habitable service to each of their citizens. This need for change will affect more citizens than before, and when compared to the past, it will be shaped for a group of people that follow global developments more closely and will not be afraid to show their reaction. National and global institutions that become more localised day by day and socio-cultural, economic, environmental and political connections of these institutions with NGOs and the civil society exhibit why urban movements should be analysed for management strategies. Revising the new citizenship, urbanites, and public ecology is essential for sustainable urban management (Zukin, 1991; Leitman, 1999; Scott, 2002; Clark, 2005). It should be noted that public ecology is proposed as a new concept. It is crucial and essential to consider all the public ecological policies carried out in terms of a more sustainable environment formation. In a matter of speaking, we might call the whole of such politics public ecology. Within these policies, community responsibility and participation should be emphasised, and in addition, local characteristics and needs to be aligned with global goals. Meanwhile, urban movements and developments can help urban governing bodies to construct a more inclusive, interactive, and participatory management approach together with NGOs, organisations and communities, and it can be beneficial for the analysis of the process (Goldstone, 2003; Cornwall, 2011; Hall, 2012).

Istanbulites experienced many things for the first time in the Pera district. Beyoğlu has a development process that follows the socio-economic structure of Turkey. Political instabilities and economic crises in the country have affected Istiklal Street, the so-called heart of Beyoğlu. Beyoğlu was the district where street lighting was first used. It was in Beyoğlu where the first apartment building was constructed. The first hint at the modernisation of the Ottoman Empire was witnessed in Beyoğlu. As this development continued, groups that were against modernisation started taking action. Beyoğlu was the address of those who defended a western lifestyle that stood against this urban movement. Therefore, Beyoğlu was a region that gave rise to urban movements and became the home to this movement. The coffeehouses and taverns in Beyoğlu were where the next steps of the internal affairs of the palace were discussed but were also transformed into places where discussions of solutions sought against social problems. Although Beyoğlu had lost its vitality for a period due to the painful events at the beginning and the middle of the 20th century, it never lost its significance. Especially the student movements that developed in the '60s changed the face of Beyoğlu, and most specifically, Istiklal Street. The workers' movements that evolved in addition to the student movements increased the vitality of Taksim Square. Beyoğlu had now become the central point of urban movements due to the spaces and squares it offered.

Urban movements hold more meaning for the 21st century than the future. It emphasises more long-, mid-, and short-term changes. These changes require more localised planned coordination and cooperation. For the purpose of ensuring ownership of each desired and targeted sustainability concept within the urban area, local cooperation and coordination should be directed towards the communities, and participation at the neighbourhood level should be ensured. However, cities located in developing countries are neither prepared nor have networks for each sustainability stage. Therefore, instead of making long-term plans and creating visions for cities, it may be more appropriate to make adjustments and arrangements that will be valid in short- to mid-term. In these cities where change is essential and widely experienced, the future vision may cause new limitations. When considering the conditions of developing cities, emergency action plans and prioritised topics can be more effective and productive than long-term activities. In doing so, movements, ideas, and reactions of the urbanites can be measured, and urban movements can be tracked. Making decisions about the future of the city and its inhabitants and doing so without informing or consulting the next generations will cause the emergence and prevalence of urban movements to be more intensive and far from being beneficial.

Therefore, urban movements cannot be considered distant from local, national and global interactions that impact the city, its dwellers and the urban space. Especially under the conditions of the 21st century, urban movements are shaped and transformed according to the characteristics of each city (Harvey, 2015). Changes in morals and content and how they will continue to contribute to making the city liveable are significant for the 21st century that will become the age of urbanisation. The subject area of this study will be how urban movements that may be considered the beating heart of the city are formed and in what ways they keep the city alive, and to see what factors trigger such movements (Sennett, 2013). The role and importance of urban movements in constructing a more participatory and sustainable city will also be investigated in the scope of this study. The transformation of urban space and the effects of the process of change make it necessary to investigate urban movements in this study (Lefebvre, 1991).

2 Contribution to Knowledge

This book attempts to reveal the motivation behind the demands, requirements, and challenges of new urban landscapes that shape the city and the rising concept of the urban dweller in urban studies. The reason why urban movements occur more quickly and frequently in cities compared to the past and what developments await cities where many more citizens will be living in the 21st century will be investigated. The study will also examine the phenomenon of civil society of transforming and developing cities by investigating whether urban movements can be evaluated as not just a means of conflict but also as a means of participation and exchange. An attempt to contribute to the scientific world will be made by questioning how challenges and rights of the 21st-century urbanite shall be sustained in which environments and under which responsibilities and whether these provide an opportunity for the city. Social movements have survived to our present day as a concept that has been accepted by the scientific world and effectively studied. However, only the right to urban and reasoned actions, events and movements provide clues about the 21st-century lifestyle, and urban movements are now more individual-based but socially driven. The reasons and differences of this finding may be considered among the contributions of this research which will include information and findings that may be regarded as holding a variety of innovations in terms of the scientific world.

The Spirit of the Time for Cities

1 The Birth, Rise, and Spread of the City

When we dissect the concept of the city, we witness the surfacing of the concept of civilisation. The English word *civilisation* has survived today, carrying its correlation with the Latin word *civitas*. Defined as community or congregation, *civitas* gives life to the word *city* that we use today. However, Romans were not the first-ever civilisation that connected and conceptualised community, culture, and civilisation with the 'city'. This interaction began with the Mesopotamian civilisation, and urban culture was deemed the equivalent of civilisation (Cartledge, 2009: p. 2).

The word *city* also has a connection with another word used by Romans. The Latin word *Urbis* gave life to the word *urban*. When we analyse the word *Urbis and burg,* its German equivalent, we find that the word means a place where people gather rather than a space. Just like the word *city, urban* also means a gathering area for its inhabitants where the emphasis is placed, rather than of a spatial nature. What is essential here is not inanimate spaces but cities that are defined as the spaces in their entirety that ensure the communication between the living. For this very reason, the population is essential for the city. In addition, cities must also bear a purpose. From this perspective, the city is not a location but a phenomenon. While spaces remain where they are located, cities are places where many living beings congregate and meet. Cities are nothing without their citizens (Kennedy, 1996: p. XIII).

The city is a concept and a school of thought derived from *Polis*, the name of political ancient Greek cities. The city where recommendations and solutions necessary to sustain the city life were discussed continues to exist in an integrated manner, and all the necessary processes for its existence are called *policy,* that is, politics. Akin to the relationship between the concept of civilisation and the word *civitas* in Rome, the correlation between it and citizen *civis* that is, the urban dweller, is essential since the city is the meeting place for its citizens, and the city is unimaginable without its inhabitants. Urban dwellers living communally are concerned and nourish hopes about the problems and future of their city. Therefore, their participation in the political processes is essential. It is this participation that led Aristotle to form the sentence "man is by nature a political animal". According to Aristotle, man is an animal inclined to live in a city, that is, the *Polis* (Aristo, 2009: p. XI).

According to Aristotle, a city is a secure place established within safe boundaries, and that would allow the organisation of public meetings. Aristotle considered it essential to meet these needs within the city without the presence
of any supporting elements. Such needs and concerns are still valid today.
However, developments in transportation and communication tools exceed
the dimensions and boundaries of the city. Aristotle believes that the city does
not accept a sovereign power. Under the conditions of the day, only men could
participate in public life, whereas today, everyone can participate in public
life regardless of gender. When considered from this viewpoint, cities are not
places under the ownership of tyrants or dictators, that is, the land reigned
by fear and terror. On the contrary, they are spaces dominated by liberty and
where the idea of freedom comes to life (Aristo, 2009: p. xi).

Civilisation arises from the citizen shaping the space based on their lives.
Humans bear the role of the subject in developing civilisation. However, there
is a sense of belonging to space that the human transformed into lebensraum
just like they have a sense of belonging to the civilisation they established. This
way, a solid and unbreakable bond forms between the urbanite, the subject
that played a role in establishing civilisation. Therefore, the space as the visible
aspect of the city that is the core of the civilisation ceases to be a passive object.
It gains vitality by becoming the host for relationships of its inhabitants, and
it is transformed into a subject itself as it guides change in the individual that
created it. The relationship between space and people, that is, its inhabitants,
is more potent, especially in eastern civilisations. While space continues to
exist as an object, it guides and hosts both the change of humans and the city
(Söylemez, 2011: p. 7).

Acting as the link between civilisation and the dwellers, the city reflects
itself in the language in eastern societies, as is the case in western societies. The
words civilisation and city come from the same root. The word *medina* means
the city, while the concept that reveals the cultural network developed by the
city is *medeniyet* (civilisation), as it is now used in Turkish. Due to this relationship, many concepts are derived from the same root (Söylemez, 2011: p. 15).

Therefore, it would not be difficult to figure out that the city is the heart
of civilisation. Munford also saw it in this way. The unions formed by the cities and the city itself help the inhabitants find life around a particular culture. This created cultural changes and developed every day. The culture that
matures over time extends the city's periphery and expands its area of influence. As a result, unity is formed by different cities and cultures, behind which
lies the origin of modern states. The impact created by the regnum stems from
the city's atmosphere and grows, develops, and disseminates thanks to the
network it establishes with other cities. Each inhabitant not only identifies

themselves with this culture but also helps the development of the culture to which they belong to the extent of their imagination and abilities. Thus, the city becomes the centre of development, the place of belonging, and the home of the future (Sit, 2010: p. 285). In the example of Islam, we see that even religion comes to life, grows, and develops in the city. It spreads out by using the ancient unity it establishes with cities.

Toynbee perceived that the city's history is a part of the relationships formed by the inhabitants between each other. Urban life is the entire phenomenon determined by the processes and forces that its citizen restricts and liberates within political economy and culture. We see that the indivisible unity of the city emerges as a product of all the experiences that have emerged from the temporary relations of the pre-urban settlements to the constant information and communication network of today. Therefore, specific priorities come to the fore in understanding the city. The way social relations in the city change to date according to time and place bears significance. When considering the differences created by this change, what the transforming activity structure of the city is made up of is essential. Also of note are the production and social relations that we encounter due to the activities carried out in and between cities (Rivet, 1973: p. 41). When the changes that occur due to these priorities are investigated, we observe that it is the city that produces the sense of community and enthusiasm of its dwellers that create the social relations within that space. As well, it is this unity of emotion and excitement that begets and revises the city (Geddes, 1949: p. 123).

The sharp changes supported by the city's core reveal the milestones of human life. Gordon Childe and the 'Neolithic Revolution' he advocated show us which stages humanity completed and established the urban environment that vitalises today. We need to understand how the emotion and excitement that created the city transformed us from a hunter-gatherer community to an agricultural settlement, then how we evolved into a productive society using our creativity. Findings in Çatalhöyük and prior in Göbekli Tepe show us how vital community unity and social enthusiasm are for the establishment and development of a city (Schmidt, 2012: p. 11).

The evolutionary process that took place in the history of the city points to an era in which people's relations are connected, and cultural changes take place. By using their intellectual abilities, people have assigned new tasks to their physical activities over time and continued their creativity and productivity around the emerging culture (Childe, 1948: p. 25). The city was borne out of nature as a reflection of it. Having learned to dominate nature, human beings developed actions on how to sustain themselves and enabled the start of urban life. This ability for sustainment brought about the first revolution.

Humanity established the food chain and created an urban ecology within nature. They did not end their communication with living beings, and while including living things in the food chain, they started to benefit from them in activities other than production. This is called the *neolithic revolution* (Childe, 1948: p. 66). People engaged in the intense activity and enhanced their organisational skills. The order became a part of urban life. Activities that culturally gained order not only touched on the matters of daily life but also issues about astronomy. In fact, the connection between daily life and the universe was resolved, and experimental approaches to this issue increased. The city became the focal point of life, not only as a centre for production but also in intellectual and experimental areas. This is called the *urban revolution* (Childe, 1948: p. 140).

Urban revolution also means the construction of society. Society was essential for human beings. It would not be possible for human beings to produce their own food alone. They would need support. Moreover, there was a need for a division of labour and an action plan for production. The industry should also have been established to create and facilitate agricultural production. In addition, there were other needs such as protection and shelter. Society had to consist of workers, guards, administrators and teachers. Therefore, an economy was founded, and added value production began. Human life was thus developed and facilitated. The city created its own geography. The climate and geography in which it was born are essential, but the city's lifeline also changed as soon as its own ecology began to form. Social structures began to form. There was a transition from a congregational structure to a societal structure. Traditions were established, and culture began to take shape through creativity. The cultural structure shaped the phases of sovereignty, and political structures began to form. Then the institute of state emerged. The connection between society and prosperity strengthened. Social life and civilisation gained a lasting run with public works. The concept of *Ümran* (infrastructure) found its place. Established relationships took place in the city and shaped its future. It became the home of new relationships. The bond of "asabiyyah" (social cohesion) within the congregation slowly transformed into a bond of being an inhabitant, a bond of citizenship (Ibn-i Haldun, 2013: p. 31).

There are three stages of a society that establishes the city: the primitive life stage, the formation of state stage, and the urban life stage. In the primitive era, the city was merely taking shape, and people lived in a tribal environment. Traditions and basic requirements were formed but were not legislated. During the period of establishment of the state, the city was established, and traditions were transformed into culture. Science, industry, and creativity developed. Interaction with the environment, culture, and cities began, and even the sovereignty era was ushered in. Laws became fundamental to city life, and order was established. In the urban era, settled life was developed, and institutions were established. Cities also followed and applied the traditions and developments of other cities, in addition to their own, as a result of the relationships they established with other cultures. Wealth increased. Creativity developed. Entertainment and social life became diversified. Science advanced, and culture thrived (Ibn-i Haldun, 2013: p. 31). Man is innately civilised, and therefore the city has been a product of its inhabitants since its establishment. Social life is inevitable for humans, and therefore, urban life is essential for them. *Ümran* is urban life, and the city itself is the person within the society (İbn-i Haldun, 2013: p. 121).

In general, cities are public areas of large, dense, and permanent settlements used for economic, administrative, and religious purposes. Cities also offer a variety of opportunities for shelter for people of different social strata. Cities assume a central function that dominates the areas around them. These are the areas where the necessary resources, goods, and human resources are gathered to maintain this function. However, not every city may fit this description completely. Some cities also have dominance over others within their periphery. In addition, there are specific regional, temporary, and cultural forms that separate cities. However, cities have two invariable critical qualities. The first of these is the form and permanent structure of the city, and the other is its function due to its centralised location (Farrington, 2013: p. 9).

The increase in economic added value naturally led to a rise in non-agricultural interests and the emergence of class segregation. It also supported added value initiatives and shaped intra-community and intra-settlement trade and exchange. The struggle and fight for fertile land and available water sources were also a result of added value. While added value also gave rise to the existence of an elite community emerging in the city, this community sometimes sought to establish a superiority that reached the peripheries of the city and even other cities. This led to a more prominent class struggle and became more visible in the city. The differences between affluence in the city can be easily understood from burial remains. While personal luxury items were found in the graves of members of the elite community, no items were found in the graves of the lower-class urbanites (Sit, 2010: p. 17).

Today's studies have shown that the beginnings of cities can be found over vast geography throughout the world. The pioneer in this geography is Mesopotamia. However, in addition to Mesopotamia, the banks of the Yellow River in China, Central America, Inca, and Maya also took initial steps in the development of cities. It appears that cities in these areas developed independently of each other rather than in dissemination. When environmental, economic, and cultural conditions are considered, the emergence of cities in the pages of history can be viewed as a natural phase in the development of society. However, cities impact each other in regionally close locations, and there is interaction. Sumerians had interactions with the Akkadians and Egyptians. They have also influenced Greek cities. The impact of Greek cities on Roman cities is also apparent. When we look at the city's history, economic, religious, technological, and social events impacted the emergence of cities in the geographies where these cities first emerged. Factors such as water supply, grain production, climate, and soil fertility not only affected where cities were founded, but these cities also influenced the emergence of other developing cities (Hammond, 1972: p. 9). This is most evident in Mediterranean cities. The Mediterranean urban tradition continued, be it agricultural, military, administrative, political or commercial. While Greek cities established their own new urban administration and city form, they were nevertheless influenced by cities of civilisations that emerged in the Middle East and Near Asia. Earlier, Egypt was influenced by the cities and culture of the Sumerian civilisation. Anatolia became the cradle of Greek cities. A new structure for a city created by the Greek civilisation became the core of Roman cities that emerged in Italy, North Africa, and Europe (Hammond, 1972: p. 153).

During their course of development, cities started to produce added value while creating a surplus in production within society due to the evolution process towards non-agricultural activities. The diversification of production and added value production was the beginning of class structure and led to the emergence of a community that ruled over the working class. This process occurred more rapidly and significantly in large, agriculturally efficient cities and was of greater volume. The formation of these different communities in the cities revealed the protective space that elites created for themselves and the relationship they established with artisans, tradespeople, soldiers, and slaves – those that enriched the life of elites to which they had become accustomed. This new space was shaping as a new settlement emerging within the established urban environment. This new settlement area had a protection system like the one found in the city and walls that separated it from the rest of the city. This type of development can be seen in almost all ancient cities, and class segregation occurred with almost identical characteristics in almost all of them (Sit, 2010: p. 24).

Every settlement centre where class segregation emerged, and a division of labour was present became urbanised over time. This process caused the urban economy to become more complex and diverse and separated inhabitants from their villages, towns, and similar smaller settlements. Due to the urbanisation process previously mentioned, cities were undergoing necessary economic development and expansion and paving the way for rural development. In plain words, cities had a different division of labour compared to villages, towns, and similar small settlements. Moreover, cities had a more significant number and variety of jobs than other settlements. As the city developed, it expanded to its surroundings and attracted new settlers to the city. Due to the added value gained through agricultural production, it was able to accommodate more people while witnessing the emergence of different classes. Added value and multiplying impact of the city created different needs in the city and created new areas of commerce due to the welfare environment created by the added value. New areas of developing commerce turned into new production mechanisms; the city was now increasing the added value it produced with the creativity it had developed and expanded its area of influence. The city could now have completely urbanised its production and life culture and was continuing its development (Jacobs, 1972: p. 56).

The village environment that was the first area of settlements is different from cities due to the process mentioned above. Villages are generally closed communities with their own facilities and weak external connections. Small scale settlements continued to exist within this compulsory situation since the livelihood source of these settlements are the lands they are located in, and the food chain is primarily from their own produce needed to meet the basic needs of their own inhabitants. However, the city is not able to support itself as such. For the urban dweller to sustain itself, there is a need for the rural settlements, that is, it requires the area of influence of the city. The city divides its human resources into other business sectors, serving only the craftspersons, businesspeople that market the produce, administrators, religious officials, and military units that do not work towards their own needs. This is what happened to cities since their separation from smaller settlement areas. It goes from being a centre that is not self-sufficient, and which requires a means of settlement to meet its needs to one which provides for itself by employing the goods and authority it produces within the city. In other words, to be able to talk about a city, it needs to influence the region it is located and its surroundings, and it must have developed a high level of social activity to ensure just that (Kienitz, 2014: p. 60).

When considering the urbanisation process of cities where social life continues in a complex organisational structure, urban structures can be tackled in the following way: Cities are political centres. Cities are settlements that emerged from a robust tribalistic life, a place where a rising community reigns over others. If we assume that this reign also extends to surrounding settlement areas, cities then become the centre of the state. Cities owe their sovereignty and sustainability of domination to the palace that is the government's centre and religious affairs. It is the political and religious rituals and functions that provide the high-level activity structure in cities and their superiority over other cities (Sit, 2010: p. 59).

The construction and physical mass that develops in parallel with the social structure of cities is of importance. Cities developed in the direction of four cardinal directions. Cities were shaped like a square or a rectangle accompanied by city walls. In general, while the most important buildings were built towards the southern end, the main entrance and almost the entire city were designed to face the south. The city's sprawl was generally in the direction of the south and north axis. Cities were generally established close to water sources and constructed above ground level. The raised land compounds often comprised the foundations of the political and religious structures. Cities were designed with specific areas in mind. There was a centrum, and it was usually surrounded by walls. Palaces and important buildings were situated in this area. There was a second area outside the central area usually enclosed by city walls. This was where craftspersons, industrial buildings, residential areas, commercial areas, markets, and sometimes agricultural areas or gardens were found. It has been observed that ditches were dug outside this area, that is, along the edges of the city walls. Considering the construction sequence, we may note that cities were primarily the hosts for palaces. Religious structures, commercial areas, and residential buildings followed them (Sit, 2010: p. 95).

When considering all the cities of ancient times, it is evident that some cities were in the centre of their settlement areas. Their central position stemmed from the abundance of their human resources, the grandeur and density of their physical structures, the strength of religious relations, and the level of influence of the administrative centre. Due to their human and production resources, these cities became centres of attraction for many dwellers and developed into the administrative centres of their surroundings (Farrington, 2013: p. 11). Ancient cities were able to maintain their central position by organising their region in terms of labour and resources by expanding and distributing their production activities due to the political, administrative, and religious roles they played, and by doing so, they gained added value in return. This production and political expansion also extended their areas of influence and led to an increase in their resources. These leading cities had a central position in their proximity and used their networks to become economically, politically, and socially superior. Social diversity was another characteristic feature of ancient cities. Cities maintained their existence through an urban framework and future investments by sustaining a class-based structure that established social relations with a wide variety of elite and non-elite communities (Farrington, 2013: p. 12).

To maintain and improve their central position, cities were obliged to follow the developments around them and embrace the development architects. In addition to each city having its own culture, they also adhered to their own traditions. Nonetheless, ancient cities' characteristics were that they could find room to accommodate innovation and skills developed by other new settlements within their own diversities. Not only did they conquer fertile lands, but they also incorporated the newfound crafts and their representatives. This pursuit and acceptance led to urban culture's diversification, growth, and development. The nurturing of the diversity of people also reflected itself in the variety of goods produced. Furthermore, the development of commercial networks also became possible this way (Farrington, 2013: p. 19).

One other main feature of ancient cities was symbolism. The symbols that represented the cities' own culture played a role in establishing the city. Just as symbols were an expression of the city's culture representing the economic and political functions regarding its establishment and development, its religious existence was also a source of symbolism. When analysed, four significant factors were found to have governed the urbanisation of cities. These were divination and astronomical precautions, the cardinal points and alignment, the symbolism of the centre, and parallels of the macro and microcosmos. These primary factors were observed to shape the urbanisation process, specifically in the example of Incan cities. These factors also shaped social life, class structure, and the cycle of production (Farrington, 2013: p. 366).

Symbolism was of great significance, not only for the city itself but also for the surrounding settlements. As clearly stated previously, the city could not survive without interacting with the regions in its surroundings. As a settlement, each city centre is considered with its outer regions with which it interacts. Settlements engaging in agriculture acquiring goods and services in exchange for their regional produce that they offer at the marketplace is a type of transaction not possible within small settlements only. The outer regions of cities and the commercial and administrative responsibilities each hold reflect a centre's needs. With such an exchange, it is clear that cities with a large population need large outer areas to maintain their livelihood. Thus, the population had an important place in the existence and development of cities. In fact, when we consider a comparison between cities in terms of population, it is possible to find out the distance that separates the two (Faroqhi, 2010: p. 113).

Since the ancient era, cities gradually expanded, increased, and approached their own era based on these values and principles. Over time, the unions formed by cities developed into states. As a result, it is clear that prominent cities underwent changes under the domination of sovereign states. Military needs were especially the reason for the changes occurring in the architecture of cities. By the 17th Century, military ceremonies, marches, and strategies became essential milestones in the design of cities. Wide boulevards, streets, and squares that merged at the centre became the elements of the city. Thus, public powers gradually started becoming more apparent in the appearance of cities. This military approach later gave way to industrial needs. The industry had now become the dominant factor that dominated the appearance of cities (Mackenney, 2004: p. 31).

According to Adna Weber, the following are among the political reasons for urban growth from ancient cities to the present: legislation promoting free trade, legislation allowing freedom to migrate, a centralised administration that reflects in the representation of the city, and political advocacy of land reform and freedoms of using of the land. The social causes of urban growth are as follows: education, recreation, high quality of life, attraction to scientific institutions, an urban environment, and the values brought about by urban life attracting attention (Weber, 2012: p. 76).

The evolution of the urban city continues. Since their establishment, cities have built upon what is already constructed. Cities that have evolved due to the industrial revolution have kept up with the new era. Labelled as 'the white coal', electricity creates cities' new faces and symbols. Looking at the impact that coal and industry have had on cities, it would not be difficult to estimate the capabilities of the new age. Many changes are to occur, from the changes in forms of production to the emergence of new divisions of labour. The impact of energy on today's cities is quite significant (Geddes, 1968: p. 46). This new age is divided into two eras, as was the case in prehistorical times: *Paleo-technic and Neo-technic*. This distinction will change the structure of cities today just as it separated the structural development of ancient cities (Geddes, 1968: p. 60).

Another characteristic that shapes cities of our era are diversity. Assuredly, cities were diverse in the past. In fact, this is the reason why cities exist and are established. However, diversity has become more pronounced and intense today. Cities are changing and developing by adding new cultures to their own cultures with the impact of globalisation and westernisation. On the other hand, Western cities continue as the locomotive of westernisation and gradually incorporate eastern cultures with the effects of globalisation. Global diversity is increasingly becoming an essential element of cities of today. For example, while 37% of the population of the western city of New York City are immigrants, this rate is 96% in the eastern city of Dubai (Brook, 2013: p. 5).

Cities are not only hosting a large number of people, but they are also hosting many different kinds of people. People living in the city are not alike. At the beginning of the establishment of cities, there were similarities among its dwellers. The people living a tribal life are like each other. They almost bear similar thoughts. It is not possible for people living within the same tradition and culture to differ. The same is true for larger areas of settlements united for military purposes. Persons supporting each other cannot manage to harbour different thoughts or diversity. Upholding a common purpose causes the inhabitants to resemble each other. However, as the population and the diversity of cultures living in the city increase, the urbanisation process will also expand in parallel. The city emerges as a settlement where different views, identities, cultures, and people come together (Aristotle, 2009: p. 40).

The new urban mix that emerged today causes an increase in what inhabitants can do. The city bears witness to the mobilisation of the labour force, the possibility of transportation to distant cities and regions, the establishment of communication with distant lands in terms of space and time, the progression of urban services transforming into megaprojects, the expansion in the provision of social services, and the development of agricultural productivity, or rather, the development of the food production chain (Mumford, 1961: p. 30).

The city consists of individuals with different identities, personalities, and appearances. Those that live alike cannot form a city. There is no one superior of language, religion, colour, or race in cities over the other. Everyone may live their life as they desire. Dwellers transitioned to settled life after the nomadic period. This stage is followed by establishing cities and inhabitation in the city. Cities are, in fact, not made of private institutions. As cities are established for the commercial and benefit of society, cities bring about the formation of large structures and buildings. So, who guides cities that are the owners of such development in the process? Architects, of course. The Turkish word for the architect ('*mimar*') comes from the Arabic root word 'ümran'. The word *Ümran* is translated into Turkish as public works, progress, prosperity, happiness, and civilisation. Another word derived from the same root word is '*imar*' (development), which means '*mâmur*', that is, 'construct' or 'prosper'. Thus, what we understand of the meaning of '*mimar*', that is the architect, is not only those that solely construct and design buildings. In the broader sense, architects are professionals who bring prosperity and welfare to a city and contribute to improving individuals and living environments (Bilgili, 2011: p. 294).

When we look at cities built by architects, we mainly see a distinction: western cities and eastern cities. In the case of eastern cities, Islamic urban historiography comes to the fore. Although it is not among Max Weber's descriptions, this field of study is considerably influential. Weber defines urban citizens as an independent community having a unique spirit of collective identity, and he argues that this identity is formed through evolution and is therefore meaningful only in western cities. Weber characterises Islamic and other non-European urban areas in contrast with European cities and as lacking a distinctive urban culture and tradition. He argues that Islamic cities were governed by bureau-cratic representatives of imperial reign and not by political autonomy, as is the case in European or even classical Greek and Roman cities. Furthermore, he emphasises that different clans and tribes compete rather than unite under a common civil interest in an effort to create an identity belonging to the city in Islamic cities (Eldem, 2012: p. 11).

In dealing with the city's architects, this would be an incomplete definition. The architects of Islamic cities assuredly designed different cities compared to the architects of western cities. Yet, it must be borne in mind that cities emerged from the east just like where the sun rises. The emergence of different urban identities should not be taken as one is superior to the other or that one should be waved aside over the other. When we look at their architects, there are, of course, different types of cities. Some place more emphasis on spiritual life compared to the physical world. Some come across as more independent than others. Some reflect a higher urban cohesion than others. Some place more emphasis on commerce rather than the administration. Some establish communities around religious buildings while others around market squares and town squares. Some have a higher level of ethnic diversity compared to others. These examples of city types can be multiplied. However, ignoring a particular type of city or similar cities should be avoided. In any case, every city has its architects, and the identity of each city differs from others due to this difference (Eldem, 2012: p. 17).

The architects of cities are also the directors of the city. A look at the present day shows that reforms have taken place in the city administration. This is especially apparent in our observation of Ottoman cities. The classi-cal Ottoman city administration style based on the Islamic faith and politi-cal understanding was grounded on the Muslim individual and congregation but did not recognise legal persons. For this reason, the service functions of the city were not defined individually by administrative units but rather by religious, ethnic, and professional communities. The administrators who were the city's architects did not just deal with the city services. There were also various administrative responsibilities. For instance, the existence of a hier-archical administrative structure was in place in that the administration of the Grand Vizier ('Sadrazam') was responsible for the happiness and welfare of the capital and its inhabitants. However, the real authority in the admin-istration of the city as well as in judicial affairs, including real estate matters, was left to the Islamic Judge, or Qadi. From this perspective, there seems to be confusion in authority while a sharing of authority was seemingly present. While the administration left the major zoning activities concerning the city to the greater administrative authority, the issues concerning civil life were considered the responsibility of the lower-level administrator. For instance, many tasks, such as determining the height of buildings or the width of the streets, were the responsibility given to Qadis. In contrast, large scale projects such as transporting water to the city were under the command of the Grand Vizier (Çelik, 2015: p. 51).

When considering the Ottoman cities, the smallest administrative unit in the cities from the pre-*Tanzimat* (meaning political reform) period was the quarter. The main gathering places of the quarters' residents were the mosque and the neighbourhood coffeehouse. Local issues were discussed in such places. Under the leadership of the *imam* (Muslim clergyman) that represented the Qadi at the suburban level, the neighbourhood residents used to organise basic local services such as cleaning the streets and security. In non-Muslim suburbs, the neighbourhood leader was again the leader of the relevant religious congregation. In the areas of trade, the guild presidents took the place of the imams. As previously noted, basic municipal services were performed by the neighbourhood residents in the classical Ottoman system as opposed to municipal administration. In addition, when we look at the municipal codes and regulations, it was not possible to rule by law in classical Ottoman cities. Administering the city was conducted with various written but mostly unwritten resources such as imperial decrees, judicial decrees, customs, and traditions. However, this structure started to change with the *Tanzimat* period. According to the Tanzimat philosophy, reforms would introduce law institutions, systematisation, and control. Every task would be set in writing and carried out by specific units from then on. City services were to be carried out by professionals based on the citizens' demands. Increasing population and diversifying social structure necessitated this. Instead of the *decentralised* Ottoman city administration, a structure managed by centralised public officials emerged (Çelik, 2015: p. 56).

The reforms implemented by the city administration were also a manifestation of economic conditions. The shaping of the new economic structure was directly related to various infrastructure changes coming about in the developing regions of the city and the new institutions. The increasing prevalence of capitalism guided the new spaces in the cities. Banks, insurance companies, the stock market, and countless other small business ventures in the second half of the 19th Century were all concentrated in certain regions. All these developments required a more efficient organisation and more effective use of urban space. When considering Istanbul, the municipal organisation, public transportation, and urban services first began developing in Galata. The urban and social landscape in Galata was systematically re-designed. Apartments, arcades, shops where all kinds of imported goods were exhibited, hotels, clubs, pubs, theatres, art galleries, and schools changed the structure of Galata, and new behaviour and consumption habits were imposed on its inhabitants. By the end of the 19th Century, Galata and Pera had the appearance of a European city, significantly different from the other districts of Istanbul. These two districts in the process of westernisation could only barely provide the services needed by the residents, and in fact, there were many shortcomings. The city was entering a new development process, not just like its European counterparts. However, it could not carry out this process effectively due to its history. This city, which had the appearance of an eastern city and with its particular habits, could not fully reflect the technological advances and the new urban sociology within itself (Eldem, 2012: p. 244).

It was a clear reflection of the cultural and intellectual division in the context of tradition and the real economic, social, and political factors, which seemed exceptional in the urban development of Istanbul in the last era under the Ottoman rule on the physical topography of the city. Deciding where the residents of the city would reside and continue their lives was now no longer just based on socioeconomic criteria but increasingly shaped by the cultural values of the districts. The desire for an urban Muslim citizen that reached an adequate socioeconomic status to relocate to the westernised parts of the city was due to a cultural preference. Changes in the city's peripheries were due to interaction with westernised districts. While one portion of the population concentrated in certain districts due to cultural reasons was increasingly benefitting from social and urban services, the remaining regions of the city were, unfortunately, making do with the old-fashioned structures of the old system. Tensions began to emerge between the districts that had noticeable cultural and socioeconomic differences. Every residing urban dweller wanted to benefit from the services as a citizen but was not in acceptance of any cultural discrimination. These two divisions and the gap between communities were a common concern among their members at that time. However, deprived of many advantages in terms of technology and economy, Istanbul had become a city where segregation sharpened, desperation increased, and tensions arose (Altınay, 2011: p. 63).

The concept of '*âdâb*' ('manner') present in the city gradually lost its regard. The origin of the concept of *âdâb* can be traced back to the philosophy of Aristotle. While new ones replaced the city's old structures, rules and traditions that previously existed in the city were becoming frowned upon. While the new buildings symbolised the new era, the city's inhabitants gradually lost their past. Identities were losing their soul, and existing structures that had become the city's identity were disappearing. Istanbul had received its share in this process. However, urbanisation beyond *âdâb* was not just a reflection of westernisation activities. The architectural elements of the mosques built in the Peninsula extended out beyond the Peninsula in the last days of the Ottoman era and were evolved into a different design by the administrative buildings and their communities. While buildings belonging to the Sultanate attempted to preserve their former splendour, they did not go beyond copying what their ancestors had done. However, there was a sense of respect. A homage to the past. However, private construction initiatives were gradually losing this sensitivity to âdâb. High-rise buildings, non-morphological structures, and an urbanisation void of identity. This type of development would also guide urbanisation during the Era of the Republic. Especially after the 1950s, Istanbul began to witness a new era due to the increasing population and crowds that were not accustomed to urban culture. This was a period of a process with which most western cities were not unfamiliar. These developments had also placed western cities under pressure almost a century prior. Now, it was Istanbul's turn. The ecology, sociology, and culture of the city were transforming. The socioeconomic and socio-cultural gap between citizens that was unable to adapt to the changing rules led to an increase in tensions (Necipoğlu, 2016: p. 40).

Today, when cities exceed the threshold value in terms of population, this case is not valid for every city. This is more so the case for old cities. While some cities have a migrant intake due to their central role in the network formed by cities, others experience emigration. Emigration causes cities to become less populated and leads to a loss in some of their capacities. Places that became abandoned due to emigration were increasingly ghettoised and began developing a new identity with the cultures of their new inhabitants. While migration movements in big cities become a concern and distress for the city, they also maintain an advantage and a sense of hope. However, migration in small cities poses a challenge for the city. People cannot provide the necessary order to organise their lives and become self-sufficient. Small cities responsible for meeting particular needs of larger cities can satisfy most of their needs thanks to trade with big cities (Faroqhi, 2014: p 39).

Humans learn through experience. Experience is the source of development. The history of the city is an excellent example of this. Cities develop by learning lessons from their past experiences. Their current identities come to light along with their past. The city has become a destination to escape and a haven for freedom. Cities developed rapidly immediately after their establishment. Their inhabitants began looking after their cities, and they expanded their areas of freedom over time. The concept of the right to a city emerged, and the city was now considered a living organism. Subsequently, the rights of citizens became a current issue, and citizens made further progress regarding their gains. However, the urbanisation process has not always been merry progress. There have been standstills at the end or between each period of development. Just as the case when in the process of decline, the city also shows rapid development after periods of stagnation (Geddes, 1968: p. 266). So, at what stages does the city become stagnant? Is the decline of cities inevitable? Or does the city show a rapid re-development due to the stagnation periods? We will attempt to seek answers to these questions in the following chapter.

The development processes of cities are not always at the same pace. From time to time, there exist periods of standstill. Moreover, due to such periods, the city and the union of cities had to collapse. In some cases, cities escaped decline by restoring order during standstill periods, and there were even examples of rapid revival at the end of such periods. Cities sometimes experience periods of famine. In other cases, they are affected by climate conditions. There are also times that they experience economic bottlenecks. And sometimes, social explosions and cultural regressions occur. What are the reasons for these periods that await cities? What is the reason for cities to experience these periods, and how do they overcome them?

2   Decline or Progress?

Revival predicts collapse. Therefore, before conducting research and explaining the decline, it is necessary to define revival. When we look at the history of the city, the following caused the collapse of the division of city unions that is, the separation of states into smaller units, the seclusion of urban centres in part or their complete desertification, the loss of the role of central cities or their central position, the collapse of the regional economic system, and the loss of civilisation culture and ideology. However, collapses rarely result in the disappearance of the inhabitants of the dominant civilisation or the loss of the dominant traditions (Schwartz and Nichols, 2010: p. 5).

The reasons for the demise of cities are varied and are under debate. Results of the research suggest various reasons for demise in addition to the ones mentioned above: invasion by another civilisation or union, external factors such as climate change, frequent droughts, and stagnant economic conditions that cause agricultural products to enter a period of famine for urban communities in need of added agricultural value. One of the most common reasons for the decline is when an increasing population in cities places pressure on the environment to maintain the city's needs, and the environment cannot respond to this demand by exceeding the ecological threshold. Cities that have lost their ideological influence also result in collapse due to such loss. Suppose the state or the ruling authority does not place importance on undertaking their required responsibilities. In that case, inhabitants lose their faith in the sovereign power and show less loyalty to the system over time. The increase in economic difficulties and suffering of citizens due to economic policies also lead people to lose their faith.

Another factor that causes decline is the discontent and stirs that emerge in most of the society due to conflicts between the dominant or ruling power and the dominant communities. Especially in communities that cannot rise above equal values or where communities that support the ruling power withdraw their support from the administration, unity of power breaks down. However, traditions and the dominant culture created during and after the decline do not lose their influence. Even the political system continues to exist in this transition period in the cities. When considering ancient civilisations and the cities that created them, civilisation's ability to re-organise due to various social activities is observed to limit the boundaries of collapse and accelerate a re-building process (Schwartz and Nichols, 2010: p. 6).

The decline of cities is a remarkably complex process. It points to the end of a grand regional unity and political domination. The timing, progression and impact will vary according to the characteristics of the co-existence of cities. Based on previous research, following the deterioration of the dominant urban unity, new control points are formed in the peripheries of the cities or somewhere in the periphery of the union. Thus, the revival that occurs during or after the collapse comes to life in various forms. The dissolution of the central political system causes the dominant city centre to lose its central role, but the culture and traditions it created re-appear in another city that once existed under its control. During this reformation, there was an emergence of a new political, economic, and social organisation. During the decline, it is often observed that local congregations undertake the responsibilities of the new era. In this process, the dominant traditions of the declining civilisation are strongly sustained and are given importance by the local communities. The newborn culture rises from the ashes of the previous dominant civilisation. While rising cities adopt a simpler lifestyle, the developments that abandon the ruins of the disappearing city gradually enrich this simple life. However, as can be observed in some cases, a completely different city structure and unity may emerge due to the changes created by the collapse (Schwartz and Nichols, 2010: p. 100).

As already mentioned, the decline is a political process. Although the collapse is generally observed in areas such as economy, art, and production, it basically takes place in a socio-political framework. Urban societies enter a rapid collapse, and significant losses occur at the core levels of socio-political turmoil. Losses that occur at fundamental levels are significant. Within this scope, the collapse is evident in some cases. Such cases can be listed as follows: low degree of stratification and social differentiation, a weakening in the professional and economic specialisation of rural areas, urban communities and urban dwellers, reduced central control, and observed weakening of the order and integration of the various economic and political groups established under the leadership of prominent communities, weakening of systematic regulation and behavioural control, stagnation of investment in fields such as architecture, art, and science, and a decline in investment in subjects that define the culture of civilisation, the decrease in the flow of information from the city centre to its periphery between political and economic groups and among the citizens, disruptions in the distribution, trade, and sharing of resources, reduced coordination, interaction, and organisation between communities and individuals, and problems of integration of the city as a political whole into the smaller rural areas. Before the collapse, communities appear as a scale in the dimension of complexity, and any community with a heightened or reduced complexity begins to collapse (Tainter, 1988: p. 4).

Complex societies are problem-solving organisations. Different types of communities, a higher number of social differences, more inequality, greater centralisation, and control emerge in complex communities. The increased complexity is characterised by little, homogenous, and equal access to resources, intra-tribal leadership, unstable political structure, minimally different communities, and there is a transformation towards a more extensive, heterogeneous, socially differentiated, the class structure established, controlled resources to sustain life not distributed evenly (Tainter, 1988: p. 37). As a result of this change, collapses occur due to the rapid decline in the basic established complex structure (Tainter, 1988: p. 38). Cities are cultural systems of complex societies. Cities become visible with the presence of complexity, and its absence drives them to decline. Complex societies are the cradles of civilisation. A civilisation established in the city disappears only with the disappearance of the complex structure which prevails in the city (Tainter, 1988: p. 41). Cities with a complex social structure maintain the continuation of the social structure at a higher cost compared to cities with a more straightforward structure. In societies of higher complexity, more networks are established among urban dwellers, and the hierarchical control necessary for the sustainability of this established network is shaped within the order. Centralisation increases, and control of the ruling power (that is, the centre) increases in the flow of information. In this process, the needs of the specialists directly involved in the production of resources increase, and they experience problems in executing and maintaining their work (Tainter, 1988: p. 91).

Fundamentally, the collapse of cities happens instantly. The collapse occurs due to significant losses at the level of the established socio-political complexity. During the collapse, cities suddenly transformed from complex communities to small, simple structures with less class stratification and limited social differences (Tainter, 1988: p. 193). The city transforms into a settlement where the level of expertise is reduced, and there is less central control. The flow of information is reduced, trade drops, interaction decreases, and coordination between communities and individuals becomes limited. There is a high-level decline in economic activities, and financial activities come to a near standstill. Artistic endeavours lose importance, and aesthetic values are lost. The population gradually decreases, and cities are abandoned (Tainter, 1988: p. 213).

Therefore, cities are born, develop, and collapse. But what decides the result when the city enters stagnation in this process? Why do the movements that predominantly occur in the urban community happen, and what are the consequences of this process? What are the reasons for the movement in the social structure? Do these movements point to the growth of cities within a more complex social structure? Or, instead, is it an expression of an eminent collapse phase? If this is the case, the urban movements that reflect the structure of the cities and the current developments, how they are born, and what results they give rise should be investigated.

Urban Movements in the Time of Urbanisation

Urban movements are reactionary organisations that date back to the birth of cities. It is even possible to deem the possible reactions given before urbanisation as the beginning of this process. However, as urbanisation advanced, the inhabitants' right to speech and voice increased in parallel. Urban movements have been observed in many geographies, cultures, states and cities. However, it has been a cornerstone for three periods. *The Age of Enlightenment* has been a crucial turning point in the lives of people and cities. Before the 18th century, a plethora of uprisings and rebellions took place within the states. However, these movements were born with a raison d'être arising from rural issues rather than events concerning city centres but soon disappeared. They disappeared from the stage of history without causing much change in society (Zagorin, 1982). Among these uprisings and revolts are, of course, those that occurred in big cities. *Patrona Halil Rebellion* which took place during the *Tulip Era* of the Ottoman Empire, is just one of them. However, like every revolt before it, it broke out suddenly. It partially succeeded, but, as a result, it lost its importance in the period it occurred and could not take a significant step forward (Altınay, 2010). Among the reasons that caused this revolt is noted to be the economic and political policies implemented by the Ottoman Empire during the establishment and growth phases that were replaced by policies that did not please the public (İnalcık, 2016). As a matter of fact, the uprisings developed in this way. There are also examples within the Ottoman Empire. The community led by *the Young Turks* resorted to violent methods, the first of which was an armed raid and the other a military coup, with the involvement of different organisations in the change of power that they could not achieve by creating public opinion. This uprising that could not lead to any of the changes they wanted to make in the short term of power partially lost its effect. However, the fact that they were a city-centred organisation has left significant traces in the history of Turkey. When it comes to the history of westernisation and democracy, this period witnessed policies that gained momentum (Mardin, 1962). In fact, the pioneer of this uprising was the uprisings that previously took place on the European continent before.

Cities began to grow in Europe in the 18th century after the Age of Enlightenment. The number of people living in cities grew, and the urban identity has spread within a new culture. Individuals who migrated to the city from different small towns and rural areas wanted to have more say in the city and sought their freedom. This realm of freedom was not only political but also cultural and economic. This process lasted until the beginning of the 20th century. The achievements have spread all over the world. Organisations that now could form public opinion could easily partake in challenging struggles to impose their wishes on the government. The state had completed its formation but was receiving reactions to rectify its deficiencies for the construction of individuals (Poggi, 2014). The rights of the citizens continued their human rights-based course with the gains they had made. This was the second turning point of social movements. This unity carried out by the communities organised in the city was entering the third period in the 21st century. Now the individual who gained the urban identity within the city wanted to live and develop their most basic rights without encountering any obstacles. These identity and culture-based movements were born entirely within cities and pursued urban desires. Social movements were reaching the city just as they had at the beginning. For this very reason, we will call the movements occurring in the society the urban movements.

Urban movements arise from the responses of urban communities to the obstacles that affect their lives. Urban movements are actions that occur out of city needs and concerns. "A movement was an urban movement only if it oriented towards a higher order" (Topçu, 2017: p. 22). Otherwise, it would not be any different from the uprisings that have an example in history. "But there is no social cause that had the triple truth lying in its foundation: Man, nature, and economy. Therefore, this was not purely a spiritual and moral issue but a whole human issue. In this sense, the name of its moral cause would be 'the morality of rebellion'" (Topçu, 2017: p. 19). This morality of revolt, that is, the actions that knew why and how and for what purpose, were being formed in the cities. Thus, the city was transformed into a morality of rebellion for social movements, and urban movements were happening.

Cities were now hosting an increasing number of protests, demonstrations, and movements. Anxieties triggered by the events that occur due to the city's growth and way of living give way to urban movements. The protests develop within the scope of growing frustration and economic inequality. Injustices, cultural restrictions, and economic inequality in urban areas have brought urban movements into our agenda even at an increasing rate (Piketty, 2014: p. 237). In recent years, human rights violations and injustices observed in police behaviour have raised concerns in the urban environment. While the urban movements organised by unions occur due to working conditions and low wages, other movements organised simultaneously progress under the leadership of communities operating in many areas, from the lack of services in the city to the search for identity. The practices of security forces in urban areas also trigger urban movements. The events in Tunisia, which progressed on the day of the police and the Tahrir Square movement, appear as urban movements that include these reasons mentioned above (Tilly and Wood, 2013: p. 1).

The citizens of the city that began reorganising worldwide in the 21st century are responding to the movements taking place in their cities by giving voice to an international call. Urban movements are being organised and manifest an increase to create a counterweight that will act as an equipoise to the oppressive forces against the inequality and injustices occurring in the cities and make a call against the calamities (Tilly and Wood, 2013: p. 3). The history of these movements has deep roots dating back to the 1750s. As a result of the increasing rate of urbanisation leading up to the American and French revolutions, the citizens had some gains. The right to a campaign that reaches the target authorities with joint claims and actions and enables the organisation and continuation of the public effort is at the forefront of such rights. Other important rights are the rights to meetings, ceremonies, vigils, assemblies, demonstrations, petitions, speeches, and associations that have been obtained as a result of the formation of associations, institutions, and coalitions established for a particular purpose included in the agenda within the individual forms of political action. And the realisation of the form of solidarity, which the participants decided on unanimously, with the units of solidarity, value, union, number, and commitment, are the other gains (Tilly and Wood, 2013: p. 4).

For the movements in the 18th century, the value of the action, the union of the participants, the number of participants, and their commitment to each other were significant. The actions organised by this union were called social movements for the first time in history (Von Stein, 1959). Social movements spread to other regions, primarily in England and then Europe and North America, in the 18th century. And it has brought along many related changes in this flow. Such changes as weakened kings in the face of states that gained power, organising citizens that voiced their wishes in cities against states and pursuing these wishes, elite communities running for the political system taking over the administration as a result of election by the citizens, expansion of transportation and commercial relations among individuals dwelling in distant lands, and lastly, communication opportunities spread worldwide, led to the formation of urban communities that are distant in terms of location, but that gather under a single goal (Markoff, 1996: p. 45).

As a result of the increase in urban movements, a series of reforms commenced in Europe. Legal recognition of guilds, communities, religious denominations, and regular representation of common rights in parliament began. Common rights are protected by law. Local authorities were mandated to enforce and respect the law. Recognition of selected institutions by the authorities for the public representation of common wishes and complaints was made mandatory. The relevant authorities could not ignore the requests and suggestions made by the selected institutions. It is out of jurisdiction for the authorities to oppose and prevent joint movements. It is out of the question to impose illegal obligations on individuals and institutions that have come to power through elections. All these steps were achieved due to the movements that took place at the beginning of the 18th century (Tilly and Wood, 2013: p. 20).

As a result of the Seven Years' War, a heavy burden came about in the cities of the countries that entered the war. Especially the surplus taxes imposed on rural areas have deeply affected urban life. North America, which lacked electoral and representation rights, has gradually begun to break away from the United Kingdom. Increasing tax burden and trade inequality compelled America's intellectuals to a series of actions. Then, in another country, France, increased taxes and meddlesome politicians drew the public's reaction. Increasing complaints resulting from these insensitive and indifferent policies have led to the emergence of urban reactions. The movements and actions that started in Boston and New York led to the American Revolution, and the riots that took place in the streets of Paris brought about the French Revolution. During and after this process, the right to representation was accepted, and the citizens gained more rights by gradually expanding. War, parliamentary representation, capital gains, and workers' actions have led to gradual growth and gains in urban movements. The mobilisation required for the war and the financial expenditures that were a burden for ordinary people were made due to the decisions to be taken jointly with the established society organisations that were in contact with the state organs and officials and were able to hold meetings after this time. The difficulties encountered because fewer people had the right to vote in the elections have been alleviated to some extent by accepting the right to vote of every citizen. In fact, the term 'every citizen' is a bit wrong. Although there was more comprehensive participation than in the previous period, gender discrimination hindered the elections. However, geographically unrepresented regions obtained representation rights. Freedom of political action has been handed over, and freedom has been brought to the actions of elected people. As a result of the development that occurred due to the capital increase, the direct intervention of the merchants with the associations and organisations they established in national policies increased instead of being the material credit sources of the kings. After this area of emancipation, the economic policies of the sovereign power have changed, and new public benefits have emerged. Improvements were made in the working conditions and duration of the employees. Employees' right to organise has been partially accepted and allowed. The way for employees to represent themselves in political life has been paved. The liberation of workers from the out-of-control treatment of their bosses, owners, and sovereign authorities has taken place. These reforms also led the bourgeois and elite communities, who were dissatisfied with the dominant power, to gain more control over the administration. The representatives of the bourgeoisie and the elite community, who want more place in the administration, have gained authority by cooperating with society's leading organisations. As a result of this cooperation, rights such as the right to assembly, representation, and discourse spread throughout society. While the unity of opposition aristocrats, radical bourgeoisie, resentful petit bourgeoisie, and workers allied together made room for urban movements to occur, the rights to protest and action were publicly recognised (Bercé, 2003; Tilly and Wood, 2013: p. 27; Bookchin, 2017a).

The gains obtained from the 18th-century movements caused the urban movements to rapidly spread, multiply, and gain importance. At the turn of the 19th century, the movements that started in France quickly spread worldwide. The urban movements that began in France in 1848 later spread to Switzerland. It was repeated in France in 1875 and 1877. Urban movements were observed in Denmark in 1849 and 1915. The actions that surrounded Greece in 1864 were seen in Chile in 1874 and 1891. The United Kingdom witnessed urban movements in 1884 and 1918. The movements that emerged in Norway in 1898 were observed in Finland in 1906 and 1919. Sweden witnessed two long-term urban movements between 1907 and 1909 and the other between 1918 and 1920. The actions that broke out in Portugal in 1911 and 1918 spread to Argentina in 1912. Urban movements that emerged in Italy between 1912 and 1919 were observed in the Netherlands in 1917. In 1918, Belgium witnessed urban events. Germany was subjected to movements in 1918 and 1919. While Uruguay was under the influence of urban movements in 1918, Spain became a country with intense activity in 1868, 1890, and 1931 (Collier, 1999: p. 23; Bookchin, 2017b).

The 20th century witnessed the revival of urban movements with the effect of the demonstrations in France. The movements that started with student complaints and protests in 1968 spread worldwide quickly. These actions, which were influential in the United States, resonated all over the world. These movements, which required representation from all segments of society, were also anti-war. Urban movements that consisted of an environmentalist struggle also wanted improvements in the conditions of the workers. They demanded that the administration become more inclusive and participatory. These movements were born in a geography that we can call the Western civilisation over time and grew throughout the world. Soviet and communist countries, on the other hand, would feel the effect of this wave more in 1989. With the fall of the Berlin Wall, the Soviet bloc was collapsing, and the citizens wanted to have more say in administration as citizens. Cities resounded with equal sharing and participation slogans, and crowds stirred cities. Urban movements spread rapidly in China, Soviet Russia, and the countries they penetrated (Tilly and Wood, 2013: pp. 68–79).

In the 21st century, effective changes have occurred in the relationship between authority and urban movement activists. In this century, as in previous centuries, urban movement participants deemed the police and local authorities their enemies, still complaining of atrocities and repression. However, the legal framework and environment have entirely changed in the 21st century compared to previous centuries. In cities where urban movements occur regularly, the authority still requires permission for meetings and demonstrations. Suspicious organisations are requested to be registered, and these organisations are monitored through surveillance, leaking, prosecution of plots, or tax assessment practices. Removing restless and discontented people from the media, protecting public figures from possible attacks, and keeping them away from fraudulent interventions that opponents of the urban movement may cause are also among the acts of authority. Ending the demonstrations, seeing the participants of the urban movement as those planning to overthrow the government and imprisoning them, and banning the opposition organisations show us another aspect of the relations between the participants of the urban movement and the modern regime (Aydın, 2006: pp. 174–5; Tilly and Wood, 2013: p. 82).

Urban movement organisations in the 21st century can find new ways for themselves, despite all the obstacles of power holders and ruling communities. At the helm of these new ways are digital media tools. Digital media that plays an active role in the organisation, proliferation, and spread of urban movements also adversely affects urban movements. Communication, which is crucial among the participants of the urban movement, causes a weakening of the established network compared to the intensely communicating movements in previous centuries due to digital media. By incorporating local issues into the movement's discourse, it increases the effects of local participants on the movement's identity, but then it weakens the accepted central identity. The individual belonging to the dominant ideology within urban movements weakens. Such effects of digital media cause urban movements to be very fragile in terms of regulation, interaction, control, and commitment (Tilly and Wood, 2013: p. 107).

Bearing in mind the changing position of urban movements against the authority and the effects of developing communication tools, urban movements have gained a different form in the 21st century. The events described as *the Arab Spring* that occurred in Egypt, Tunisia, Libya, Iran, Syria and Yemen are proof of this. Also, *the Occupy Wall Street* movement that originated in America and spread to major European cities followed a different structure compared to its predecessors, just like the movements in the countries we have mentioned. The urban movements in Brazil also witnessed the kinds of actions that we will include in this class (Tilly and Wood, 2013: pp. 112–117). Urban movements occurring in Turkey, on the other hand, also belong to this classification, but they have unique content. The turmoil in Turkey spread in several cities from Istanbul to Ankara, and the foreign press pre-judged the events by describing them as the Turkish spring. However, this definition does not reflect the facts and has difficulties understanding the most basic concepts of Turkish political life. The Arab Spring wanted the Arab countries to transform the existing dictatorships into democratic, transparent governments that foresee equal distribution. However, the demonstrations in Turkey were not held against fair elections but against the policies of a government that had won successive elections and managed to keep the majority with the incompetence of the opposition parties. The events were not a struggle waged by the secular community against religious sections as broke out by the foreign press. The protests were a movement against the urban policies of the ruling party that has been in power for years and those wanting to implement these policies without consultation (Fuller, 2016: p. 223).

Movements that occurred specifically in the Middle East were not just for political reasons. Economic reasons were also of significance. The ongoing drought in the region before the protests and the famine that followed it caused the emergence of urban movements and impacted the severity of the protests. It was not the first time that climatic events triggered urban movements. As history shows, climatic events can sometimes be the leading cause of raids, conflicts, uprisings and riots in cities. The pressure of increasing population accumulates over the centuries and creates a general crisis. Population explosions that occur due to major disasters or significant rises during the process increase the pressure of the population on the economy. The agrarian-bureaucratic states of the early modern era could not respond to the population pressure and climatic changes in their regions, resulting in revolutions and rebellions. Ming-Qing dynasty change, the English Civil War, and rebellions in the Ottoman Empire resulted from such conditions. Like in history, climatic conditions have affected urban movements in the 21st century. It may not be the main reason, but one (White, 2011: pp. 28–29).

The already-defined concepts of old urban movements and new urban movements are meaningful in themselves as conventional meanings. While new urban movements adhere to identity, cultural, political, social, and economic foundations, old urban movements were struggles based on social, economic, and political dynamics of the 18th and 19th centuries (Chesters and Welsh, 2011: pp. 1–5). Many organisations and bodies born in the 20th and 21st centuries are among the new urban movements. Prominent ones are Alternative Globalisation Movements, Anarchism, Antagonistic Movement, Anti-Movement, Anti-Nuclear Movements, Anticapitalism, ATTAC, Autonomy, Biographical Availability, Black Power Movement, Capacity Building, Civil Rights Movement, Claimant Movement, Cognitive Praxis, Collective Identity, Computer-Mediated Communication, Counterculture, Countermovements, Culture, Cycles of Contention/Protest Cycles, Defensive Social Movements, Direct Action, Disability Rights Movement, Disobbedienti, Earth First!, Ecology of Mind and Ecology of Action, Emergence, Emotions, Environmental Justice Movement, Environmental Movement, Feminist Social Movements, Frame Analysis, Free Riders Problem, Friends of the Earth, Global Civil Society, Global Social Movement, Green Movements, Greenham Women, Green Peace, Health Social Movements, Identity Politics, Indigenous Peoples' Movements, Indymedia, Knowledge Practises, Latency Period, Leadership, Lesbian, Gay, Bisexual and Transgender (LGBT) Movements, Lifeworld, Marxism, Moral Action, Movement as Media, Multitude, Network Movements, New Social Movements, Offensive Social Movement, Old Social Movement, Peace Movement, Peoples' Global Action (PGA), Political Movement, Political Opportunity Structure, Poor Peoples' Movements, Power, Precarity, Protest and Disorder, Reclaim the Streets, Repertoire of Action, Resource Mobilisation Theory, Scientific Social Movement, Situationist International, Social Movement Organisation, Social Movement Society, Social Movement Unionism, Students for Democratic Society, Subvertising, Urban Social Movement, World Social Forum and Zapatismo (Zapatistas) (Chesters and Welsh, 2011).

1 Why Should We Call the Term 'Urban Movements'?

When we sift through history, we see that cities' cultural and political context throughout their evolution helps us comprehend the importance of events called social movements. In addition, the same process shows us what a significant role those urban problems play in the formation and organisation of joint mobilisation. The close relationship between the city and the people proves that people are the builders of cities and that cities are also sources in the formation of human experiences. When we examine the development of history, it is revealed that the form and formation of cities are prone to social changes. The evolution of cities causes social protests in the process, and the construction and expansion of cities prove that social objections develop in the same pattern. Since the city is the gathering place of individuals, that is, the citizens, where people attain a social life as a community, objections, protests, riots, and uprisings created by the communities cannot be called social movements. It is the city that causes them to occur. Since people have achieved a communal life in the cities and the differences have increased during the progress, they started to mobilise. Since not every citizen of the city benefits from the services provided by the city equally and this difference and deprivation occur in the same space, complaints arose and gradually escalated and became occupied by the society at different rates. Therefore, the city is the area where differences and thus grievances arise and rise. Of course, the field of struggle may expand to the rural area during the development process, the fight may progress in the rural area, or it may host the beginning of the events that escalate the differences in the city when the relation of the rural area with the city is considered. However, the idea and widespread struggle of the movement is city-centred and city-oriented. Then, the necessity to observe the objections, protests, uprisings, and riots occurring in the society as urban movements arise. The city is the cause and host of change, diversity, difference and the struggle that emerged afterwards. Therefore, it is necessary to call this struggle an urban movement (Castells, 1983: p. 67).

While the opinion that the social explosions that emerged so far are events far from the cities has been dominant, it has been overlooked that these events were urban-oriented or city-oriented. However, as mentioned, all of these movements were city-oriented and city-centred. For some of the events, especially those that took place before modern history, the starting point may seem to be outside the city walls; however, the continuation and management of the movement were entirely under the control of the cities. So, in any case, the city is there, and the events take place in the city's centre. So, these are urban movements. In the example of the Castilla events in the 16th century, it was not a political mobilisation but one that occurred due to the crises in the provision of housing and urban services. Then, even for the movements in the distant past, this proves the existence of urban conflicts, that is, the disputes arising from the inability of everyone to benefit equally from the services offered by the city, and that these events are urban. It is also observed that the source and existence of these movements do not belong only to today. Especially the housing-oriented transactions that we can predominantly note among the increasing urban issues appear as a problem at all times in history. Issues such as expulsions, exiles, unhealthy housing conditions, the vitality of the urban real estate market, the changing nature of housing rents, and the gradual decrease in the number of affordable housing observed before and after the urban renewal have caused conflicts and reactions of the citizens in every period of history.

In addition to urban renewal, accelerations in population growth also cause some movements in the city. The inability to provide city services on time and at the desired level is one of the cases observed during the periods when the urban population increases. And the deprivations that occurred during these periods are manifested as the reason for the cities to revolt and seek an order other than the current one. To overcome such reactions, new plans are made in regions that are seen as *morbose*. With this planning, not only the residents of the region are expelled but also urban designs that can accommodate the city's law enforcement officers are being undertaken and made use appropriately. However, the history of these actions has created a reflex to react in advance to such renewal plans of the citizens. Creating not only new places but also new communities to settle in causes reactions to these designs as well as economic problems. For this reason, the urbanisation process directs the distribution of profit-oriented production and urban services that stand against the collective action that socialises the conditions of consumption. However, every new citizen coming to the city is harmed by this order and moves to the cities to live in better conditions and open a new page for themselves. The reaction to this profit-oriented development is like turning into a part of the profit machine and willingly falling into its hands. Because cities are the factories of this mechanism. However, the citizens who settled in the city see many citizens like themselves and are informed about this system that destroys them in the process and does not allow them to open a new page in the city. The reactions that escalated due to this enlightenment made the organisation natural due to the freer behaviours and ideas of individuals born as citizens and allowed reactions to occur within the cities. Therefore, besides its task of increasing profits as a machine, the city also hosts nurturing ideas and reactions that would assist in urbanising the communities and in growing cities by providing equal rights for each citizen (Castells, 2005 p. 69).

The rise in the number of crowds hosted by the cities, in other words, the increase in the population, causes a growth in the number of marginal groups already existing in the city. In addition to the crowds drifting in pursuit of new lives in the city, new opportunities pursued by those born or grew up in the city give rise to conflict among the citizens. Since the urban services cannot respond to the increasing population and the threshold value of the new population is not sustainable in terms of the city's opportunities, the possibility of looking at and reacting against the city increases. When we consider the population increase in the city, it is observed that the higher the speed, the greater the marginality among the urbanites. The deprivation of some services and opportunities increases, and successful people's material and moral values at the same rate improve. The existing difference within the city is expanding, and diversity is increasing. Still, if we need to draw a symbolic circle, the area of the circle in the centre increases, more circles are formed, and the area covered by these circles also increases. Although the circle in the centre is growing, the percentage it covers is decreasing. This regression is greatly expanded in other circles. While the interpersonal difference gradually shrinks, the difference in the other circles increases in the central circle. In fact, we see other circles more, but the opportunities and urban services that the citizens, living in these circles, have are becoming more and more similar. This unites the circles and creates tension between them and the central circle. Increasing circles appear to indicate the cultural marginalisation that occurs after the assimilation.

In fact, the service they receive and, therefore, their complaints are the same, but their reaction to this habituated situation is different. This change in the characteristics of objections due to cultural and social diversity not only increases the number of circles but also leads to an increase in the marginality in the city. So, unless the population is managed sustainably, it creates cultural diversity and is shared between different marginalised groups in possible difficult times and under incomplete and mismanagement. Individuals who are not included in the city services and the economy produced by the city are organised given their cultural and social values at the time, and they react to put a stop to this process. Diversity is the tastiest fruit of cities, but under unaware administrations, this diversity gradually rots while rotting every fruit and progressively leads to the city's destruction. The rotting diversity benefits from intervening in this process with an equivalent number of reactions, and explosions begin. Administrations that do not monitor and analyse them well face the collapse of their cities. However, when these reactions are carefully examined, the increased marginality circle can turn into healthy circles that display beneficial diversity as the city should have (Goldstone, 2016: p. 33).

Urban movements occupying the news today are not on our agenda for the first time. It is one of the main issues raised, especially at the beginning of the last century. In fact, it was called the uprising of the masses because the foundations of the movement were not examined.

> There is such a phenomenon that today, for better or worse, has taken on the greatest importance in the public life of Europe. This phenomenon is the complete domination of society by the masses. However, by definition, the masses should not and cannot manage their own lives, and it is not

their job to dominate society. Therefore, Europe has fallen into the most severe crisis that can happen to societies, nations, and cultures. This is a crisis that has occurred several times in history. Its face, as well as its results, are familiar. The name is also familiar. It is called *the uprising of the masses.*

GASSET, 2017; p. 39

This definition denies the name given to movements that preceded it. Revolution. So, what is revolution? "Revolution is not a rebellion against the pre-existing order; it means establishing a new order that overturns the traditional order" (Gasset, 2017: p. 86). So the masses come together when they rebel against the order that cannot manage them. So, what is it like?

There are various reasons for the formation of the unique qualities and characters of the masses. The first of these is this: the individual in the mass gains an invincible power by abandoning himself to the instincts that he can only restrain when he is alone merely with the feeling of multiplicity and excess number. Because the masses are nameless (anonymous) and therefore without responsibility, they always distance individuals entirely from their sense of responsibility, which plays a restraining role everywhere, and more easily surrender them to their instincts.

LE BON, 2014: p. 29

In that case, the masses have a common attitude when they find people who think like them, worry about the same problems, and have the same concerns as them. This is a characteristic that the city has given us. Urban residents who increasingly have the same type of income and quality of life in the city complain and react when they see the privileges of the other section. This reaction is a necessary tendency for the society to meet in the equal distribution and gain that it deserves. The city citizens see that the administration works that go wrong in this way should be stopped and what kind of solutions can be produced. It is expected, then, that urban movements emerge over time.

The unity, harmony, and partnership that constitute the socialising forces must be interrupted by distance, competition, and alienation to form the fundamental structure of society. As the real builders of the society, or for the reactions and developments of the effective organisational forms that emerge or build the society as it is to come alive with successive concessions and resistance, they must be constantly disturbed, destabilised and pushed aside by individualistic and disorderly forces.

SIMMEL, 2017: p. 11

The first effective revolt in sharing and managing the city's earnings came from the bourgeoisie. The bourgeoisie, which does not have any sacred or social privileges, has achieved success by inviting every layer of the society to struggle for its own right to become the city owner. "A corresponding political advance was accompanied at every stage of development of the bourgeoisie. While it was an oppressed group under the rule of feudal lords, it became a self-governing armed society in the communes, now an independent city republic" (Marx and Engels, 2018: p. 54). But the bourgeoisie was reluctant to take the necessary steps to share this gain fully. While it was one of the voices of the machine it created, it gave up the search for a new partner and did not accept a stakeholder.

> Bourgeoisie has subjected the country to the rule of the towns. It has created enormous cities, has greatly increased the urban population as compared with the rural, and has thus rescued a considerable part of the population from the idiocy of rural life. Just as it has made the country dependent on the towns, so it has made barbarian and semi-barbarian countries dependent on the civilised ones, nations of peasants on nations of bourgeois, the East on the West.
>
> MARX and ENGELS, 2018: p. 57

However, let us go back to the issue of population growth, which inflames the urban machine. It is mainly population growth that causes cities to grow and the bourgeoisie to raise both its economic and political position. If we look at the history of Europe, the increase in population caused the interests of the cities to grow, then the population of the towns to rise, and then the expansion of the rights of the bourgeois that was the most profitable segment of this growth.

> Due to the absence of statistical data, no precise numerical estimates can be made anterior to the 15th century for sure; but perhaps we wouldn't be making a big mistake by admitting that between the 12th and 15th centuries, the urban population in all of Europe was not more than one-tenth of the entire population.
>
> PIRENNE, 2016: p. 72

We know only one-thousandth of what historians can compile about the urban population movements of the 16th century. But it is possible to make almost reliable diagnoses about the whole. All the facts point to clear and continuous increases until the end of the 16th century. Nothing unexpected happened in the 16th century; in this period, we see that all cities became active at the same time. It was general progress at that time, and population growth marks all urban environments.

BRAUDEL, 2017a: p. 518

"Considering the beginning of the 17th century and the end of the 16th century, we observe that there were movements in the cities of the Mediterranean region and that their number grew" (Braudel, 2017b: p. 561). This population increase has completely changed the order of the cities. Towns that were now more active and larger were actually gaining the status of a newer city. And the bourgeoisie was growing, benefiting from the labour and purchasing power of the growing poor.

At the end of the 17th century and throughout the 18th century, it fought to participate in the government and gain its rights. Of course, this struggle existed before. This is because this growth and development have been observed in Europe at an increasing rate since the 9th century. However, after the years when the industrial revolution occurred, every individual living in the cities started to see themselves as an urban and a citizen and did not hesitate to fight for their rights.

> The urban opposition, the predecessor of our liberals today, included the rich and middle bourgeoisie, and a section of the petit bourgeoisie, larger or smaller, depending on local conditions. Their demands never went beyond the limits of the constitutional ground in any way. Whether it be a right to supervision on town administration and town council or through public representation (grand council, public committee), they wanted to participate in the legislative power; they also wanted a restraint on the nepotism of the patricians and the few family oligarchies that emerged more and more openly among them.
>
> ENGELS, 2018: p. 46

The increasing demand in the society and the perception of the public changed the aspect of the seat occupation in the grand council quiet differently. Emerging success of the elected citizens in the grand council was realized through the party supported by the disaffected nobles and the poor. The success that came through this party, which formed the majority in the local council and guilds, had radicalized the opposition of the nobility and council supporters. However, the group that oppose the emerging new paradigm was now a small minority.

We shall see later that, during the movement in the sixteenth century, this 'moderate', 'legal', 'wealthy', and 'intelligent' opposition played the exact same role as its successor, the constitutionalist party, in the movement in 1848 and 1849 and with the exact same success.

ENGELS, 2018: p. 46

In the previous section, we attempted to present the urban movements until today, after the Industrial Revolution. So, when we examine the movements before the industrial revolution, what is the role of cities and what kind of movements have occurred? And why they should be called urban movements? For example, the reaction to the wars that broke out in our age is widespread. Of course, the effects of these reactions on the beginning of the war are beyond our subject. However, it is indisputable that individuals living in cities are more against war due to their urban consciousness and civilisation experience. But did such urban movements exist in the past? Of course, it did, and it was observed in the cities in a non-unusual manner.

In May 1409, while the war was still going on, when the hungry people took to the streets shouting 'Peace! Peace!', the administration, whose mercenaries attacked the people, killed two hundred people at once. Thereupon, using the words peace and the war was forbidden with the death penalty, and even the priests were ordered to say 'Give us calm (dona nobis tranquilitatem)' instead of 'Give us peace (dona nobis pacem)' in prayer.

BURCKHARDT, 2018: p. 43

So, if this extreme example is seen in the previous centuries in our history, how far back do the urban movements, which are considered the beginning of economic conflicts, go back?

The Ciompi proletarian uprising of 1378 was quickly brought under control by the employers, who implemented a lockout that turned the rebellious workers into a mass of hungry and homeless people. And when this army of hungry vagrants turned the rebellion into a bread riot and marched menacingly towards Signoria, the upper guild workers under di Lando inflicted a heavy defeat on them.

BRAUDEL, 1983: p. 512

"As Schevill (1936: 308) observes, the struggle in Florence in the 14th century marks the beginning of the modern conflict between capital and worker, and the relatively easy victory by capital demonstrates the difficulties that anti-capitalists have had to face ever since" (Arrighi, 2016: p. 162).

Of course, if the Renaissance was born in the lands where Rome was founded and developed, it is because the cities played an active role in this geography. And for this reason, the closest examples of urban movements to their contemporary counterparts emerge in this geography. There are older examples from our previous example, and they are as follows:

> Vocational guilds have created a significant model that brings together men of the same profession from different neighbourhoods under a single roof. Guilds were established not only by merchants, doctors, pharmacists, jurists, and notaries but also by ironmongers, drapers, butchers, bakers, furriers, carriers, leather dealers, and suchlike occupational groups. In this respect, they completely reflected the social structure of Popolo.
>
> BOOKCHIN, 2014: p. 181

The occupational groups that were made up of only wealthy merchants and professional craftsmen constitute the oldest public organisations whose records survived today.

> They not only oversaw their own craft and proceeds, but they also formed armed groups to control the commune. Not long after, clashes broke out between Popolo and Nobilta. These conflicts began in Brescia in 1192, in Piacenza in 1198, Milan in 1201, Cremona, Assisi, and Lucca in almost one-year intervals, and finally in Pistoia in 1234.
>
> BOOKCHIN, 2014: p. 181

If we go back to our previous section, that is, closer to the present day, we can better understand urban events. This century began with the urban movements seen in Iceland and Ukraine. In fact, these are the most effective of many activities. However, the Arab Spring is the turning point of the 21st century. This urban movement has taken the Arab region by storm. When we look at the essence of the complaints, which are the central axis of economic and political reasons, it is sure that we can see the level of deprivation of the cities by the administration. In addition, in these geographies where religious matters are applied sensitively, many urban reasons encourage rebellion, unlike political and economic issues. It is usual for this geography, which is tied to religious practices and traditions, to seek its ashes in the past during its Renaissance stage, and the fire of these ashes actually paves the way for the explosion of urban movements themselves. According to the power holders in this geography, the opposition is unnecessary and even a betrayal. However, the reverse has also happened in the history of this region. When we look at the early periods of Islam, the following may come out:

> Unless such propaganda turned into violence, the caliphs of the period did not consider them a political crime and even allowed these people to express their opinions openly within the framework of vast tolerance. Just like in the example of the Caliph Hazrat Ali (r.a.) responding favourably to those people, although he heavily criticises himself for the practices of those who have external thoughts and hints at his blasphemy while he was delivering the sermon. Again, as in the example of Caliph Omar H. Abdulaziz ordering the Kharijites, who disagree and rebel, to be treated with kindness if they do not resort to violence.
>
> AKALIN, 2016: p. 53

In fact, the sentences describing the Arab Spring exactly came from Ibn Khaldun centuries ago.

> In this regard, Ibn Khaldun's comment on the subject is remarkable: If the invader is administrating the state with a praised policy per the provisions of religion and the laws of justice, it is permissible for them to remain at the head of the state administration. Otherwise, the Muslims will resort to methods and persons who will oust the invader from the administration of the state. In this way, their damage is eliminated.
>
> AKALIN, 2016: p. 109

Another explanation is as follows:

> The third approach on the subject is not to abandon the principle of enjoining good and forbidding evil. Instead of leaving an unjust and tyrannical power completely unattended, it is to attempt and strive to be effective at this point by creating social pressure. It may not be afforded to dismiss the administrator who is in the bond of power. Or, it may not have been deemed appropriate to engage in armed struggle for fear of sedition in the society. But this does not necessitate giving up the struggle altogether. At the very least, this can be challenged. Warning and reminders can be used. Society must strive to be influential on the ruler.
>
> AKALIN, 2016: p. 145

In that case, it is safe to say that starting from the 6th century, urban movements took place in the cities in Islamic countries, especially as seen in the examples, and they occupied the societies' agenda. Just as is the case in the 21st century. So, what are the characteristics of the 21st-century versions of urban movements that emerged from such a region where no one expected a reaction at the beginning of the century and spread all over the world, and why should they be described as urban movements? Let's try to bring clarification to these matters.

Capitalism has spread to the world in a different strategy since the last half of the 20th century. With the initiatives it has made, it has renewed and expanded its influence in a way to occupy not only the economic life of every potential consumer that are urbanites but also their every possible moment. Capitalism now attempts for us to consume not only the materials we need but also almost any materials that come to our minds. Capitalism, which turned to our products of necessity in the past, now markets every product it produces as if we needed it. This marketing strategy is not only based on economic fundamentals. An attack that includes not only religious, national, or identity diversity but also all kinds of social and cultural values is directed at today's urbanites. However, the centres of this collective movement have not changed. It has changed shape and is becoming denser. Of course, the existence of states and their dominance in political matters can still be discussed. However, as a phenomenon that started in the last century, global governance changes not only states but also societies. In particular, the rise in the number of cities and citizens has made it essential to manage capitalism as a potential customer on a global scale. Urbanites, who are increasingly similar to living in cities but still differing, are directed to the same type of consumption worldwide, and this strategy does not appear to be just economic. Therefore, this strategy must also have cultural and political centres. Undoubtedly, although this transformation affects the life of the citizens in terms of consumption, it mainly affects transportation and access to urban services.

With the protests that started in 1968, the masses divided among the urbanites no longer directed their targets to the state forces or powers in power that were supposed to rule the cities, or not only to these authorities but also to protest the global organisations. In fact, the intensifying reaction is now against these organisations. Among these organisations are the United Nations, WTO, IMF, World Bank, International NGOs, and Multinational Companies. These organisations and companies have expanded their activities that were once focused on specific regions and cities in the past to now worldwide, and they diversified their strategies, which focused only on particular issues, especially on economic status, by reducing them to more cultural and social issues, thus aiming to reach every citizen they want to reach. The reason for this can be given as the fact that people around the world have started to live in cities at an increasing rate day by day, and the citizens living in each town are socially differentiated even though they are increasingly similar to each other. Cultural and social heterogeneity has now become the lifeblood of capitalism (Martin, 2008: p. 164).

Social heterogeneity interacts with certain forms of collective identities. In the past, movements emerged from among homogeneous social groups. We observed that urban movements were steered by specific periods and economic class or ethnicity. Undoubtedly, we are not talking about just one or two groups, but an assortment of parties as diverse as today is not in question. As the proportion of the population living in the cities increased and the social and cultural production of the city expanded, more and more different and more diverse groups emerged among the masses compared to the past and became more prominent. Therefore, there is a more heterogeneous structure. However, having the concept of 'we' in such diversity does not mean that it will be more difficult to establish than it used to be. On the contrary, considering the social elements that were more difficult to organise in the past, it is observed that groups with very different identities and cultures can quickly unite when the time comes. Although differentiations such as gender, religion, class, generation, race, and environment distinguish themselves from others in terms of quantity, they are similar in quality in the struggle for rights in this cooperation we may define as the meeting of discourse. Despite that different groups have different types of both actions and activists, they know how to support each other when the day comes and try to be a group that embraces differences. Compared to a period in which the borders were determined, and participation was very uniform within the left tradition, as in the old times, in an anti-capitalist or anti-liberal understanding, this combination is among the visible differences of the 21st century (della Porta, 2005: p. 200).

Such organisations affect the distribution of social and physical resources in space, or the diversification of activities related to spatial arrangements and accelerate the development of the community. The sudden tallying sensitivities of the different groups mentioned above against urban policies lead to social and spatial consequences. Although groups sensitive to such issues as regulating the ring roads passing through a region, resisting land use, activities to increase local cohesion, and gathering against the affordable rent and housing problem seem to separate themselves, in fact, all the different groups we mentioned above can become a single force in such activities. The desire to be included in this decision-making process and a participatory urban management approach prove that these are called urban movements. Regardless of the subject, whether economic, political or cultural, all of these movements originate from the city. This is because these groups, with the activities they organise and the awareness of the activists they organise, emphasise joint action on ecological, cultural or political issues in cities and try to increase their role in urban change or transformation. Communal profits, that is, shared benefits, which encourage this participatory city management approach, help form institutions and organisations belonging to the city within the society. In other words, the city unites the communities, helps them to organise for their benefit, and encourages the citizens to institutionalise for a shared future and participatory democracy (Hasson, 1987 p. 1).

The innovation that emerges in urban movements is not only in the methods of opposition but also in all areas of participation. Instead of the actions of low-income groups in the past, innovations are occurring in the activities and involvement of the same groups and the citizens belonging to this group but feel belonging to different groups at the same time. This difference, which came to light after the 1960s, became visible in every aspect of the protests that took place in the city. For example, the movement called the poor people's action is not just a movement against the economic order. Against the standards of the life of neighbourhood where they live, against the state, that is, the injustice in the distribution of urban resources, and against deprivation such as not being able to take part in the decision-making process, the same group again engaged in protest actions and realised their discomfort with new methods and new participants compared to the past (Tarrow, 2011: p. 5). When we look at the actions that took place in the past, left-leaning tendencies are observed in general, and they are carried out with minimal resources. In addition to limited resources, the scope of these actions is also minimal. In fact, due to political limitations, many citizens who were suffering from the complaints voiced by these protests were excluded from these protests. However, over time, political and economic constraints have become obsolete. When we examine the participants' identities, we see that the transitivity has increased. However, the fighting spirit and belief of the previous years are contracting. While the protests involving limited groups were more prolonged and more violent, we find that the protests have become shorter and more peaceful in the years nearer the present.

It has been determined that more citizens in the city are involved in the process with different understandings and interpretations, but they participate outside of particular organising or organisation. It is also apparent that these actions broke out suddenly and had a short lifespan. Since the participants come from different groups and opinions and reject the leadership of one individual, the initiation and development of movements are easy. Still, it does not turn into a long-term struggle necessary to reach the result. However, a large number of participants and the formation of groups with the participation of different circles have a broader impact on the public. This causes the actions to take place frequently, although they are short-lived. Unfortunately, no authority will force the political power to make changes in a short time due to the lack of confident leadership and the deprivation of organisational structure. Over time, political decisions can be affected due to citizens raising awareness, but this does not affect the power immediately. Although the essence of the protests includes political expectations, since the participants' self-description, that is, their identities are not based on a political language, it is not possible to see urban movements as a political formation in the 21st century; more accurately, to transform these movements into a political formation. As a result of some movements, although the movement participants have taken on political formations with the name their movements have adopted by the public, the influence of the movements in the political arena is not very strong. However, the reflections of the movements gradually create interaction among all the citizens of the city, which leads to a political transformation. However, this transformation cannot be as fast and effective as the movements intended. Still, it is observed that the parties, which are the founding and main elements of the political system, benefit from the effect created by the movements (Schuurman and Naerssen, 1989: p. 6).

It is claimed that global interactions, that is, globalisation, are also effective in igniting urban movements. The reason for this can be manifested as urban life, in which the tremendous local area of joint action is the actor of political, economic, cultural, and late modern perspectives. Locality, even extraordinary locality, has begun to be seen in cities and even in the regions of cities, as opposed to the increasingly observed globalisation. It is possible to overlook the local dimension of the event since the element that reveals the results of the urban movement stem from globalisation. Still, the locality is a critical factor in the organisation and effectiveness of urban movements. As observed in the dimension of local and global relations in the cause-effect paradigm, the relational model of change causes us to rethink the structure of the forces imposed by globalisation. It is also crucial for the formation of urban movements that the asymmetrical power relations of community, culture, nation-state and international organisations cause local transformations due to globalisation. While globalisation stands as the sword of Damocles as a significant pressure factor on cities, the scales of the blindfolded representative of justice are urban movements organised locally. And by using the advantages of globalisation, the movements that occur at the local scale suddenly spread to the national dimension, and even this expansion becomes regionally responsive. As with the phenomenon of globalisation, cases in which these movements are effective on a global scale from time to time are also becoming common. Thus, movements organised on a local scale transform into national and international actions and organisations, as well as global movements find a response on a regional scale (Hamel et al., 2000: p. 2).

According to Immanuel Wallerstein's systematic point of view, as globalisation spreads, it also creates, awakens, and develops its opposite. In this respect, urban movements are the key indicators of change. Urban movements are making progress in reversing the harmful changes to the citizens for the benefit of the citizens. For this reason, urban movements play an essential role in balancing the factors that block the city during local and global crises. Urban movements show us at least a dual division within the system. In today's world, where the changes and transformations affecting the cities, especially in the division of labour and capital ownership, are increasing, the differentiation that exists in the cities and is rapidly progressing continues its struggle to open up a wider area for itself and proceeds its way with a new skin (Hamel et al., 2000: p. 5).

When we examine the urban hierarchy, with the effect of globalisation, global economies that manage and coordinate the network between cities with their cross-border activities have gradually become the strategic areas of central regions. This power relationship has evolved in this way throughout history, and today it has become an intolerable whole with a more intense version of globalisation. When we look at the cities in general, it has been determined that the number of citizens benefiting from these existing inter-city network relations roughly corresponds to twenty per cent of the total. This figure is higher than the proportion of urban elites who are much less. However, the number of citizens who cannot benefit from this blessing created by the cities is still 80 per cent. Nonetheless, when the cities are considered one by one, it is observed that not every town has these rates. While specifically, the percentages in cities that benefit significantly from this urban network are decreasing among urban elites, that is, it is observed that wealth and privilege are intensified, these large cities experience greater deprivation in poverty rates and income inequality. So, again, as in our theory, urban inequality is more valid for cities that deserve the concept of the city, and this problem necessitates that urban movements are observed more in these cities; that is, the movements should be called urban. This is because power is growing in these cities, but so is inequality. This inequality spreads to every area of the city and narrows the space of the deprived citizens. However, the city's attraction causes the migration of people living outside and wishing to live in this city, further increasing the problems of deprivation areas in the city.

The problems of gentrification, displacement, congestion, pollution, and many more are increasingly affecting the lives of the citizens, especially the innocent citizens who are not privileged. In this environment, the masses, who have begun to lose what they already have in the city life left in this environment and that is taking shape, are gradually becoming conscious and integrating. Even if they are from different mentalities and cultures, the reactions given with the concern for the common future are similar and become more frequent. They start protesting against the problems mentioned above and many others, and they try to stand up and expand as much as they can against the system that has formed. They derive activities against the problems that cause them anxiety and try to develop creative solutions. They want to prevent their cities from being formed only for minorities by the great powers. The idea of a shared future, which has many stakeholders considering ecological concerns, causes the masses to come together and turn into frequent but not long-lasting actions. Even if these explosions do not exist, they prevent big investors who shape cities from seeing cities as centres of attraction. In other words, urban movements are beneficial in shifting the forces that will cause cities to form asymmetrically (Hamel et al., 2000: p. 9).

Nonetheless, since the same urban movements highlight the current understanding of democracy and the legal order in cities, they also make their cities attractive to investors because they are accessible environments. However, the cities with neighbourhoods deprived of urban services and where the number of urban residents damaged by urban renewal projects increased included almost all cities. Cities that lack central funds to compensate for the deprivations and damages arising from these and similar activities are not only faced with economic and social exclusion. At the same time, these cities are faced with spatial exclusion. Because of this exclusion, community-oriented protests and uprisings have increased, especially since the 1960s, influencing municipalities to apply for revitalisation and compensatory programs (Hamel et al., 2000: p. 10). The fact that the common future cannot be sustained due to the developing urban network and increasing human consumption has caused the protests in the cities to occur at a more local and global level. Crowds who are hurting more in the face of this ever-increasing challenge of man against nature and who have already begun to feel the damage express their objections that this order needs to be changed in almost every setting.

Global competition and the local competition created by the city within itself have brought up the right of urban citizenship, that is, the right of the citizens, and has made the right of the citizens to be questioned and the right to the city. The feeling of being excluded from the city by urbanites has brought the concept of social garbage to the fore, and the crowds that are uncomfortable with this concept want to have more say in their cities, contrary to the said concept. For this reason, the concepts of citizenship and being urban have been among the main problems of our age (Hamel, 2000: p. 26). In addition to these, other problems such as poverty, homelessness, job loss, and marginalisation triggered by these problems are causing more and more complaints. The social security and job perspective, therefore, plays a key role in the formation of new urban movements. While these problems are occurring, ongoing social issues are also conducive to new urban movements' formation, revival, and development (Broadbent and Brockman, 2011: p. 35).

Social problems, that is, the issues arising from the relations that occur in the city play an essential role in the occupation of our lives by urban movements and the diversity of urban movements. Concerns about urban problems raise the demand for new citizenship for the urbanite. This is because, as in the past, struggles occur in an environment where only leftist views, workers' movements, or purely democratic reasons are presented. Of course, the places of these movements are included in the current movements. However, they are a part of the urban movements due to the concerns of many factors. Nevertheless, the main factor that occupies the urban movements at the moment is the concept of citizenship, that is, urbanity. Social justice, human rights, global responsibilities, gender equality and diversity, and democratisation are among the main issues that constitute the complaints of the current urban movements. Of course, political and economic factors are among these issues as triggering factors. Global justice, local democracy, and respect for life choices are at the centre of today's complaints. Urban movements demand to expand the citizenship rights that the state considers every living person entitled to without mentioning ethnic structures, without racial and gender discrimination. Therefore, being an urbanist and having a say in the city is the primary desire of urban movements. When the development of cities is considered, it can be observed that cities are the main element of development, and every citizen who is a part of these development engines should have equal rights. The necessity of living conditions and quality to be free from privileges and as fair as possible for every citizen brings a new understanding of citizenship to the agenda with the awareness of urbanity (Jacobsson, 2015: p. 39).

As A. Touraine points out, our society is evolving from a vertical society where class differences are constant at the top and bottom to a horizontal society where everyone lives on the same level but where there is a divide between the periphery and the centre (Hamel et al., 2000: p. 61). Globalisation is a phenomenon that has occurred in different periods of history. Still, in its latest form, globalisation first increased the creation of the upper class and gradually aligned the lower classes. The solutions found by the economic and social structures to the current problems and the innovations created by the increasing communication technologies have aligned most citizens. However, in this case, they have created a centre with privileges. These privileges did not give birth to the nobility as before. However, it has created a certain segment that is more invisible and violent than that. This urban hierarchy was formed through the breakthroughs and initiatives following the Fordist era. The differences in the cities that have determined their place in the network of cities and gained more income have been less, and the existence of classes concentrated on a parallel line has been observed. Those who are at the centre of the community living on this parallel can, of course, benefit more from the production of the city than those on the periphery. And for this segment, the living space is not just their own city. We see the network of cities on a parallel day by day. There is a differentiation between the cities in the centre of this parallel and the cities on their peripheries, and the inhabitants of the cities. Exclusion and polarisation are observed more in the new system. This is because there is no transition between classes.

The benefit obtained from the city's production is important, and those who profit from this benefit change from time to time. However, the group that collects the main profit maintains its position in the centre. And day by day, the masses in a row on the horizontal plane began to polarise as the centre and the ends. The conflict between the centre and the periphery creates the conflict necessary for urban movements, and the tension is growing day by day. Because the number of people living in the city is increasing and the everyday life in the host city environment is rising. However, there is a differentiation of living space among the citizens sharing the same city, which happens openly. Such unfair sharing that occurs in the lives of the masses who are aware of each other causes the masses to organise around their circles and the eruption of urban movements. Local changes are, therefore, significant, and the progress of local democracies and their greater involvement in urban life is essential for the common destiny of the city (Hamel et al., 2000: p. 140). When we analyse the urban movements, it is possible to observe that it has changed a lot since 1968. Especially after the 1990s, urban movements were realised within the framework of the features mentioned above. Today's urban movements are more complex, more diverse, and heterogeneous. Starting from the existing small settlements within the cities, the urban movements diverge from each other. The forms and types of action gradually change when it comes to metropolises. However, movements occurring at these different scales have a lot to learn from each other. The restructuring of the city, regaining its form, and urban transformations reflect differently on the settlements within the city and produce different results. However, since each result brings more harm than good for the majority of the citizens, the common side complaints increase, and the reaction is not delayed (Hamel et al., 2000: p. 142).

The high position of the cities and the intense competition between the cities require the change of shape of the business centres in the cities and the expansion of the area that we can define as the centre. In fact, we observe that more than one centre has emerged in the city, and they are gradually swallowing their surroundings. The city is growing and expanding its borders. This expansion makes the situation for the citizens already living on the city's outskirts very difficult. In addition to this, the fact that the city's borders are surrounded by a natural border which is also surrounded by a natural environment, has made the situation of the disadvantaged people living in the city even worse. The masses living in the peripheries were further excluded and had to move to other areas. In fact, communities living in the city's centre and trying to compensate for the disadvantages some cities bring are displaced by urban design elements such as gentrification. They will add new ones to their problems. Increasing business centres and the urban settlements built for the users of this centre that developed around it attract foreign investors. These investors are increasing areas similar to these centres and building new sites to serve these centres. This investment increases the general income of the city as is supposed but does not necessitate a change in income for all citizens. As we see that this change is not for everyone, municipal activities that should take initiatives to eliminate this difference cannot fully fulfil their duties. On the contrary, the municipality spends its budget to carry out the infrastructure and similar services of the new investors. One reason is to attract more investors.

Municipalities that are supposed to operate for all citizens provide services to specific areas for certain groups and appear as a source of existing and increasing diversity. With the newly arrived population, displacement is growing, and the city is becoming an increasingly polluted environment. Consumption is also observed to increase, but this does not mean that the whole city consumes. Modern castles built in the city create their own observation points and walls. And the number of beneficiaries in these areas is gradually decreasing. This creates a contrast among the growing population and is a harbinger of an increased reaction. Citizens do not like that the city grows like a stain by spreading to green areas. The city's deprivation areas increase, and the city centre sees itself as an autonomous structure. For example, the municipality that produces temporary solutions to solve the heavy traffic in the city centre usually makes all its investments in these regions and the parallel campuses that feed these regions. However, there is no service provided for displacement, and worse still, for those living in the periphery while living further on the periphery. These people, who already have limited livelihoods, can only reach their workplaces by changing more vehicles from further away, provided they have a job. If we consider other versions of this example, it is unacceptable for us to stay away from the existence of a countermovement, that is, urban movements, starting from the city peripheries and spreading towards the city centres protected by imaginary towers. The existence of a struggle against the privileges and inequalities born and growing in the city is thus confirmed by the wrong steps taken (Hamel et al., 2000: p. 143). Seeing that foreign investment has changed cities so much, the city's citizens organise around informal organisations and try to create an economic and political resistance. Non-governmental organisations are trying to fix the current order by bringing healthy nutrition and development methods into question in the face of these investments that cause obesity disease in cities. Especially since the 1990s, when they could not find an answer to the problems in this third party, the masses tried to announce their reactions to those in power by using the mass media, which develops entirely independently of a leader or organisation, and actually tried to become a partner in the government (Hamel et al., 2000: p. 147).

Urban movements are not uniform social actions involving homogeneous social actors. Urban movements do not have to share the same vision or make the same radical claims. However, it is common for them to take a stance against the direct interventions of the state or city power in the city. For this reason, urban movements are actions against the new cultural politics of identity, differences, and marginalisation of the city. Considering the increasing population of cities, a different version of the familiar social solidarity emerges in urban movements in the face of diversifying problems. Instead of the concept of solidarity made in a narrow field, as in the past, there is a social agreement such as an unambiguous and understanding identity agreement. The actions of rooted urban communities concerning values progress towards democratisation by integrating with institutional innovations and encouraging new socio-economic and political processes. These joint actions and common goals cause urban movements to be more different and colourful than in the past (Hamel et al., 2000: p. 158). This ongoing restructuring has other social implications.

Opportunities that arise due to responses to changes in the conditions and quality of daily life in all local environments, from social exclusion to social inequalities, are products of these effects. Apart from the ethnic and religious protests and uprisings, especially in the 1950s, it is a whole of activities that are also not far from them from time to time. Today, cities, especially metropolises, host crises and conflicts due to the multiple meanings attributed to the urban environment and the growing complexity of these meanings in opposition to each other. The symptoms of the problem that began appearing in the society gradually became the character of the cities. These conflicts, which are observed as problems occurring within the society, are essentially the city's problem and arise from the city's administration. So the question should be directed to the city, not the society. Therefore, the Urban Question is noteworthy, and more contributions should be made while slanting towards it more (Hamel et al., 2000: 159). Solutions to the city's problems can be found not with a view from above but with steps taken on a local scale. Therefore, local economic development appears as a complex and multidimensional process and is observed as the complete opposite of one-dimensional economic development directed at cities.

The creativity of the urban environment emerges as a result of the synergy of each concerned actor and socio-economic sector. Therefore, social and economic success follows an active and responsive civic democracy. Hence, in response to urban problems, participatory and democratic city management, starting from the local, is essential for the city to create a success story regionally and as a whole. It is also a condition for every citizen to adopt this sense of social justice (Hamel et al., 2000: p. 160). Therefore, urban movements play an essential role in such a success story. Today's urban movements rise for more participatory city management, which is necessary to fulfil services that are not valid at the local scale. Furthermore, these movements highlight the public interest by limiting the steps taken by the private enterprise for the restricted segments. For this reason, movements are in favour of more inclusive and democratic city planning and city management. Moreover, by wanting to defend their rights to take more part in decision-making mechanisms, they wish that public policies should be shaped for the benefit of every citizen. Therefore, they organise urban movements with and for every segment of the society (Hamel et al., 2000: p. 160).

When conflict and innovation arise, the complex field of struggle transforms into a coalition-building environment among self-emancipating participants. The practical experience of contentious opponents and radical activists helps guide values, priorities, strategies, and political projects. The emerging fight and the type of fight help strong institutions and liberating movements raise awareness of the participants in the field and produce alternatives in daily life. For this reason, socio-political activism is the address of leading initiatives in the fight for common sensibility against opposites. Over time, those who enter this fight, and their actions lead the decision-making mechanisms to take steps for social change (Laxer and Halperin, 2003: p. 122). Urban movements are, therefore, a vital element of civil society. Student protests, feminism, peace, and environmental actions in the city since the 1960s indicate the existence of new wave urban movements. Generally, urban movements are loosely connected formations but take direct action like a campaign tool, unlike traditional parties. This is because urban movements consist of desirous, angry, and idealistic communities who want social change rather than being a means of socialisation.

Urban movements are like a cycle now. There are newcomers and those who have already joined and transferred their duties to others. People who participated before but did not participate later but came into action again one day are also among these communities. While the participants of urban movements are like this, so are the urban movements. While certain urban movements operate in specific periods, more giant explosions are observed in some periods. In environments where the city administration or the central government do not include citizens in decision-making, big explosions are observed after a long silence. In more democratic environments, where there is little interference in political participation and decision-making, urban movements continue, albeit on a small scale, to become more peaceful, and big explosions are observed in periods when these features are narrowed. The context of collective action is, therefore, the political opportunity structure. If the will of the ruling minority to share power diminishes, urban movements struggle to seize their opportunities. And this struggle takes shape in the form of local, national, and global conflicts (Purdue, 2007: p. 6). For this reason, urban movements turn into complex and sequential trans-geographical events. Local neighbourhoods usually appear as physical spaces where the movement is clustered, and mobilisation and virtual space will expand with macro and micro spaces. In addition to the centres where the economy and political activities are clustered, we observe that the activities against this clustering suddenly exist and cluster. The paradox of space arises because the centre that shares these contrasts is the city. The reason for the activities is the city, and its opposite will be there. If there is an effect, the reaction will undoubtedly be found in the same place (Purdue, 2007: p. 222).

2   Sociology of Urban Movements

Urban movements haul and bring change to the agenda. However, urban movements can also be formations that try to prevent change in a subject (Uysal, 2016: p. 1). Psychological explosions and rebellions during the French Revolution led to the initiation of studies on crowd psychology. According to the common assumption in crowd psychology theory, it is claimed that there is a mechanism that causes participants in urban movements to behave differently and strangely than they usually do. The term used for such crowds is the madding crowd. According to this theorem, collective action and urban movements are based on social psychology and differ from other actions (Uysal, 2016: p. 4).

Resource mobilisation theory is another theory. It stems from the micro-economic assumption that urban movements operate like a market-ruled economy. According to this theory, grievances and resentments always exist and are everywhere, but these negativities do not turn into urban movements instantly and every time. The main reason for the participation that enables complaints and anger to turn into an urban movement is the ability of urban movement entrepreneurs to use their resources effectively in line with a goal. For this reason, this theory emphasises the importance of participation in urban movements and the functioning of urban movements. According to the resource mobilisation theory, the basic unit of analysis is the urban movement organisations, which are considered just like commercial firms in the economic market. These organisations can be foundations, associations, and clubs. The theory examines how urban movement organisations find their resources and how urban movement entrepreneurs continue the process by using the resources they find effectively and rationally. In other words, resource mobi-lisation examines what resources are suitable for urban movements, what is effective in finding and producing new resources, and what influences the effective use of existing resources (Uysal, 2016: p. 6).

Another theory that concerns crowds in urban movements is the Discourse Analysis Theory. Explaining material and cultural struggles, this theory deals with how social relations are constructed. Discourse Analysis has developed a more holistic approach by eliminating the deficiencies of the resource mobili-sation theory, which overly addresses the processes within urban movements, and by bringing complaints and emotions back into urban movement activ-ities. This analysis explains the personal lives of individuals and social life itself and defines the schemas that enable individuals to interpret. With this theory, the process of creating a bond between the individual and the urban movement organisations is discussed (Uysal, 2016: p. 11). The discourse process can be described under four headings. These are discourse amplification that highlights the cultural aspect, discourse linking that combines two different discourses, discourse expansion that directs the target of discourse to a more effective target, and discourse transformation to replace an unsuccessful dis-course with a new one. These processes in the discourse analysis will justify the urban movement operating on a particular subject and will help obtain participants about what needs to be done. The discourse will also ensure that the view put forward by the urban movement is adopted by the society (Uysal, 2016: p. 12).

Collective behaviour is disorderly, oppositional, instantaneous rebellion, and prone to violence. The transformation of many individuals into a crowd leads the participants to act, feel, think, and act differently by engaging in a new collective mindset that they usually do not do. Individuals lose self-control in the crowd. Crowds begin to act with simple group logic. Participants who show cooperative behaviour in ordinary situations begin to act with the crowd leader in a group and fall under their direction. Led by the leader, they act on their most straightforward impulses and pursue higher ideals. Human behaviour in the crowd becomes contagious. While the crowd is acting under the leader's leadership, the participants become open to influence so that they will adopt every course of action that the leader puts forward. Participants behave aggressively and thoughtlessly in the crowd (Le Bon, 2001: p. 20).

It is observed that the reactions given to stimuli during participation in urban movements vary according to the environment in which the participant is located. The element that determines how the given reaction and action will occur is not the stimulus's physical quality but the stimulation's effect on the stimulated person and the participant's interests and priorities. It is established that the symbolic interaction emerges when participants act based on the meaning they attribute to the action and objects and that these meanings emerge through interaction. It can be stated that the attributed meanings change with three main assumptions that they are created, maintained, and transformed in the process of interpretation (Mayer and Tarrow, 1998).

The role of secondary organisations is essential for the protection and continuation of social order and democratic political systems. However, as the Frankfurt School stated in the formation of mass society, the masses gradually came under the influence of extremist groups and became the subject of the influence of demagogues. The fact that individuals are open to mass movements due to their alienation from business environments, local community, and politics and that the absence of independent organisations and institutions between the family and the state have caused individuals to be inclined to mass movements. That the existence of social mobility in modern societies and the fact that heterogeneity and centralisation have weakened the previously existing ties have caused individuals to turn to mass organisations and mass media more. In this respect, it seems that mass culture blunts individuals' mental structure, thinking ability, and acting potential. Individuals are becoming more and more politically ineffective and passive. For this reason, individuals have increasingly become a product of mass culture, with mass public opinion and media directing political feelings.

Upon analysing the mass society approach, it was claimed that resentment and reaction against the society would occur due to the loss of social ties and the weakening of relations such as kinship, union, and neighbourliness of alienated individuals. And for this reason, it has been argued that individuals will quickly participate in collective behaviour. However, the resource mobilisation approach states that, contrary to the definition of disconnected individuals, circle of friends, religious and sectarian networks cause individuals to adapt to protest actions more quickly. This understanding argues that there are always complaints, concerns, and resentments in society, and therefore resentment and complaints are not very effective in forming urban actions. According to this approach, the main determining factor is the abundance of the resources produced by the urban movement organisations and the efficient use of the obtained resources. The number of staff, time and money are essential resource topics for organisations, and these resources come before complaints and resentments. When the necessary resources cannot be collected or used effectively, the movement's effectiveness decreases, and the failure of challenging and opposition movements comes to the fore (Uysal, 2016: p. 45; Alver, 2017: pp. 14–5).

Urban movements that focus on the public interest often encounter the problem of free use, which negatively affects participation. The reason for this is that the citizens sometimes think that participation is unnecessary because they believe that the benefits that everyone can use will arise due to the participation activity, and they feel that they will benefit from it like everyone else. Knowing that they will benefit from the results of the actions, even if their participation is not in question, reduces participation in urban movements. Urban movement organisations use awards to honour those who participate in the movement to tackle this problem. The existence of citizens that are not willing to pay the cost of the public benefit of individuals has led to this result. The individual that believes that the return will be low in matters that reflect the benefit of a large part of society avoids the necessary trouble. That is why the use of optional rewards is vital for increasing participation. Identity also plays a vital role in such incentives. Movements that gain identity are more successful in reaching concrete targets by spreading their existing culture with such incentives (Melucci, 1996).

Resource Mobilisation Theory, which tries to explain the activities of social movements with the economic model with profit-loss and supply-demand models, is based on the idea that the main success of urban movements lies in generating resources and using the produced resources efficiently. According to the theory, urban movements have to develop a discourse and strategy according to the demands, needs, and problems of the segments of society to obtain the appropriate resource. Again, according to this theory, it has been argued that people participating in urban movements act rationally as in other social actions and act according to the profit-loss principle. This theory saw urban movements as part of the social order and deemed their activities within the system rather than outside it (Johnston, 1995: p. 220).

The new urban movements differ from the old urban movements by focusing on the general interest of the society, giving importance to the culture and understanding of the society, and aiming to improve the position of some cultural segments in the society rather than gaining a share and defending the interests of a community. Traditional urban movements, which have a deprivation-, resources-, and opportunity-oriented approach, think that only opportunities and resources are sufficient for the functioning and success of urban movements. However, the new urban movements advocated the need to address the cultural dimension and these elements. This approach is Discourse Analysis, which both produces and consumes and complements other perspectives in terms of social context and opportunities (Gamson, 1995: p. 92).

Opposing communities in society affect each other's activities and their chances of making change. Just as it is normal for urban movements to be brought about by a community, it is also typical for an opposite action to emerge. Some segments of the society, predominantly governing elites, may perceive the change that affects their political, economic and cultural interests as a threat. Some social segments and the state apparatus may create a movement against change, and formations with different forms of cooperation and support against urban movements may also occur. However, the relationship between the state and counter-movements is quite complex. The activities and discourses of movements formed against urban movements do not occur randomly either. The reason for this is that the counter-discourse development process is not only dependent on the discourse of the urban movement with which it is fighting. At the same time, the discourse developed by the countermovement is also influenced by historical and cultural elements (Swidler, 1995: p. 31).

Urban movements use the courts to seek justice to achieve their goals of change, the national assembly for appropriate legislation, and the media to make their voices heard and influence public opinion and the agenda. Mass media undertake many functions in terms of activities of urban movements, directly or indirectly and intentionally or unknowingly. The media plays a vital role in persuading the public about possible solutions to problematic situations and influencing the public's point of view. The media emerges as a more compelling topic even from the courts and the parliament that urban movements try to influence (Smith and Fetner, 2007: p. 16). With its informing function, the media enables the urban movements to be aware of the issues they are uneasy about, spread the issues they are angry about, and inform the public about the movement's activities. The interpretation feature of mass media also has an important place for urban movements. When a different demand and development arise with urban movements, the media usually creates an agenda by commenting on this issue. Although not every individual agrees with the comments, since it contains social information and everyone will care, it will affect the change struggles of urban movements (Jasper, 2007: p. 73).

Mass media can deliberately connect people far away and unaware of each other. Bringing the issues that are the subject of complaints to the agenda in the media and giving place to the activities of the emerging urban movements cause the formation of an organisation for people with similar complaints to reach a unity of belief and cooperate. On the other hand, the media's negative coverage of urban movements causes the movement to disperse and reduce its impact. International urban movement organisations that continue their activities, especially with the connection of national borders, try to overcome the distance problem they encounter as a challenge with internet and satellite technologies. Contrary to the traditional structure of the media, they take care to use new opportunities (Castells, 2004: p. 107). For this reason, mass media fulfil more than one function. They obtain the opportunity for the movement to introduce themselves with the information function, while the propaganda function helps the movements have activities that will help them; on the other hand, they can also pave the way for actions, and the connection function provides the unification and integration of disconnected individuals and segments of society. With these media functions, the success of the urban movement that breaks out in one place can be taken as an example and set as a model in another place. Considering that these functions are in the hands of both urban movement organisations and opposing groups, the media can be a resource that can be used by both the ruling elites and urban movements (Uysal, 2016: p. 113).

Urban movements fulfil three main functions to achieve their goals: recruitment, mobilisation, and effective strategy selection. On the other hand, culture concerns these three main factors partially or entirely. During the recruitment period, both the movement culture and the shared culture are essential because, while establishing the social bond in a new way, the newly developed discourse is established through cultural elements. Culture also enables the participants of the urban movement to communicate with people from different segments, such as authority, adversaries, and potential members. In this respect, culture has supportive and restrictive functions for urban movements. The elements of culture can be open to new interpretations, or they can be closed. Conflicting values within the shared culture can complicate and facilitate the discourse and activities of the urban movement. Urban movements often use pervasive socio-political culture to articulate their presence and demands against counter-movements. Through culture, urban movements struggle to define the controversial issues and gain public support. The concept of discourse development, also described as culture construction, is used to understand and explain this struggle (Uysal, 2016: p. 133).

Urban movements generally try to create new meanings in society and explain situations using existing cultural codes. In this respect, urban movements demand change and try to reach each potential participant by using their activities and demands from existing cultural elements. Even the most radical movements have to consider the existing cultural codes in the society and not become alienated from the society. They should explain to their potential supporters the justification of the discourse they developed in this way and neutralise their opponents. For this reason, the more the demands of urban movements resonate with society, the more successful they will be. They need to convince them of the movement's agenda against those who will hinder the urban movements or at least have a serious interaction with the mainstream culture to neutralise them. Otherwise, even the simplest demands can easily be judged as disruptive or destructive (Johnston and Klandermans, 1995: p. 6). It is vital to utilise culture for urban movements, as conflicts within the society in post-industrial societies revolve around culture. Due to the concept of the central conflict, we now see identity conflicts instead of class conflicts in the city. Since urban movements have turned into lifestyle struggles, new urban movements that emerged in post-industrial societies do not stay away from cultural elements and develop their discourse among developing socio-economic and socio-cultural groups (Touraine, 1988: p. 141).

Instead of seizing the state within the existing culture, the new urban movements want to disturb it and influence the state with local actions. New urban movements seek to reduce the role of the state in the system that aim to develop civil society. These movements appear as more local, decentralised, and anti-bureaucratic. The new urban movements do not want to take advantage of the state. On the contrary, they often come into conflict with the state authority. Therefore, participation in urban movements itself has become a goal. Urban movements aim to establish an egalitarian community within the framework of consultation created within the movement. However, seeking consensus in the decisions taken and ignoring individual differences enables everyone to express their opinions openly and causes very different voices to be heard. This polyphony also prevents the movements from being long-term. Urban movements propose establishing an egalitarian and non-violent society that attaches importance to ecological balance. For this reason, new urban movements want a change that will shake the dominant traditional culture. Values, ideas, and culture as a type of action became both the purpose and the means of these movements. While movements want to live with their own identities in modern society, they also want to make peace with the existing culture. These discussions and interactions with culture determine the strategies necessary to accept their feelings and reasons for existence (Epstein, 1991: p. 144). When analysed in terms of methods, urban movements do not want to seize power with revolutionary and reformist practices but rather to increase the cultural impact of a civil society consisting of conscious individuals. Movements want to be involved in decision-making processes in economic, cultural, and political institutions by protest methods outside of official ways.

3   Conflict and Collective Movement

All of the movements that took place in the past are events that care about the needs of minorities or occur as a result of issues that concern minorities. Movements outside the city are self-directed, independent movements created by the vast majority within the interest of the vast majority. These closed mobilisations formed by the majority without urban mobilisations remain as a periodic reaction rather than a result. Unfortunately, every step the majority would take without being supported by expert urbanites has been ineffective throughout history (Marx and Engels, 2008: p. 16). Every change that takes place in the economic establishment sooner or later causes the transformation of the entire enormous structure. When this transformation is studied, it is necessary to distinguish between the material transformation of the economic conditions of production and the legal, political, religious, aesthetic, and social changes. While the economic variability radically changes the structure of the society, it also changes the other factors mentioned and creates a struggle within the society. This struggle deeply affects the decisions of the communities that will be in conflict (Marx and Engels, 2008: p. 18).

While a social movement suddenly takes place in cities, it is affected by the revolutionary transformation and is influenced and inspired by the slogans, names, language, spirit and participants of the movements before it. For this reason, it will not be difficult to claim that every movement is a continuation of the previous one. While the Paris movements of 1789 carried the symbols of the Roman period, the Paris movements of 1848 existed with the symbols of 1789. However, it is impossible to say that the new urban movements are entirely similar to those in the past. Although past movements influence each movement, they create their own languages, costumes, and expressions. This language created over time can forget its past reference and evolve into other states while not ignoring the references it had at the beginning (Marx, 2008: p. 19).

Actions in the city can cause anxiety and pain in society. As a result of the actions that have taken place, the concerns of the members of the society, unfortunately, dissolve the culture of solidarity. The culture of solidarity is gradually being erased because the changes in the distribution of social functions cannot meet the needs of the society or because natural talents can no longer be evaluated by the society (Durkheim, 2008: p. 22). The inequalities that arise in the distribution of functions and talents in society blunt the solidarity of the society. The principle of equality in the external conditions of conflict ensures the commitment of individuals to functions and the interdependence of functions. With the principle of equality, individuals own each function one by one according to their abilities, while each function creates harmony among each other and ensures the healthy continuation of urban services and social structure (Durkheim, 2008: p. 24).

The definition of the crowd typically refers to the gathering of individuals regardless of race, nationality, specialty, or gender, and whatever the chance, to lead to unity. Crowd inference has a different significance from a psychological point of view. The new character of the community formed by individuals that provide unity under certain conditions may be different from the owners of the formation that creates the community. The identities and personality signs of the individuals who have joined the formation for a particular purpose are erased in the actions that each individual continues in only one direction and a certain unity of thought. The ordinary mind and identity are increasingly coming to the fore, and the general identity is embraced. For this reason, individuals that came together gradually gained a better form of expression and evolved into a more organised and psychologically sensitive crowd. The crowd gained a single personality and turned into action with the law it gained with the spirit of unity (Le Bon, 2008: p. 36).

Urban movements can be defined as a joint step to establish a new orderly life. Although it is possible to take the unrest as a starting point, it derives its motivational power from the dissatisfaction with the life in the current order on the one hand and the hopes expected from the new order or life system on the other hand. The urgency of new order life can portray the career of urban movements. In the beginning, urban movements appear as shapeless, disorganised, and formless. Collective behaviours are primitive, and interaction mechanisms are done at lower levels without thinking. While urban movements are developing, they take on the character of the society from which they emerged. Urban movements are gradually improving their organisational ability, gaining shape, advancing customs and traditions, establishing leadership, and developing a new life order in terms of cultural and social organisation (Blumer, 2008: p. 64).

We can divide urban movements into general urban movements, specific urban movements, and expressive urban movements. When we mention general urban movements, we think of workers' movements, youth movements, women's movements, and peace movements. In the past, such movements brought about gradual and widespread changes in the value of society, and these changes caused cultural deviations. The cultural deviations in people's ideas, in general, led to a reconsideration of rights and privileges in society. Over time, people come to the fore with their new visions of the future, and society brings a new perspective to itself. This perspective cared about the urgency of the newly established values and increased the number of people waiting for the necessary steps to be taken for their own lives. Examples of cultural deviations may be noted as increasingly developing health activities, belief in accessible education, the importance given to children, the gains of women, and the prestige of science (Simmel, 2008: p. 31).

The spirit of unity (Esprit de corps) is crucial for urban movements. It shapes the movement by showing that they care more about group goals than individual interests by increasing the commitment of individuals to the concepts, ideas, and goals that emerge within the group. The unity's feelings and belongings to other participants are essential for mutual support. The spirit of unity enables the participants' sense of belonging to the current movement and their emotions to grow. Each individual focuses on in-motion interaction and tries to benefit from this interaction. The spirit of unity is essential not only to develop solidarity but also to bring solidarity to the movement (Blumer, 2008: p. 68).

Private urban movements can be classified into two types: reform and revolutionary movements. It seeks the effects of change in social order and existing institutions in both types. The life cycles of both types appear to be nearly similar. Nevertheless, there are specific differences between the two. The scope of their purpose is where these differences emerge. Reform movements seek change in private areas or, to a limited extent, within the existing social order, like eliminating child labour or reducing alcohol use. On the other hand, Revolutionary movements have broader goals and aim to completely change the social order (Gramsci, 2008: p. 56).

Differences in positions between reform and revolutionary movements bring together important distinctions in general procedure and tactics. While the reform movement entrepreneurs move forward by creating public opinion for the purpose they want, they continue their search by creating public opinion and creating discussion. The reform community is viewed as antagonistic by interest communities and the idle majority. Reform movements, therefore, need the support of individuals that are not different and do not belong to interest groups to convey their message. However, revolutionary movements do not primarily care about influencing public opinion but consider transforming it. Expressive urban movements, on the other hand, do not seek to change the social order, institutions, or objective characters. The inferences caused by tensions and unrest do not seek to focus on social changes and achieve the cohesiveness that movements often seek. Expressive urban movements are generally revealed as reactions observed in individuals as a result of crystallisation occurring during events and as ongoing actions following the character of the social order (Blumer, 2008: p. 71).

The wealth of mass movements characterises mass societies. Other types of societies come to the fore with different varieties of urban movements. Urban movements rising within common communities are traditional movements in character. For example, resurrection movements tend to be traditionally oriented. It shows the characteristics of the common societies where the movements have risen. Urban movements that develop within pluralistic societies are typically reformative. For example, workers' movements are reformative movements with a limited or specific scope that seek changes in working conditions. These movements want to reach their goals in the constitutional dimension by creating public opinion. There is only one kind of effective movement in totalitarian societies, which is developing in a way that supports the regime (Kornhauser, 2008: p. 77; Erdoğan, 2015: p. 21). Value-driven action is a joint venture that restores, preserves, changes or creates values in the name of generalised beliefs. Such beliefs are necessarily involved in every stage of action. Beliefs consider the revival of values, the redefinition of norms, the reorganisation of individuals' motivation, and the redefinition of situational possibilities (Smelser, 2008: p. 83).

Independent professionals such as lawyers, journalists, artists, writers, professors, physicists, and students who continue their education under their influence easily participate in protest movements and volunteer. These people that can use and create educational and economic resources in line with their intellectual and organisational skills can easily direct and manage actions due to their current economic and social status. In fragmented societies, the standing up of these few professional groups and their members may be blocked due to societal discrimination and attribution factors. If a social structure is open to opposing actions, these professional organisations and their members can easily reach political authorities and direct them as they wish due to their experience and economic power compared to ordinary people. If these professional organisations and their members are put under pressure and pushed underground, they will not be left with much choice, but it will not deter them from their actions. The rewards and expectations of the opposition then become more attractive than ever before and more attractive than any other alternative would provide. As can be understood here, oppression causes groups with voluntary and economic status to stand out rather than intimidation. In addition, such professionals and members of associations can avoid any punishment or psychological pressure more efficiently than ordinary people and limit their sphere of influence. The corporate identity and sizeable organisational structure of professional organisations give their members many powers as well as powers that they do not have when they act on their own. For this reason, the risk and reward ratio works differently for such professional organisations and their members due to the opportunities that ordinary people do not have. Members of the profession voluntarily face and cope with difficulties that many ordinary people cannot tolerate. Due to the advantages of an organised structure and the personality characteristics of the members, the course of actions and risk-reward analysis change (Oberschall, 2008: p. 103).

Some emphases are central to the perspectives from which it develops. Studies on collecting resources (material and labour) are essential for understanding urban movement activities. This is because resources are essential for engagement in social conflict. Resources have to be collected for common purposes. The collection of resources entails some minimal form of organisational structure. Therefore, overtly and implicitly, our work will be more directed toward urban movement organisations than works directly from the traditional perspective. Apart from the unity offered by urban movements, the importance and recognition of the involvement of individuals and organisations help to make calculations about the success or failure of the movements. Obviously, the supply and demand model can sometimes be applied to the process of flow of resources around and outside of specific urban movements. Within the urban movement activities, individual and organisational attachments are of great importance in terms of cost and reward. As a cost and reward centre, it is affected by the structure of the society and the authorities' activities (McCarthy and Zald, 2008: p. 107).

The new perspectives emphasise the ongoing movement and institutionalised actions, the rationality of movement actors, the strategic problems movements face, and the role of movements as agencies for social change. Specifically, these new analyses make the following discussions: the rationality of the movement's actions, whether the different lines of the actions can respond to the cost and reward model, what are the main goals of the movements defined by the conflicts of interests built into institutionalised power relations, and whether the success of the movements is achieved by the collective decision-making of strategic factors and networked political processes (Jenkins, 2008: p. 118).

Social ties are crucial to collective action. It is accepted that people participating in urban movement organisations are employed from previous social ties. Mobilisation occurs when members of the beneficiary population are associated with social ties; otherwise, it does not occur when social ties do not coincide with the interests of the beneficiaries. While the questions that come to mind are which social ties are essential for joint action, what kind of social ties are relevant to the subject, and whether social ties bring more people together or mobilise at less cost, they also reveal why social ties are essential for urban movements (Marwell and Oliver, 2008: p. 133).

4   Political Transition for Transformation

> The 'people' who exercise the power are not always the same people with those over whom it is exercised; and the "self-government" spoken of is not the government of each by himself, but of each by all the rest. The will of the people, moreover, practically means the will of the most numerous or the most active part of the people; the majority, or those who succeed in making themselves accepted as the majority. The people, consequently, may desire to oppress a part of their number; and precautions are as much needed against this as against any other abuse of power.
>
> MILL, 2014: p. 15

The limitation, therefore, of the power of government over individuals loses none of its importance when the holders of power are regularly accountable to the community, that is, to the strongest party therein.

> This view of things, recommending itself equally to the intelligence of thinkers and to the inclination of those important classes in European society to whose real or supposed interests democracy is adverse, has had no difficulty in establishing itself; and in political speculations 'the tyranny of the majority' is now generally included among the evils against which society requires to be on its guard.
>
> MILL, 2014: p. 15

The state has been a subject of the opinion of thinkers since ancient times and has become a symbol in which the views of the notables about the need for their existence in the life of the society are put forward. The state should know the needs of the society that created it, be able to meet them, and arrange measures for its future needs. The state should guide the person that takes over the power for the well-being of every living person, that is, every citizen, and preserve the common good (Plato, 2017: p. 29). Happiness depends on the activities in the cities, and the link between the cities depends on the policies of the states. Farabi expresses the relationship between happiness and the city as follows:

> The highest good and the greatest perfection can only be attained in the city, and not in a community that is less than the city. However, since good, in the real sense, has a feature that can be obtained by choice and will, and evils are only the products of choice and will, it is possible to establish the city as an entity where people help each other to achieve some evil goals. Therefore, it may not be possible to achieve happiness in every city. A city, then, in which people aim to help each other in those things through which genuine happiness is achieved, is a virtuous, perfect city (madına fadıla). A society whose people help each other achieve happiness is a virtuous, perfect society. A nation where all their cities help each other with the things that bring happiness is a virtuous, perfect nation. Likewise, a virtuous, perfect universal society only emerges when all the nations it includes help each other to achieve happiness.
>
> Farabi, 2017: p. 98

Therefore, caring about the citizens' happiness is the primary duty of the citizens. It is the state that mediates this task. "The sultanate continues with blasphemy, but it does not stand out with cruelty and brutality" (Nizamül'l-mülk, 2017: p. 15). In other words, the state that will prevent society's happiness and limit society's reaction to help each other is decaying and disappearing. A contract is therefore needed to ensure the relationship between the happiness of society and the state.

> Find a form of association that will bring the whole common force to bear on defending and protecting each associate's person and goods, doing this in such a way that each of them, while uniting himself with all, still obeys only himself and remains as free as before. In short, the person who attaches himself to the society will not be tied to anyone, and since no member over himself does get the same rights that he gives to others,

everyone gains precisely what he has lost and more power to protect what he owns. When this crowd of people is thus united as a whole, whoever attacks one of the members attacks the whole, and whoever attacks the whole attacks the members. Thus, their duties and interests force the contracting parties to help each other mutually, and the same people should try to combine all the interests of these two relations according to this relationship.

ROUSSEAU, 2017: p. 14

The state is the fundamental element that will keep this contract owned by the society an everlasting one. Therefore, it is necessary to organise joint actions and subsequent demands for society's benefit; society assumes ownership of this need and the state undertakes the implementation.

People cannot easily act together. People petition, assemble, go on strike, march, occupy facilities, stop traffic, set fires, and attack others to the point of harm. These movements stem from cultural elements and social contact rather than religious rituals, civic celebrations, or ongoing politics. The meeting of learned conflict is part of the public culture of society. Urban movements are the vault of the experiences of certain routines in the history of society. These experiences help weak and disorganised movements overcome the deficiencies in resources and communication (Tarrow, 2008: p. 146).

Far from gaining support for their policies, states are an often-framed issue that competes with the meanings placed in the public sphere by movements. Movements that gain meaning through struggles can be forced to endure disadvantages brought about by the competition with the state in situations in which they often get involved. This is because states not only manage the control of oppression, but they also try to destroy the importance of instruments for meaning construction. For this reason, the struggle between states and movements does not only take place in the streets but also continues to compete over meaning (Melucci, 1996: p. 147).

Continuing policies are produced when the political opportunities are broad, the potential for unity is demonstrated, and the vulnerability of dissidents is taken into account. Urban movements crystallise when debates become intertwined with social connections and unifying structures, in the production of collective action discourse, and when supportive identities gain the ability to sustain discussions with solid opponents. Urban movements become the focal point during the transformation of external opportunities within resources. Discussions, social connections, and cultural discourse are all the more important when the cost of bringing people together in collective action comes down, and the crowds more widely accept the meaning of claims and they realise that one is not alone. If these three factors come together, the historical position of urban movements becomes central and affects the dynamic processes of political and social changes (Tarrow, 2008: p. 148).

When we begin to analyse urban movements, we encounter more complex and tamer connections of politics rather than the single environment created by social actors and their opponents. It is a cycle of challenges, movements, alliances, and hostilities in the size and creation of political opportunities when debates begin. In this respect, movements cause the criticism and re-creation of policies in waves and cause social changes to be the subject of struggles for power at the national level. The structure of reformed local governments and the gradual transfer of policies to municipal institutions increases and reduces opportunities for minority and marginalised groups. Minorities to gain representation gets complicated in terms of experience, and they also live far from an effective administration in achieving a place in the system. Reform administrations take steps to facilitate the lives of minorities and marginalised people against the difficulties encountered (Eisinger, 2008: p. 158).

Protests are destructive acts resulting from the rise of collective manifestos. It is the political process that powerless people use to voice their own needs as leverage. Protests are collective actions and mean that people with concern speak out according to their capacity to represent the issues they need. The sudden power created by the crowds that take action with the gathering of the driving forces turns into protests due to the growth in needs, the rise of complaints, and the increase of troubles. It is observed that mass movements are not competent in resource use. The fact that the protests are usually sudden and lack order also limits their sphere of influence. Protests appear as an opportunity for the leaders of the movements to express the needs of people who have not found a place in the political system. An action that will reduce costs in expressing the desired demands, protest is more common in environments where resources are insufficient and representation is impossible. Political protests need to be distinguished from acts of violence. Violence is a state of atrocity that occurs as a result of the reflection of the psychological state of individuals to the masses rather than expressing the needs of the people. Political protests are situations where groups in a problematic state complain about the position they have been struggling with up to that point, the rights they could not gain or have not achieved, or the fact that a particular segment of the society continues to live in a privileged position. The only method that minority communities, alienated groups, and marginalised identities resort to for meeting their legal rights and needs in society is to protest. Groups whose ability to create resources is limited due to their situation are also excluded from the system in terms of representation.

The masses that cannot defend their own rights get agitated and resort to protests to raise their voices. Rights that cannot be won or obtained but not implemented cause resentment in individuals, leading them to evaluate radical choices while expressing their complaints. Expressing fears but not being able to respond leads to the disappointment of the masses. In this case, according to the psychological state of the people participating in the protest and the treatment of the forces on the opposite side ready to intervene, the level of anger of the crowds changes, and violence occurs. Protests grow due to the inability to find a response point in the face of increasing complaints in the system, the closed application routes, and the insufficient opportunities in the city. The increase in complaints in cities compared to rural areas is actually since the identities, habits, and lifestyles that emerge in the city are different from those in rural areas. The increasing needs in the city and the social, economic, and cultural differences between the segments also affect the decision-making processes of the steps to be taken in the city. For this reason, the complaints of those who cannot be involved in the decision-making processes are ignored while growing the problems of those deprived of the city's opportunities. Protests are increasing to meet their need to be included in decision-making processes (Kriesi and Wisler, 2008: p. 165).

Urbanites experience deprivation and oppression with precise adjustments, which does not happen at the end of an abstract and extensive production. This experience also plays a vital role in shaping the discontent of the citizens, which comes to the fore with concrete complaints about specific targets. When we observe the daily experiences of the citizens, it is manifested that the factors that shape their complaints lie in their measurable demands and directing their anger towards particular targets. The institutional template puts mass actions on the agenda by shaping the collective activities that fuel protests. Institutional life brings people together, shapes group identity, and helps urbanites organise the arrangements that cause collective activities to explode. In a factory, men and women come together, receive training, gain experience, and live in a shared activity. Again, employees and managers are united under a common purpose and identity, even though they are in different positions. Institutional roles are essential in defensive decision-making of strategic opportunities, and resistance turns into daily protests against rules and authority. Primarily the actions organised by the employees are the most effective resistance. The reason for this is that these activities result not only in stopping the means of production but also in the occupation of the streets. However, the actions of the unemployed do not go beyond the occupation of the streets by the crowds filling certain areas (Piven and Cloward, 2008: p. 175).

It should be noted that the probability of success of the revolting crowds increasingly depends on the nature of political opportunities. Two main facilitating effects can be distinguished. The reduction in power disparity between the rioting crowds and their opponents helps improve the chances of urban protests succeeding. Neither does the efficiency of extensive urban processes serve the foundational structure of the entire political system, nor simply that an increase in the strategic position of the single challenger changes the result, which appears as a rise in the political leverage exercised by the insurgent crowd. The practical effect of this development leads to an increase in the probability that rebel crowds will dominate confrontation with groups opposing them in terms of interests and goals. Nonetheless, this possibility of encounter will not be valid for every conflict the rebellious crowds face. Even in the context of the advanced bargaining position, the revolting crowds are at a definite disadvantage in the confrontation process with the political members of the establishment. In summary, this means: The increasing political power of the aggrieved population advances the bargaining processes of the rebelling crowds and nevertheless creates new opportunities for the joint pursuit of the common goals of the crowd (McAdam, 2008: p. 180).

We need to make a distinction. When we observe the general phenomenon, we try to explain the actions of organised, sustainable, and rational challenges against existing authority. This challenge is faced by state administrators and authority owners of a wide variety up to prominent society leaders. When considering urban movements, generally, national administrators are faced with a challenge. When such urban movements are considered, the development of nationally elected policies and the proliferation of established associations that can be regarded as tools for joint action has increased national urban movements. Urban movements, which came to be a model with the accumulation of movements that had occurred before, caused the actions to be shaped at all levels and turned into a real challenge to the leading leaders of the society instead of the leaders of the national administration. Urban movements vary in their character structure and history, and their activity schemes and structures change according to the authority they challenge. By the 19th century, national urban movements had crystallised and were rising; however, urban movements were becoming more and more similar (Tilly, 2008: p. 186).

Western democracies are becoming more and more active societies day by day. Urban movements have become routine and institutionalised in these communities. The right to petition that became evident with the rights to demonstration and referendum has led these communities to lead to urban movements over time possibly. Moreover, movements have become a core part of ordinary politics. However, urban movements are not a forum or a method for political expression, or manifestation, as it is thought, but rather an activity between ordinary sessions, parties, legislative works, and elections. In fact, urban movements constitute a part of the social structure and environment that shapes the sessions, legislation, elections, and parties, which are instrumental in gaining importance in some way. It has often been shaped by protests and traditional political actions, not only in individuals but also in organisations. Urban movement organisations sometimes act as protest groups and even organise protest actions. At other times, urban movements seek an occasional exchange of information while also providing recommendations and advice to incumbent authorities and carrying out their ordinary lobbying activities. From time to time, urban movements are organised like political parties and seek votes for some political leaders (Goldstone, 2003, p. 2).

Urban movement actors and actions intersecting, penetrating, and intertwining with traditional political participation and political parties are not a new development nor a practice seen only in Western democracies. The main labour movements that began in the 19th century in Europe indiscriminately organised activities by arranging protests and building labour parties, finding votes and electoral representatives for them (Abendroth, 1992). In the United States, in the 1930s, the Roosevelt welfare program developed as the Democratic Party split with the worker-centred and reformist urban movements that would spearhead protests and traditional political mobilisation, jointly with the labour movements' legacy of long-standing participation permeated Democratic Party politics. To give an extreme example, Nazism also started as an urban movement but continued as a political party (Goldstone, 2003: p. 5).

Social protests and ordinary political participation are complementary in many ways. Organised politics is, for many ordinary people, a highly discontinuous process focused on electoral periods. However, protests and association actions are organised more frequently, going beyond seasons and years. While most traditional political participation only allows for choices to be made equitably, it can turn into an activity where different positions can be held, such as standing out as the opposite of a candidate or party. Protests and association activities, on the other hand, can address more specific issues, and they can influence party behaviour by placing greater emphasis on actions. In fact, the protests also enable political parties to look at the highlighted issues more urgently and with greater emphasis. Short protests and urban movements draw attention to current situations and problems so that ordinary voting behaviour and political party participation are difficult to focus on (Goldstone, 2003: p. 8).

Those who describe struggles for democracy as urban movements often question what factors influence anti-regime mobilisations, such as potential unions, paradigm-shifting policies, and changes in the gravity or probability of repression. The level of mobilisation does not actually tell us much about the process of regime disintegration carried out by the protests. This is essentially an event related to the stages of transition to democracy. It is necessary to analyse the conditions under which the protests bring the regime together with the overwhelming opposition. We see that democracy-based movements emerge in cities with two different action styles. The first is state subversive actions that equip themselves with violent struggles. The second is the urban movements that want reform, which usually come to the fore with events that stay away from acts of violence (Meyer et al., 2002: pp. 28–9).

5   Globalising Movements in the Age of Urbanisation

In the last twenty years, conflicts seen before in western societies have increased rapidly. In many aspects, the reason for these conflicts is the disruptions in socio-economic sharing by deviating from the welfare state line. These new conflicts then appear outside the realms necessary for the reproduction of economic output. It is observed that political parties or organisations do not channel them. And after that, it cannot reach its target in the form of compensations that mitigate the effects of the actions to make it suitable for the system. Now, new conflicts are found in areas where cultural reproduction is realised, and social integration and socialisation occur. While the parties to these new conflicts continue their actions with the activities of an institutional but deep wave, the parliament is protesting in excess forms. The parties to these conflicts identify the relevant gaps by addressing the commodification of the means of communication necessary for action. However, necessary steps cannot be taken to close the gaps identified due to the money and media of power, and measures cannot be strengthened. The primary and robust side of the origin of conflicts is the lifestyle. While the inconsistency and injustice observed in distribution and sharing maintain their importance, the main starting points of new conflicts are the lack of respect and tolerance for lifestyles. In short, it is observed that the problems that cause new conflicts to shine are not due to sharing but to the dissatisfaction with different living spaces (Habermas, 2008: p. 201).

When the studies done by the humanities are examined, it is found that the majority of the publications produced emphasise new concerns and new movements as simply disconnected and discontinuous actions. In these studies, new urban movements were named new protest movements, new politics, new populism, new romanticism, anti-politics, unconventional political behaviour, and irregular politics. Else, they described the conflicts of the movements that came to the fore with the new paradigm as unusual. In the meantime, the citizens who participate in the movements that have emerged in a new style with new concerns call the movements they contribute to new policies or alternative movements. The participants observe these definitions as positive and equal content, and depending on the situation, the definitions are replaced by expressions such as anti-economic, anti-institutionalisation, and anti-public. However, these movements and protests are the product of a universal action coding that classical liberal theories cannot easily explain, and it is observed that they are not in the form of a dual fiction. According to classical liberal theories, every action is divided into two separate classifications as private and public. However, new urban movements are deployed in a place that oscillates between these two headings (Kriesi, 2002: p. 158; Offe, 2008: p. 208).

When we analyse the new urban movements, we see that the most destructive aspect is that the codes of self-recognition and identification of the people participating in the protests are not based on right or left political views or distinctions such as working-class/middle class, poor/rich and urban/peasant, as in the past. The codes of universal political conflicts are now coded by factors such as gender, age, locality, residence, environmental problems, and passive stance, unlike in the past. Whatever it is, the elements observed in the old social movements are not given much attention in the new movements. They become distinct in the form of appearing in numerous forms due to broadening by disintegrating, just like differences occurring in the city becoming differentiated. And in this respect, these movements are called urban movements, and they are constantly improving themselves in terms of innovation. Although its social basis is a matter of concern, new urban movements involve three different segments of the social structure. These are; the new middle class working in the service sector and public institutions, the old middle class, and citizens that do not fall into the scope of the working class, such as the unemployed, students, housewives, and retired persons (Hamel et al., 2000: p. 196; Offe, 2008: p. 211).

Although urban movements are less socio-political, they become more socio-cultural with increasing speed. While the distance between civil society and the state is growing, the distinction between private and public life is disappearing. The continuity from urban movements to political parties is disappearing; political life is becoming a depressed area between the state, which is strengthened by the changing international conditions, and socio-cultural movements. The main risk at this stage is that, in the past, political parties connected and balanced the movements, but now the movements are left alone with the state on a global scale. In this case, urban movements can easily split into branches when public life is dominated by post-state or anti-state views, and they can be forced to seek their identity or defend minorities. Environmental demonstrations spread from Germany to the United States are an excellent example of this statement. Accompanied by these pioneering historical movements, new urban movements can finally achieve a high capacity for political action, as in the case of the Greens. However, there may also be a different evolution. This is because anti-state actions can be sharper and more concrete than socio-cultural urban movements. Weak unions, short-term strikes, and violent riots mean that the actions in the grievances of workers and the confusing mix that occurs in industrial and pre-industrial cities witness the defiance of some groups living in the city against the city government or the central government, that is, the power (Touraine, 2008: p. 215).

While drawing attention to the forms of actions related to individual identities and daily life, it marks a boundary between the actions of today's movements and political activities, unlike the traditional one. Urban movements now increasingly distance themselves from the political system. Today, when individual needs increase, and the pressure of the political innovation network is formed, movements choose the middle path, that is, the customs and place themselves in the middle of social life. While political parties see the necessity of resorting to innovations to increase their existence and influence, they ignore individual needs and move their roots away from the socio-cultural basis. Due to the crystally clear nature of urban movements, social conflicts can become fruitful and effective only if they remember the mediating role of political actors. Considering this repulsive and triggering role of urban movements, it is observed that the political system can only change through institutions. However, the ability of the actions in which the typical demands are expressed depends on whether the political actors are explanatory by making the necessary transformation to democratically guarantee the demanded wishes and expanding the solutions to the said needs (Melucci, 2008: p. 219).

So, where do we put today's movements? Through the growing mix of economic structures, complex communities witness the production of political arrangements and cultural agencies. Products are produced by information systems and global symbolic large organisations. Scientific cooperation and certain symbols are used to produce and distribute the material. The conflict, therefore, shifts from the industrial economic system to cultural aspects. Transactions and actions now extend to personal identities, the life of time and space, and the motivation and codes of everyday behaviour. Today's conflicts reveal that the actions of leading actors and forms in this process are different from the conflicts of the traditional industrial age or groups in conflict. It is observed that new production and reinterpretation of meanings are at the core of today's conflicts. This understanding requires explaining why urban movements need to be redefined, and their appearances changed (Mueller, 2008: p. 226).

The most significant key aspect of the new urban movements' practices is that it increasingly emphasises their autonomy. The relationship of traditional actions in the past, which was considered in the political arena, that is, in the eyes of political parties and the state, was more dependent and related. Although this state of autonomy is exaggerated, especially among the romantic thoughts of today's thinkers, it is in a development phase that has solid roots but is constantly changing by renewing itself naturally. Another key is the role of cultural elements in the constitution and actions of movements. The cultural form is essential for describing and understanding new movements when considering the analysis of economic and political forms. The cultural weight causes the diversification of the participants and the differentiation of the demands at an increasing rate. As a result, it causes movements to move away from the events in the memories in terms of formation, development, and conclusion. Nevertheless, movements are still economic and political struggles, but their cultural aspects are gaining more and more weight (Escobar and Alvarez, 2008: p. 240).

When the participation in the movements is analysed, the form of the actions is discussed in a wide range from complaints to sabotage. In addition, when we examine the participation, the belonging that seems part-time can be one-time from time to time. However, the number of participants who devoted themselves to the movements is not at all insignificant. The perception of cost and gain varies according to different actions. When this perception is considered, and when individual participation is analysed, the selective perception appears and varies from individual to individual. In addition, the change in perception seems to differ regionally. In fact, the change in perception differs even while the movement continues, which is a crucial element in mobilisation declarations. When we look at the rational choice discourse, it should not be understood that the idea that feelings, emotions, and contemplation are unimportant. As a matter of fact, the number of participants that emotionality and feelings add to the actions increases exponentially and strengthens the belonging and loyalty of the people who take action. When emotions come into play, reasoning changes, and expectations transform increasingly. Faith, on the other hand, emerges as a separate element. When we analyse today's movements, the necessity of being sensitive about the lack of belief comes to the fore, while the presence of belief for the unity and continuity of the movement is essential. In fact, the common goal of urban movements is the common good. Reaching and achieving the common good may not always be possible with a spirit of unity that will be formed with the contemplation and imagination of individual participation. This is because the involvement of more rational potential participants in the process seems possible if it is not selective and encouraging. Encouragement of rational participants to actions depends on their directing and referring them to more specific goals (Klandermans, 2008: p. 249: Beinin and Vairel, 2011: p. 144).

Volunteering in urban movements can be defined by the functions of the perceived charm or repulsion of the results expected from participation. The function of volunteering in participation in actions can be addressed in two aspects considering this. First, expectations of participation in action help produce the common good and the value of the common good. Second, expectations of participation in action generate the value of choice cost and benefit analysis as well as cost and benefit analysis. Compensation for social motivation can be achieved when these expectations, distinguished from important reactions, are selected. Expectations are rewards for motivation, while most are included in the cost and benefit analysis, most of which are not social. The combination of expectations and values produces specific results in multiplicative ways. These are; if valued social change is not believed, or if the change is not valued but helpful, the value of the common good is nullified. The second result is that the negative evaluation of the changes or the increase in the belief in the retention of the valorisation of the social change causes the value of the common good to be negatively valued (Snow, 2008: p. 250).

Cognitive approaches are rooted in rediscovery, and their informal form within urban movements has embodied initiatives for opinion generation. We can easily say that urban movements are the whole of actions that have occurred due to the combination of cognitive praxis and have been changed by clustering in their historical process. The current forms of opinion types of urban movements vary from movement to movement. While environmental movements are shaped by nature and technical issues, they appear as a set of actions consisting of theoretical knowledge, including ecology and technology; actions that arise as a result of the interest in civil rights, religious and moral issues are associated with more social and human activities (Eyerman and Jamison, 2008: p. 272).

When the urban movements and social movements are analysed, we observe the emergence of three different elements. The first of these elements is the nature of coercion and political opportunities confronting movements. The second is the form of activities available to the rebels. The last one is the collective processes of social construction, quality, expression and interpretation that ensure the harmony of opportunity and action. These three elements can be expressed in summary as the design of political opportunities, mobilisation structure, and discourse process (McAdam et al., 2008: p. 279).

Movements undoubtedly produce emotions, but they are not a set of actions that revolve around emotional ideals and whose members succeed in this way. Emotions are used to encourage, awaken, revive members, secure their belonging, protect shared meanings, and free the selective motivation of the participants. The high points of the emotions become more or less sacred, and the emotionality engaged with the movement is formed around the movement's leaders. The intensity of the emotions and their bonding with the participants create excitement in keeping the mission of each participant alive. It is a fact that emotions are essential for increasing individual participation. Increasing crowds with high individual participation mean that the attention of the media and relevant institutions is drawn to the action. However, the confrontational climate of dense crowds acting with emotions can reach more dangerous dimensions (Calhoun, 2008: p. 295).

There is a remarkable fact that researchers of humanities and social sciences have discovered in recent years. If there is isolation, non-governmental organisations, multinational organisations, and widespread urban movements reach the same point, and convergence is observed. They start to behave like NGOs in a sense. In fact, there is an international connection between these institutions and activities, and the movements have turned into a multinational activist network. This network mentioned here has spread to almost all areas. This network is about almost all social areas, from human equality, welfare, health, environment, human rights, right to housing, gender, and residents' rights. While urban movements occur at local and regional scales, some of them turn into activities that impact on a global scale. With high finishes, movements created by massive, well-funded and renowned networks can turn into mega-movements. However, less processed, small-scale, fluid, restricted, and visible actions are limited to local or regional activities (Wiarda, 2003: p. 41; Appadurai, 2008: p. 303).

Modern urban movements began to develop with the creation of nation-states, and nation-states have been the target of movements for quite some time. Although urban movements see and demand direct democracy as a driving force, institutions and actors of representative democracy have been instrumental in structuring the political opportunities of the movements and hindered the main goal by putting limits on institutional policies. When we analyse representative democracies and their actors, it should not go unnoticed that it is the most democratic end achieved since the establishment of

nation-states. Representative institutions are directly linked to the formation of shared identities. However, with the new millennium, nation-states
are faced with a series of challenges. These are current acts of terrorism, the
majority of the world being away from the pluralistic and secular rule, opposition to and dissatisfaction with traditional forms of politics, disillusionment
with the active state, the contribution to international activities and globalisation, and a growing sense of world citizenship but not realised power ownership occurring at the same rate. Even though nation-states have been losing
power since the 1960s, social, cultural, and geopolitical changes are effective
in urban movements' institutional and cultural transformation. Being named
with a political power centre structure has started to be described with a much
more pluralistic structure, and some denominations have emerged. Examples
of this are multi-level governance, world government, and global civil society.
At the same time, the balance of power is shifting from parliaments to executive authorities. Power shifted to parties that gathered for particular purposes
and gained the dominance of certain sections rather than mass parties. While
politics and administration are gaining importance locally and nationally, centres of power and influence have expanded to more international institutions
and organisations. While international organisations are signing policies at a
level that will affect the policies of nation-states, it is observed that there are
administrations that put their own will into action on a local scale (della Porta
and Tarrow, 2008: p. 339).

It is possible to see a multinational urban movement style within a multinational administrative structure. Despite all its successes and failures, the
multinational joint action, albeit temporarily, enables the parties to work
together and causes the development of a multinational activity structure and
identity discourse. Although it starts to boil into a multinational structure, the
main target of the actions is at the national level, and the organisation expands
within national borders. However, it should be taken for granted that the
actions are becoming more and more international. In addition, in order for
urban movements to be successful on a national scale, it is observed that the
discourse and activity structure produced should increasingly be suitable for
development on a global scale. This type of action leads to the acquaintance
of the activists with fellow organisations operating in different world regions,
the development of the organisational network, the establishment of the coordination of action, and the construction of global discourse and programme
(Smith, 1999: p. 346).

Mobilised movements for global equity are made possible by growing
activity within civil society. This mobilisation is possible due to the intensification of the exploding contact network on a global scale. Such movements

depend on mobilisations resulting from the joint action and communication of thousands of local, regional, national, and international groups. The number of groups whose memberships were from three different countries increased from 178 in 1909 to 4,620 in 1991. When the internationally active movements are analysed, we observe that their growth between 1970 and 1990 is one hundred per cent, while the growth between 1993 and 2000 is fifty per cent. This growth in the activities of international movements depends on the geographical expansion of the movements. When we look at the headquarters of such activities, it is observed that they are generally located in developed countries. The centres of movements are clustered in key and brand cities, such as New York, London, and Paris. Geographically, movements are generally centred and focused on the world's northern hemisphere. When analysed, we observe that the movement activities that emerged in the world's northern hemisphere between 1973 and 2000 increased from 13 per cent to 20 per cent (Montogna, 2008: p. 350: Schaeffer, 2014: 188).

Globalisation as a process ultimately affects social relations. This process is not only economic in nature but also social, cultural, and technological. Globalisation is becoming an interaction in which the northern and southern hemispheres are reluctantly involved, implying a wider circulation of capital and goods. Sociologists see globalisation as experiences of physical space that are composed of the separation of space and time and the interpretation of fundamental change. Globalisation transcends geographical distances and forces people to a specific and concrete way of life, making them swimmers of a voluntary or involuntary current. Globalisation means remote action. It is a result of the war of independence of space. Globalisation separates political and economic decision centres and allows individuals to go beyond territorial borders (Giddens, 1990: p. 352; Robertson, 1992: 103: Moghadam, 2009: p. 126).

6   Reasons behind the Emerging Urban Movements

Throughout history, people have been deploring the issues they did not like or with which they are dissatisfied. Sometimes they stop lamenting and unite with people like them and do more for change. More than ever before in our age, human beings are organised to follow the dazzling pomp of goals. We live together with strikes, or workers' movements, which also have political goals, demanding higher wages or recognition of the union or unity. In the 19th century, the 'Luddites' took action by destroying the machinery that reduced the number of workers in English factories. In addition, many revolutions took place in France, Russia, China, Cuba, Iran, and many other places.

While women's movements want to change family life, they demand the right to increase women's economic opportunities. We are passing through a period in which actions specialised in environmental issues have increased, and the number of meetings sensitive to animal rights has grown. At the same time, there is a considerable increase in the number of conservative actions and meetings. Just like the anti-immigrant movements observed in the United States since 1840, the reaction to bus transport operated by the federal governments that erupted in 1970, and the anti-abortion movements. While some of these movements sought the opportunity to assert new rights, others were born to stand in the face of an emerging tide of oppression. While some were after political and economic gains, others sought cultural and identity changes created by their living conditions and preferences. While some of them continue their lives under an organised activity, some are born in disorganised informal networks, and others occur due to instant developments such as rebellion.

Movements are regularly the result of choosing whether to be violent, legal or illegal, confusion or persuasion, extremism or tolerance, and reform or revolution. Urban movements, then, are conscious, unanimously decided, trans-institutional protests of sustainable efforts created by ordinary people to change certain aspects of society (Goodwin and Jasper, 2015: p. 3). When we analyse urban movements, we observe that significant changes have occurred over the years. In the 19th century, crowds attracted all the attention across Europe for the achievements of better working conditions, the right to vote, and other rights. Unfortunately, many people from all walks of life, even university lecturers, preferred to stay away from these events. Crowds reminded people that they have the right to do what they want to do and not do what they do not want to do. However, the idea that crowds were turning into unthinking automatons that do not think began to take hold. The work of researchers took a wrong turn, especially in the 1950s, when it was observed how the crowds could be organised for evil purposes with the effect of Nazism on people. Although more than a century has passed, the academy has begun to fear political actions that appear outside of institutionalised channels. However, after the 1960s, with this approach, demands of people belonging to the deprived segment of the society for more freedoms and progression caused the upper segments to react, which led to the development of sympathy for those. The civil rights movement can be seen as the main reason for this change. With this movement, the United States became aware of the oppression of people with coloured skin in the southern parts and confronted the past and the future. However, the hate speech in the protests drew more attention from the academy and society to the hate-related cases of the movements. Nevertheless, this movement and these years were turning points for urban movement actions (Goodwin and Jasper, 2015: p. 5).

In the late 1980s, another aspect of urban movements began to emerge, that is, the cultural aspect. Even though the economic and political administrations were the main topics of the protests, after these years, the activists started to attract new participants by creating symbols, turning people with complaints into activists, and establishing a culture of solidarity among the participants. Two cultural titles of the movements began to gain importance over the others. The first is the discourse, which brings together larger groups of people and persuades potential participants, and of course, puts feelings at the forefront. The other is the common identity, which is the necessity of being one body of solidarity, which reveals the importance of acting together and tells how disastrous the disintegration actually is. Many people involved in urban movements only with their current characteristics under the headings of discourse and common identity suddenly started to participate in the actions organised by militant behaviour and took part in the organisation. Shared identity and common discourse suddenly became one of the main goals of the movements and helped to result in an overwhelming number of crowds appearing in the city squares. The civil rights movement in the United States is an example of movements revived due to this cultural development. Discourse and common identity helped suffering citizens in the southern states organise among themselves and have a nationwide network of activities (Goodwin and Jasper, 2015: p. 6).

When we focus on the 21st century, we observe many movement actions. One of them is the Occupy Wall Street movement. Occupy Wall Street started with 2000 attendees on 17 September 2011 in Zuccotti Park, a private property located in Manhattan. The action, which did not attract much attention initially, started to set the agenda on a world scale within a week after it was covered in the media. Since the act of occupation was very pleasing, the action began to be observed in many places within the borders of the United States, of course, as in the rest of the world. By the middle of October, the demonstrations had spread to 951 cities in 82 countries worldwide. The occupation phenomenon had occupied both the media and the public for the next two months when the intervention of the New York Police Department on 15 November and the removal of the activists from the park caused a change in the news. Perhaps the invasion phenomenon was removed from the park and the borders where it was born, but the phenomenon continued its adventure in other areas. The long-term effects of this action are unknown, but it is certain that it occupied the news in a short time and changed the course of economic and political issues. And its place in the lives of its participants is definitely permanent (Milkman et al., 2015: p. 30). Occupy Wall Street is not an instant action not seen anywhere. It is a carefully planned action by a group of experienced political activists inspired by the protests and Arab Spring actions in 2011. Started in New York and lasted about two months, this action reflects three different titles. First, although veteran activists took on the instrumental planning and appeared to be around, they could attract countless novice participants who had not previously participated in political protests and demonstrations. Although these novice participants were deeply politicised, they gradually began to participate in political activism and participated in similar actions. Second, the phenomenon of occupation has moved to the centre of United States politics. It has placed growing economic inequality at the centre of public attention, highlighting those who benefit from and create inequality, suggesting that the 1% elite rich own the gains of the 99% of the population.

With the phenomenon of occupation, social class has become the central focus of political considerations. The third point is that the Occupy Wall Street communication network survived the eviction and existed in very different environments. Participants in the network continued their activist qualities by participating in many workers and community actions organised in New York. They also kept the phenomenon of occupation alive in many parts of the country and the world. When we observe the members of this network, it is possible to get some information about the participants. Although the number of participants with advanced education was relatively high, the ethnic and class differences among Occupy Wall Street participants were not that much. When we look at the economic conditions of the activists participating in the Occupy Wall Street protest, most of them were unemployed, had just lost their jobs or were under heavy credit burden. Moreover, it is observed that their age is under 30. Many Occupy Wall Street participants and supporters believe that traditional political methods fail to achieve expected social changes. This belief still held its place under the administration of Barack Obama, who came to power with cries of change. However, despite everything, Occupy Wall Street participants and supporters did not give up taking part in traditional political methods and continued their civic engagements.

The occupation of Zuccotti Park was the historical beginning of urban movements for a period, and the participants developed and expanded this action. Occupy Wall Street participants and supporters saw themselves as global parts of urban movements such as the Arab Spring and believed they had fulfilled their mission in the United States. The Occupy Wall Street action is a non-violent movement. This is due to the pragmatic nature of the participants rather than an ideal and principle. Occupy Wall Street was born as a non-hierarchical horizontal-shaped organisation. This is because the occupation phenomenon is individually conscious and politically pointing. Occupy Wall

Street actually succeeded in capturing many groups and individuals not associated with the essence of the action. The key point in gaining the support of
these irrelevant people is the rhetoric of "we are one and whole as the 99%", as
emphasised by the action. Occupy Wall Street has succeeded in transforming
national debates by making economic inequality the number one agenda in
the country. Occupy Wall Street participants and supporters often appear as
politically experienced activists. However, young participants are people with
a limited background who have not previously participated in protest movements. However, these participants have started to turn to political events
thanks to the experience and gains and have begun to work for social change
by committing (Milkman et al., 2015: p. 31).

One of the most critical problems facing urban movements is recruiting
activists and supporters. Of course, getting and keeping the pledges of the
won activists and supporters is another matter. Confronting these challenges
is crucial because it takes a long time for a movement to achieve the changes it
wants, sometimes costing decades. For a movement to be effective, it must at
least make up for the number of participants it lost. If the number of participants gained decreases and an activist to replace the lost number is not found,
the movement declines and often disappears. The fact that the people participating in the demonstration take part in the activities, join in the demonstrations, and carry out the demonstrations are usually different from the primary
reason that causes them to participate in the said demonstration. In general,
movements welcome new participation and aim to develop their activities.
Urban movement and movement organisations can either proceed with their
actions to receive the support of participants, or they may not proceed at all.
The main questions to be asked are why the reasons for participation of the
participants changed during the movement process, why they even participated in the first place, why some participants gave up their participation over
time, and the differences in the number of participants that took place during
the participation (Goodwin and Jasper, 2015: p. 101).

Potential participant gains do not actually occur until ideological com-
mitments to protest movements are fulfilled, and group causes are formed.
In addition, participants also need to believe that expected changes can only
happen through political action beyond the institution. Consciousness-raising
can be realised by strengthening the beliefs and cultural discourses in group
discussions and debates. For the continuation of participation and the formation of consciousness, it is necessary to be convinced that the belief and expectation that the problems targeted by the movement are common can only be
realised through unconventional political activities. If this belief is formed, the
movement can easily reach the potential participants and gain strength in the

participants' bond. Although the effective increase in awareness is actually a complicated tactic, it is very diligent in creating due to the anti-authoritarian position. Factors providing talent, such as political socialisation, sometimes make the participants' view of the actions suspicious and bring them to a disagreeable point (Hirsch, 2015: p. 105).

The group process within protest movements influences gaining and obtaining participants' commitment, which we may call joint power. The risk that increases depending on the current power of the challenged authority affects the participants' willingness to the movement, as the movement gains the feeling of the potential power within the awareness-raising sessions of acquiring participants. If many participants are willing to sacrifice themselves, the chance of success for the movement becomes greater. For this reason, the leaders of the movement are trying to emphasise the common good and common power. Another factor affecting the movements is polarisation. By challenging the authorities, the protests question the rules followed in the decision-making process of automatic questions, which in a way, institutional tactics cannot. The authority, which is influenced by the use of non-ordinary methods, is astonished, and the reactions of the targeted authority become uncertain due to its bewilderment. Although polarisation is generally observed as a problem, the lack of readiness for sacrifice and compromise on both sides affects the development of the movement. In fact, the separations in the movement and the polarisation of ideas resulting from the said separations cause the movement's participants to question the reasons for their participation. Unable to decide which side is right, many participants lose their engagement goals, hindering the movement. Movement representatives who gained power and could not mobilise caused negative evaluations of individual participants due to the rise of compelling tactics, and the movement declined gradually. However, in this dilemma, if a group cares about raising awareness and gaining joint power and can create a cultural discourse on these issues, the dispersal of the participants is prevented.

Activists participating in the protests are more connected to the movement with some anger rather than isolation, fear, and shyness. Polarisation can be a positive development for a movement that resulted in this way. For this reason, even if the crises that occur from time to time interrupt the course of the movement, if it does not end it, it can strengthen and maintain its course. The sacrifices made during this process increase the number of volunteers participating in the movement because people with involvement potential have learned that the possible negative result due to the movement will be jointly shared out. Strategies developed on the goals adopted by the majority inhibit uncertain conflicts, thereby preventing the movement from ending with the intervention of social elements. Participants' love for the action and the activists who express their commitment to the movement grows, and their rage and opposition proportionately increase against the other party. Adopting different ideas but making decisions with the participation of the majority leads to tolerance of differences among the participants, increasing volunteerism (Hirsch, 2015: p. 106).

7 Portrait of Urban Movements: Organisational Ability for Struggle

Until the 1960s, urban movements were believed to be highly irregular. Many of the activists who participated in the urban movements were involved in activities for personal reasons, and political reasons were left to the background. Therefore, they could be easily manipulated and exhibit irrational behaviours. Urban movements are characterised as collective behaviours instead of joint actions for these reasons. However, if politics were carried out only through ordinary institutional channels such as parties and elections, these movements would not be necessary. The main breaking point in urban movements occurred after the 1990s. Be it formal or informal. While informal organisations were realised with individuals brought by social networks, they evolved into an isolated and alienated structure but were well-integrated with society. On the other hand, official organisations continued their activities with a network of official connections and an organisational structure defined by the state (Goodwin and Jasper, 2015: p. 155). Urban movements vary in terms of how many components are within the organisation and their relationship. As an extreme example, as in revolutions, only one organisation may be leading the entire movement. Nevertheless, it is also possible that many different organisations may be driving the movement with little communication and interaction among them. Regardless of how many organisations they contain, urban movements still vary depending on their coordination level. Urban movements can be described as fragmented, polycephalic and reticulated in this respect. Each group continues on its way, separated from the others by a relatively autonomous structure, without a specific leader and as a loose link between the parts (Goodwin and Jasper, 2015: p. 156). However, when analysed, many movements such as environmental, human rights, and peace movements are organised with a network that transcends national borders day by day. These international movements are increasingly becoming integrated with the world. This is because many social problems can no longer be addressed at the national level.

The international environmental activist groups stand out as elements of pressure on states, but they are capable of doing more than that. They undertake several activities such as increasing the ecological awareness of new groups, putting pressure on multinational companies and strengthening local communities. They can be a part of emerging topics such as world civil politics or global civil societies formed independently of national states. Today, the fact that activists and organisations with complex international networks are mobilising day by day is called global equity or democratic globalisation. This global network is observed to be instrumental in enabling citizens to act with power beyond local and national communities. The coordination and formation of the global justice movement, also called the movement of movements, is facilitated by the developing technology, primarily through the internet. The number of international urban movement organisations has increased dramatically in recent years. Moreover, these organisations are not centralised but have a decentralised identity. Paradoxically, the more international urban movement organisations grow and start to deal with global issues, they are formed at smaller scales, appear face-to-face, and the similarity increases (McCarthy and Zald, 2015: p. 162).

The concept that best explains the efforts of the international activist community is world civil politics. Whenever the activists want to change the conditions without putting pressure on the state, their actions occur in the common civil life. Civil society is above the individual but below the state as the arena of social obligation. Civil society is the economic, social, and cultural arena based on friendship, family, and voluntary kinship. Although the concept starts with local-scale discussions, it would be appropriate to start from the global level (Wapner, 2015: p. 176). For example, international environmental activist groups have worked for decades to protect wildlife in developing countries. While these groups consist of participants from developed country communities, there is widespread participation from developing countries as well. These organisations take their movements to the international arena by organising locally or by supporting already organised groups. With such efforts, international environmental activist groups are not intended to galvanise the pressure of the public that directly lobbies to make expected changes in official policies or government departments. This is because their activities develop far from parliaments and executive offices with no strings attached to them. International environmental activist groups want local development realised and local capacity increased by producing sustainable development projects (Wapner, 2015: p. 181).

The notion of a network integrates the understanding of the participation of large-scale participants in urban movements at different times and places. In our world, where individuals are inclined to be involved in many different movements, many formal and informal groups conceptualise this notion and form the mobilisation structure. The key concept is that contemporary societies are becoming more and more bureaucratic or formally and professionally organised. Therefore, contemporary communities generate potential participation in social change efforts in many different fields. At the same time, most widespread and long-term movements involve more than one official organisation, the primary purpose of which is to achieve movement-specific goals. However, the movements will not just be a gathering by official organisations. In fact, when analysed, it is observed as an informal structure with an increasingly decentralised organisation. Individuals and loosely defined communication networks have informally begun to organise (Smith, 2015: p. 184). The informal movement dimension of the mobilisation structure is one of the most dynamic and essential breakthroughs for contemporary global change. As the researchers emphasise, urban movements have openly established links with informal politics, and communication-oriented political work has influenced the global social change process in the network of participants who appear on the scene. When we look at the official actors of movement, we observe that they include international social movement organisations and an increasing number of national and locally organised social movement organisations. Protest committees of other official organisations, such as professional associations or trade unions, also find their place in this organisational structure.

Movement actions lead to the creation of official international organisations that help with coordination and continue to campaign long term on specific issues. Since contemporary politics has come to the fore with the knowledge and caution where scientific evidence is comprehensively presented and various political methods are tried, it has become increasingly common and necessary for think tanks and research institutes to support urban movements with specific goals (Smith, 2015: p. 185). Expanding a formally organised and densely networked global civil society helps democratise the global political system. First, the flow of information exchange in the global and local context has accelerated, and as a result, public awareness and debate on global issues and policies have increased. Second, a structural opportunity is provided by enabling groups marginalised by official political means to emerge on the global political scene. This activity will increase the principle of publicity, impartiality, and the representation of international institutions. Third, the transparency and reliability of states for citizens and other states grow with the increase in the capacity of rapid international communication and public participation. Fourth, the concepts of fairness and equitableness gain value in the global context, and political policies gain structure based on these values due to the acceptance of international identities and shared organisational ties. Finally, with the attention of the public drawn to global problems, the impact of the work of international organisations and networks grows as a result of the ongoing efforts of global organisations, resulting from monitoring and mobilisation pressure, and their contribution to international agreements increases (Smith, 2015: p. 195).

The assembly arena is a socio-political tool, a meeting point that evokes appropriate behaviour, has precise roles, defines the situation, and discusses the dimensions of interaction. Potential participants can follow these contents in arenas throughout the movement and even support the movement by creating new understandings and spaces. While the emerging expectations affect the presence of potential participants in a particular meeting area, they direct their inquiries about the intellectual purpose of the meeting, their ideas about the duration of the meeting, the rules of executing the movement and the communication about other areas of action. The elements of the movement, its orientation, and the participants' behaviours directly impact the type and classification of the participation area. While the squares are home to dozens of people, a sit-in protest covers a small area. If the movement is to be managed with the participation of large masses, popular and large areas of the city should be preferred. Likewise, actions in such areas can also be seen as movements with growth potential. However, if the periphery of the institution and organisation to be protested is narrow, the form of the action changes, and the role of creativity emerges. Today, people participating in actions can arrange space planning and space design through interaction. So, while the action can shape the existing structure of the area, the area can also make up the general identity of the action (Haug, 2015: p. 200). Some elements can identify the form of gathering places. The first of these is membership. The meeting area may be open to everyone. Although the number of incoming and outgoing people is not precise, it may also belong to a particular group or several groups. Indeed, some participants facilitate consent regarding the right to participate.

The acceptance or exclusion of some people or groups depends on clear and immediate decisions. While acceptance and exclusion are open to those who find themselves connected with the purpose of the movement and feel close in terms of context, it does not seem easy to accept the elements that are contrary to the purpose and spirit of the movement. In addition, even if there is no difference in terms of ideas, groups that differ in method stand out from the content of the movement, causing them to be excluded from the groups in the movement. Hierarchy is another element. While urban movements usually have an informal hierarchy, they can have a formal one too. In some of the actions, certain groups may have taken the movement's lead and decided on developments during the movement. These groups determine what the participants will do and who will be involved in the process. The hierarchy among the participants is shaped according to a group of tasks ranging from how the participants will lead to how long it will take. Sometimes, people are given specific tasks and have to lead the movement compared to other participants. Another factor is the rules. Even in urban movements shaped by formal organisations, rules are carried out as informal movements. Although the organisation determines the roles among the participants, we see that they move away from absolute rules in order not to distract potential participants from the movement. The location of the selected area, the ratio of the number of participants, and the activities of the opposing groups shape the rules of the movement. The right to speak, represent, and the wide-reaching interventions in the action are handled within the body of rules. However, nowadays, we observe that there are no definite rules for actions. In the communication network, the participants express their opinions using technological tools, and the majority accept certain ideas and act accordingly (Haug, 2015: p. 202).

Another factor is control. During the movement, some people or representatives from official organisations can easily share their ideas about the course of the movement. It measures the expectations of those involved in the movement, classifies them according to their identities, examines the rights they are demanding, draws out the movement's timeline, and looks at the variety of methods employed. In fact, the movements that want to get rid of violent events wish to direct the movement by choosing specific people to limit such activities. The control of the movement can also progress within technological means. Movements that do not want to deviate from the main purpose create public awareness accordingly, while movements that want to increase the number of participants as much as possible bring up the problems and common identities that affect the majority. The last element is sanction. Participants usually participate in the movements voluntarily. The reasons for the involvement in the action may be demonstrated as having found a common denominator, that their voices can be conveyed more powerfully, and the strong likelihood of their expectations being realised. However, the movement can sometimes assume an undesirable tune. When that happens, some sanctions come to the fore. The first thing that comes to mind is the right not to speak. The speaking opportunities of the representatives or participants of the parties that would make the action undesirable are presented to society as an activity outside the limits and the movement. Many methods, such as exclusion from the field of activity, can be implemented on those who may cause problems regarding the safety of the participants. Expulsion from the assembly area, expelling those who commit acts of violence within the area and those who have undesirable relations with opposing groups from the assembly area and public networks are some of the sanctions that would be applied (Haug, 2015: p. 203).

8 Fake or Fortune: Communal Action for Identity and Dignity

Common identity construction may be possible by linking certain actors to specific events, private or public. These events have to encompass in a broad sense the experience in which they are effective in different times and places. As a result, individuals and organisations in collective action no longer pursue specific goals but instead follow the broader and inclusive process of change and even the processes of resistance to change. For example, as in the global justice movement, people who participated in the battle of Seattle and the action of Narmada Valley Dam in India support each other in terms of communication network and action process despite being in distant geographies, and they are similar movements showing us how identity construction is common (della Porta and Diani, 2006: p. 22).

Constructed or reproduced identities are essential parts of individuals' experiences and the transformation processes they go through over time. However, it should be noted that there are significant differences between the individual and the collective dimensions in terms of identity construction. On the one hand, throughout the revitalisation, preservation, and production of identities, individuals define and redefine individual projects regarding whether action is open or closed. It is observed that identities usually direct participation in movements as personal and political projects according to individuals. On the other hand, the construction of identity and the rediscovery of one's self are psychological mechanisms and a set of social processes (della Porta and Diani, 2006: p. 92).

The presence of identity and mutual solidarity makes it possible to face risks and combat the uncertainties of collective action. When the workers' movements are considered, there is solidarity among people working in the same conditions and the same places. The concept of equality brought by the socialist culture imposes the idea that participants actually have a common destiny. However, in post-industrial communities, these ties have begun to weaken gradually. It does not mean that social ties have entirely disappeared. The bonds have gained a different dimension due to the distances in between. The space of relations has become certain regions and even entire national borders rather than specific environments. For this reason, the collective actors have begun to connect themselves less and less with the local. Common identity has gradually replaced face-to-face contact with other social relations instead of direct relations. As a result of the current media environment and the electronic revolution, the collective identity for movements has gained new channels and new boundaries (della Porta and Diani, 2006: p. 94).

A similar mechanism exists in the relationship between a single organisation and movements in a broad sense. On the one hand, while organisations approve of themselves as the movement of a particular issue, they can turn into a global action in general because of their common identity. On the other hand, organisations also differentiate themselves from other activities by strengthening their identity. For this reason, organisations may, in a way, have gained autonomy and become specific, distinctive and unique, but they are also observed as spreading to the world as a product of large-scale joint efforts. Depending on the production of the movement identity, it can reach a wider audience with the help of common images. In this way, the movement can be linked to various participants and movement organisations. Moreover, even small groups can strengthen their experience with larger organisations and expand their scope of activity (della Porta and Diani, 2006: p. 99). Understanding the issue of identity and its particularity is essential when it comes to participation in collective action. However, it is impossible to overlook Olson's theorem in understanding the joint action. According to Olson, the concept of common action is possible through producing the common good. Sometimes the common good concerns those living in a particular region, and sometimes it gains a global dimension. For example, actions to reduce carbon emissions may have started at the local level. The common good is fresh air in this movement. Everyone wants the air they breathe to be clean. And this goal for a healthy life is a common denominator that everyone may share. It is also the common good that would suddenly gain a global dimension. The movement that starts in one region can easily find parties worldwide (della Porta and Diani, 2006: p. 100).

Identity construction is an indispensable part of collective action. With identity construction, actors feel they belong to interests, values, and common history. As supposed, a common identity does not have to remain closed within a specific boundary. Ethnic, regional, class, and gender identities can be included in the common identity by acknowledging the common good, even if they do not belong to the said identity. For this reason, in every field where there is a common good, the common identity was able to find support from those who did not actually possess that identity, and they could find a place in the identity construction. Identity, therefore, plays a crucial role in joint actions.

The network configuration is observed to depend significantly on the character of the environment in which the movements operate and the resource validity for the mobilisation. In local networks, resources are limited, but the density of integration and relationships is high. In national and international networks, resources are almost unlimited if used efficiently, but the intensity of communication and relations is low. There are groups with different ideas among the participants. Multiple memberships have occurred in these networks, and they have been divided into groups or subgroups, and there is a minimal connection among them (della Porta and Diani, 2006: p. 130). As a result of the organisation of urban movement actions and their connection with their activists and supporters, individuals have a series of unique social relationships. In this way, the political dimension of the action overlaps with the unique dimension, particularly bringing the establishment of subcultures to the agenda. Individuals often pursue goals not only in terms of political ends but also of individual self-expression within the network of movements. Even individuals who have these concerns and are not members of any group sometimes participate in actions and activities organised by cultural operators and service makers. Therefore, affiliation with a particular movement organisation lies highly in personal preference. Although the symbolic codes produced for urban movements have a specific target, they do not create a homogeneous group structure. Cultural codes are perceived differently by the participants in the action and adhered to varying extents. Although not desired, it creates a heterogeneous structure (della Porta and Diani, 2006: p. 131).

Another aspect is the behaviour of the activists in the movement. Individuals owe being active in actions not only to their previous connections but also to creating new connections by making use of associations and activists together. In this way, activists unite the urban movement with different organisations, political actors and institutions, and potential participants. As a result, they change and keep the urban movement industry or market alive. Participants are also very successful in using intersecting cultural codes. The participants highly affected by the real-life experience are increasingly curious about the cultural codes of the virtual world and concentrate their organisations in this area. Virtual space increases computer or mobile phone-oriented communication and opens a new era in participation in urban movements (della Porta and Diani, 2006: p. 134).

When the evolution of urban movement organisations is analysed, we do not see a one-way street. Some organisations institutionalise and transform themselves into political parties or interest groups. And some of them become radicalised and turn into protest activities that witness violence. This is observed in urban movements occurring in commercial activities and the market economy. Others turn inward and turn into something akin to religious sects. Which path to take and how to form the organisational structure depend on several factors, namely the effect of opportunity arising from the configuration of the political system, the weight of organisational culture, the role of technological change, and the interaction of rapidly spreading information and communication technologies (della Porta and Diana, 2006: p. 161). Urban movement leaders face a series of strategic dilemmas. Extracting a form from others appears as an action related to conveying messages to various public groups with various demands. While urban movement activists want to strengthen internal solidarity, communicating through the media is a separate demand. Some try to create unions to temper the form of action, and the search for partners they can trust is among the methods frequently used by decision-makers. However, not every action turns into a means of protest but reflects the activists' values. As historical events and actions limit socialisation, urban movements vary by region, country, and movement. Innovations happen with the interaction among learning processes (della Porta and Diani, 2006: p. 192).

The way of the intervention of the police force affects the character of the urban movement particularly and historically. Repressive strategies create tensions. While democratic countries enter into a bargaining process with movement organisations that are already aiming to take peaceful action through the bargaining process, the interventions of the police become more effective. While the form of police interventions depends on the identity and traditional structure of the organisation, it is also shaped according to whether it is sensitive to political opportunities. When the factors shaping police interventions are analysed some elements come to the fore, such as political institutions, political culture, the behaviour of the urban movement activists, and the unions' behaviour (Aydın, 2006: p. 316–8). Considering the cyclical characteristics of unity and conflict, the emergence of protests and the potential for mobilisation seem effective. With the interaction of the urban movement and the counter-urban movement, institutional power gains opposition, affecting the increase of movement strategies and protests. In the past, the resources created with the support of unions and left parties affected the chances of success of urban movements. The decline of mass parties and activists challenges the potential coexistence of political parties and urban movements. The concept of political opportunity is considered to play a central role in urban movements, but the assessment of reality perceptions has been paid little attention. According to contemporary research, cultural differences and divisions filter political opportunities and affect movements' strategies and chances of success. The multiple structures of media organs and the increase of moderate media organs effectively spread the movement's message and ensure its political, cultural, and economic development (della Porta and Diani, 2006: p. 222).

Urban movement mobilisation is completed in some areas by implementing some changes. Besides the policies that the public is concerned about, protests increasing on specific issues can make their voices heard within the legislation yielding legal results. However, the change is mainly shaped by the transformations in the value systems of ordinary citizens and the economically prominent groups and the changes in their behaviours. Changes in public policies and opinion lead to procedural changes, and even from time to time, decision-makers change, changes are made in relevant commissions, local administrations, and representative authority of democracy, and the involvement in the decision-making process has increased because of urban movements. Urban movements and following actions help the democratisation process and democratisation of authoritarian regimes. Its effect in representative democracies appears as a more participatory social and political system (della Porta and Diani, 2006: p. 248).

Space of Urban Movements

1   City, Space, and Time

The world's structure is becoming more and more urbanised. In other words, a significant majority of the world's population now lives in cities. This brings changes in people's living areas, i.e. the spaces. Technological developments, particularly in transportation and telecommunication, give the citizens a great deal of freedom in their location preferences. However, another development with a similar pace also takes place. Cities are gradually losing their importance, and the regions around them are gaining importance day by day. High quality and experience-intensive activities in these areas growing around the borders cause the cities' surrounding regions to gain importance. This also applies to industrialised cities. As knowledge production and experience development increasingly become the main topic of conversation, developed cities become the drivers of the economy. This development, together with the surrounding areas of the cities, points to a new Renaissance period. With the innovations gained from scientific and technological developments, the cities gradually become old. The uniformity which the cities used to have is being progressively replaced with a dispersed density. Cities spread to their peripheries, dispersing their physical and population density and losing uniform features. This is a result of decreasing transportation costs and increasing transportation networks.

At the same time, the speed of transportation is rising. However, personal transportation preferences take precedence over public transportation in today's world. Motorised private vehicles and the lack of space required for these both caused an expansion of cities and constituted a problem in their expansion. This expansion and accumulation began in the existing spaces in the city centre and gradually affected the peripheries, with the urban accumulation having an effect throughout the city with semi-autonomous corridors. New technological developments in communication have led to the emergence of a new area for cities: *cyberspace*. With this development, the issue of distance within the city has become obsolete and was replaced with a contemporary urban context. Working, recreational, business, residential, recreation and consumption areas have detached themselves from the urban context and spread to the new area. The city gained a new image after its spatial integrity was disrupted. Flexibility in terms of time and the activities gaining functionality in a context away from space led to the division of areas as well, and different centres emerged throughout the city. While this caused the cities to spread and disperse, it also caused them to gain a regionally uniform appearance (Henckel et al., 2013 pp. 7–9).

The importance of density, centrality, harmony and context is changing. Indications that change is being observed in the context of time, space and area are becoming observable within the city. Considering these changes, we see today a shift in cities from the space of locations to the spaces of flows. This change plays a key role in the city. The shape and platform of the places where the citizens of the city who have become a connected society spend time and feel a sense of belonging are changing. This is the beginning of the place's journey towards a different definition. This future gives us a clue as to how urban development will progress. The relationship between time, space and area brings up a network of relationships in the city, where the area independent of space becomes insignificant over time. The dissolution of the traditional urban rhythm and the creation of new spatial derivatives developing in connection with this are changing the lives of cities and citizens.

The relationship between the citizens trying to keep up with this change and their spaces with time is also important. The network of citizens, now a social society living at a rapid pace, wants to shape their spaces to keep up with this speed. Time gradually becomes more important, and temporary spaces become an important part of the life of the citizens. Spaces to meet, rest, work and spend time are increasingly becoming synonymous with time. In today's world, where urban lands are now handled with a new approach that moves away from the traditional urbanism approach, the function of the urban area is changing; for this reason, the spaces created, and the existing spaces are arranged and designed according to the new needs of the citizens. The relationship between space and area is becoming more "fluid" rather than static, and the spaces designed for citizens within the urban network have to keep up with this temporary and dynamic order. Now, the citizens wish to be almost in every place simultaneously, but the time spent gradually reduces. The relationship between time and space changes in proportion to the interest of the citizens. Increasing population, decreasing number of urban meeting areas and newly emerging virtual spaces are transforming the places that seem limited, putting them into a new production style.

With the developing technology, spaces shape themselves according to the demands of our era, and multiple spaces are created as a result. Multiple spaces serve citizens both physically and virtually. Business environments change, and the commercial setting transforms. Characteristics such as the sense of temporary belonging and obsession with a place also cause competition among spaces. Brand spaces emerge, and the number of citizens hosted by these spaces gradually increases; however, there are changes in terms of time. The citizens competing with time also want the places to keep up with this race. These urban changes cause individual phenomena to change as a whole in the presence of different conditions and processes. Due to the meeting of newly developed technologies with society, developments that save time and shake the foundations of spaces occur. Experience-intensive and innovative developments occurring in industrial and commercial life have brought a new era to the historical process of spaces. This structural transformation causes spaces to be concentrated in the virtual world and the physical one as well. The changes observed in places are also observed in the social time structure. Changes occurring in the city in terms of population, such as birth rates, ageing and heterogenisation, also change the city's demographics, thus transforming the structure and shape of the spaces that serve the citizens. In particular, having a heterogeneous structure and penetrating different cultural areas is becoming the sole purpose of spaces.

The spread of the support and distribution services necessary to meet the needs towards new areas of the city and the change of the spaces required for these are an example of the spatial transformation of the city, and these affect the citizens' perception of service, as well as the service spaces. The freedom required for the sense of belonging to social sharing and distribution areas and permission to access these increases the belief that spaces should be the same and ready for every citizen. Increasing social polarisation is also reflected in spaces. The number of places providing services to different communities in different regions has increased as much as the number of common areas. For this reason, the demand for the areas required for the spaces is increasing, and the urban rent is increasing. This demand and orientation bring along changes in industry and business requirements. In addition to these effects, cities are becoming increasingly globalised and are on the way to becoming an international space. For this reason, the appearances and designs of spaces have to take global concerns and innovations into consideration. Looking at the temporary topography of the city, we observe three different time changes in the urban time structure. They are vast acceleration processes; prolongation of work, operation, and activity times; and flexibility of working and service times. The loss of integrity and privatisation of urban structures develops the urban time landscape in a new way. The available processes for transition among spaces are designed to save time, and the proper positioning of spaces within the city is shaped according to timelines.

Accessibility is determined by the actions of spaces related to time. Network and new edge cities are concepts related to density. Due to the density of the spaces in the urban network, the density of the citizens decreases in the core areas, whereas it increases at the edges (i.e. the peripheries) of the city. Looking at the areas where the density of the urban population changes, we see that the infrastructure transforming relative to space also gains importance. The regional variation of the density is due to the types of service provided in the spaces created in the city. When we look at urban spaces, we observe a loss of identity of spaces as we get closer to the city centre. Transit corridors, transportation nodes and main infrastructure facilities, which may particularly be classified as non-spatial, appear as new identities. Apart from these areas far from the space, it is observed that spaces with new identities have emerged parallel to the urban movements occurring, especially in the peripheries and core of the city. It is apparent that the spaces are now spreading to the peripheries; however, it may be anticipated that this phenomenon will not continue. Noticeably, the cities will regain their core, that is, their central areas, in the medium term with the help of new economic forms, new business forms, new lifestyles and demographic changes. Spaces emerging in these areas will gain importance. The spaces expanding in these regions and gaining new identities in direct proportion to the increasing urban movements show us that the urban points of focus will again channel the area of activity towards the urban nuclei.

Decisive, general and complementary studies examining the relationship between the city and flow present us with how space changes under certain social conditions, accompanied by socially structured technologies frameworks. Social relations are an element that decides what form the space will be constructed and where it will be located. The areas where the citizens carry out activities turn into the nests of the spaces. A flow is present in the areas where the citizens of the city carry out their business, work, trade, recreation, and cultural activities. Thanks to the new advantages of developing technologies, the spaces that appear in these areas gain new identities and appearances. The density and distribution of spaces vary according to the intensity and degree of relations. Particularly, urban movements create certain centres in certain regions of the city. This does not mean that urban movements occur only in certain regions. Urban movements are observed and reflected in spaces spread throughout the city. However, the citizens intensively use the spaces concentrated in certain regions.

In addition, provided that they are accessible, some places have gained a place in the consciousness and memories of the citizens as the seats of freedom. Due to economic, social and cultural relations, places are also subject to these distinctions; however, some places incorporate all of these elements thanks to developing technology. In the light of these developments, it is seen that, rather than serving a specific purpose with certain identities, the places are structured to serve all kinds of activities and different groups. This fluid attitude in spaces incorporates physical structures in the flow of daily practices. It is important to establish spaces that do not ignore the variabilities of daily urban life. Meanwhile, thanks to all electronic means of communication, urban streets are being reshaped, and urban public spaces and urban public transport spaces are, more or less, changing and transforming between distances. Citizens, social groups and urban movements reshape the streets and the spaces around the streets to be re-transformed through mobile communication tools and social media. The use of streets changes, the meaning of streets diversifies with different identities, and the functions of urban areas and spaces vary. The concept of fragmented urbanism refers to the division of these social relations into sections due to spatial differentiation and a transition taking place. Although infrastructure services try to keep cities together, urban services are subjected to regional changes.

Since urban services are not spread throughout the city as smoothly and organised as desired, regions are formed in the city, and conflict arises among the citizens living in these regions. Due to the differences in the distribution of the urban infrastructure, the conflict between the citizens is increasing, and problems arise like never before due to the revolution in communication. The emergence of different places belonging to each group is a sign of this. However, the city administration ignores this differentiation and pursues the concept of a unitary city. The spaces of this unitary city should also be similar. This Fordist and Keynesian approach is the main target of 19th and 20th-century urbanism. However, cities have grown and transformed in the 21st century. Changes have revealed a different urban texture and a diverse urban understanding. For this reason, similar urban spaces are no longer sufficient for the lives of the citizens. There is an utmost need for new opportunities to accommodate new identities. For this reason, the concept of fragmented urbanism has emerged. However, the unitary urban structure and understanding have not completely disappeared. It is still printed on existing urban spaces. However, the city is already fragmented due to increasing communication tools, privatisation, and liberal policies. The division maximises if we include the movements that emerged in response to these.

Increasing technological innovations and social media cause the citizens to adopt various cultural and social identities in this divided city environment. This process causes spaces to change and become more and more sensitive to movements. In many of the cities shaped by the effect of neoliberal policies, the administration as a whole has become layered, privatised and competitive. Due to the changing economic conditions, economical spaces and neighbourhoods have emerged in the city. The transportation, resting, meeting and working areas developed in these neighbourhoods have caused the urban space to emerge with a new appearance. While these developments are changing the city, the activities that are unable to find a place for themselves in these areas spread towards the periphery of the cities. These activities, which shift towards different regions in the city, create a different economic, social and cultural context within the city. Of course, these regions with other infrastructure and superstructure services have not completely moved away from the centre and the main artery of the city.

The regions, which take their spot in the urban movement and unify in the company of the citizens who participate in these activities, find themselves in an immediate transition area over time, proliferating common spaces among the regions. While a higher and more widespread use of space emerges in the city's centre, this effect decreases towards the city's periphery. Open spaces are becoming valuable due to the increasing physical infrastructure and building density in the city centre. Although these areas, which are used by a denser crowd in terms of population, are an area of demonstration for the economic system that created them, they can easily turn into a place where people react to them in their own way. Because the economy is one of the primary tasks of city life, every citizen wishes to benefit from the city's production. In addition, the relationship of the separated regions with the centre has always been strong. Although the spaces created are an extension of the areas in the city core, there is less interaction between different areas. Even the relationship of different regions is sometimes realised through the centre inside the city. For this reason, the actions taken in the city centre are important. And the spaces that host these movements should be easy to access by everyone as free spaces.

Depending on the coexistence of all other global areas, equipping time and space with new infrastructure services causes the city to assume a bypass condition. Removing the factors that halt and eliminate the communication between regions means the unification of the urban nuclei and the peripheries. For this reason, *archipelagos* are formed in the city, where high-quality infrastructures dominate, and valuable economic and social settlements come to the fore. For this reason, the fragmented urban area has ventured away from the unitary urbanism approach and is divided into zones but continues to create spaces that live in harmony with each other through movements. These local organisations and the new urban spaces that emerged as a result of these organisations emphasise, nourish, and get nourished by the city's life and the urban life of the citizens. These archipelagos have led to the emergence of different centres within the city, and the number of citizens dependent on these centres has increased. The main city centre, which gained importance globally, is in communication with these centres, but they have a kind of division of duties. Although the city's economy is divided into units in the presence of centres, it also gains in the presence of centres. Although recreational areas have changed, they have become more available at local levels.

Consumption areas have grown and diversified with the cascading growth of the spaces. The corridors formed between these centres have brought a new spatial identity to the agenda. Fluid cities and citizens utilise their temporary assets in these corridor spaces. Thanks to these corridor areas, urban spaces are connected to each other. There are also global corridors. And this brings a unity that will bypass the blockages in the network established between the cities through cores. With the gains of global organisation and movements, especially the urban centre and the focal areas revolving around this main centre get rid of stagnation and end their obstructed lives. While the centres acquired by local organisations cheer up with the participation of urban movements, the centre of the city revives more with global participation. Of course, urban spaces get their share of this revival. Other local centres revolving around the more globalised city centre increase the diversity of urban identity and spaces. In this context, global-local areas, which we refer to as "*glocal*" in the city, bear fruit in a way that urban movements are not only derived from these spaces but also trigger the shaping of existing spaces in this context. In this way, urban spaces are once again divided into local, national, international and global levels. They arise in spaces where all of these are accessible, thanks to the existing connections between the centres. The network of movements between this archipelago, and the existence of spaces that serve this network, provide and maintain urban unity (Henckel et al., 2013: pp. 24–9).

Modern civilisation has always struggled to be independent of the rhythm of nature. And the city has always emerged as the area where this independence process takes place and continues. Today, the struggle against nature has turned into the concern of living alongside nature. The existence of urban movements comes to the fore in the struggle for life with nature. According to this understanding, these movements, which aim to design urban life in a way that includes nature together with the citizens, are concerned about designing the existing spaces in the city. The preservation of the current green areas in the city and the constructed areas keeping up with the environmental conditions affect the transformation of urban spaces. This transformation does not progress at the pace desired in every region of the city, and it shapes the city as an additional and sometimes even a guiding element to the existing economic, social and cultural conflicts in this urban area. In this way, the city causes another division. The city is once again divided into spaces that either ignore or do not ignore environmental factors. Just as society is divided.

It should be reminded that, in addition to the environmental spaces, there are also micro spaces living at a fast and slow pace in the city. As these fast and slow-paced places are spread throughout the city, each feature emerges at different times in the city centre. However, remembering that urban movements are an entirety of activities that continue every hour of the day, the life of the city centres designed especially in and around the city centre appears to flow fast, and the spaces can be described as fast spaces. This time limitation changes according to the type of relations between the citizens and causes the spreading and neighbouring of spaces. Generally, the city centre is an area where fast-paced places are located. Other sub-spaces assume different forms during the day as they are located in certain parts of the cities. While the fast-paced life continues for a period, it slows down during specific periods of the day. Therefore, they appear as sub-spaces, i.e. the areas where suitable spaces are located. As a result, cities are areas with a highly diverse concentration of people but where a limited number of functions and spaces provide services. However, this concentration and state of limitation increase towards the peripheries rather than the city centre. More precisely, while the concentration is high in the city centre all day hours, the number of places to provide services for this concentration is also relatively high. However, when we look at the other centres of the city, not all services can find persons suitable for them, and not all persons have spaces ideal for them. For this reason, although these sub-centres are the regions where primarily urban movements sprout, the region where they truly shine is the city centre itself. Housing areas can also be shown as another reason for this.

The transportation network between the regions generally runs through the city centre. Since the city is geographically a large area, it ensures its communication through the city centre, except for the specialised vehicle networks. For this reason, the choice of city centres is vital for the intense participation in the movements concentrated in certain regions because the city centre is more public than the spaces in other sub-centres. These areas are heterogeneous, with contradictory trends. City centres have heterogeneous spaces, as they are open to every kind of movement and every citizen. However, homogenisation can be observed when we look at areas with more micro qualities in terms of localisation. Although relatively more heterogeneous spaces are replacing these regional centres, we observe that the spaces are becoming homogeneous as we move away from the city centre towards the peripheries. Heterogeneity is critical and essential for both economic and social developments and innovation. Looking at the content of urban movements, we generally see a heterogeneous engagement, both culturally and socially. On the other hand, the heterogeneity of urban areas or the presence of heterogeneous areas is an essential condition for the city. It is also essential that spaces provide the connection by responding to these heterogeneous engagements with the same diversity. For this reason, the city centre and sub-centres grow along with such spaces.

The concepts of urban density and city are kind of synonymous. Urban density has both positive and negative aspects. Although density acts as a means to reach the level of a city, diversity is observed in the differentiation of areas and the classification of spaces in cities with urban density. Open spaces and the existence of the spaces located in these areas are among the factors of concern in the cities where the density is increasing. Urban density creates an environment where economic, cultural and social accumulations increase, and conflicts arise in the city. Urban mobility is often mentioned in cities with a high urban density and determines the relations within the city. In terms of urban planning, the expenses and costs of cities where urban density is dispersed, and population density decreases somehow are higher than those that distribute urban density to limited areas. However, urban groups concentrated in limited areas have to meet their various needs and expectations in this limited area. Urban problems such as housing shortages, livelihood and recreational issues cause an increase in conflicts and thus an intensification of urban movements. Although urban spaces attempt to serve the identities revealed in such cities to the extent possible, some groups are overlooked. In addition, public spaces that are difficult to access, which can be due to economic, environmental, technological and social reasons, make it difficult for the citizens to share areas and spaces. If the culturally diversified citizens cannot find the opportunity to share in spaces, a struggle for public space begins, and urban movements reach the boiling point.

The relations of the citizens are realised more in such limited areas, and this causes negative as well as positive results. Suppose the citizens having to share common areas in cities with inequalities do not find these areas affordable and accessible. In that case, they will feel a sense of displacement and exclusion, and this will cause complaints. The reason for the complaint is that urban spaces will be the focal point of urban movements, and urban movements will increase due to the sharing of spaces. There will be sexual, age, cultural, identity and social differences in areas with an increased urban population density. In addition to these, environmental and physical differences will also emerge. However, the sharing of these areas differs between regions in terms of density (i.e., it is limited in some regions whereas it is deployed to a much larger extent in other regions) will create inequality among citizens and cause urban struggles in the absence of ease of access. If urban land planning is not carried out to consider the entire city, spatial inequality will occur, which will trigger urban movements. In addition, physical density will be a subject of a complaint by the residents of urban centres and may cause urban movements towards trans-forming the spaces. Urban complaints and protests will increase due to rising costs and inequality if affordable and accessible spaces and conditions are not maintained in areas where urban physical density is distributed.

The urban context is a complex system that is not homogeneous; it is a sys-tem where different structures come together. Historically, the city is the phys-ical geography where density and space come together. Cities are the core of the network of relations in which cultural contexts are formed and connected within the urban structure. European cities are cities that produce this context in different, clustered corners. American cities, on the other hand, are rather spread and scattered. In contrast, the Asian and African cities are shaped in a very compact and unified way. Physical, i.e., spatial density, creates an iden-tity directly related to urban structures, poles, and borders. Population den-sity is less visible compared to physical density. In addition, unlike physical density, population density is not directly linked to economic development. Although generally accepted, population density is not a factor bringing eco-nomic density. Some cities are not dense in population but dense in economic, social and physical terms. Proximity and density are not necessarily identical but are related. The social separation of this division of labour can be seen in the organisation of civil society. Proximity and accessibility in urban space are key accessories for social density. And this relationship relies on mobility and the developing communication technologies. Communication density and the city are mutually sustainable. A high communication density enhances the increasing complexity and diversity of urban spaces. And urban spaces are diversified by the density of communication.

Social density and division of labour lie at the core of innovation, which defines a heterogeneous society in terms of production. And, of course, social density spatialises with the support of developing technological innovations and, therefore, social media. As a result, it causes the virtualisation of spaces and communication due to the developed networks. Generally speaking, social infrastructure facilities and social density can be considered the role of *urban nuclei*. And this role is a reflection of the social density that emerges in different parts of the city and the resulting physical density. Suppose the spaces located within the physical density do not conform to the diversity brought along by the social density. In that case, urban movements are revived in the city, and these spaces, offering limited opportunities, are transformed and diversified through these movements. Today, technological developments bring another density and space to the agenda: virtual world and virtual spaces. With the development of technology, communication networks and density flow from urban squares to virtual environments, and urban spaces must have a reflection in the virtual world. Unless the spaces of this virtual environment get their share of urban services and are shared by the citizens, urban movements will reflect an increase in physical spaces (Hunckel et al., 2007: pp. 82–93).

In general, social media can be regarded as a public sphere. Social media is more or less synonymous with the urban atmosphere. While the attractiveness and facilitation of the virtual world transform it into an area extensively preferred by the crowds at a rising rate, it is also transformed into a more aesthetic space with the efforts of international artists and software developers. This area has many other internal functions besides meeting and speaking of the citizens. An increasingly privatised space, the virtual world is also a public space where daily conversations occur, communication networks and connections are established, business activities and commercial activities are carried out, and various kinds of entertainment activities occur in the recreational space. Individuals use social media to contact each other and talk and chat at an ever-increasing rate. They perform all the fun activities, which they used to perform by meeting in person, through the applications offered by the virtual world, and they even do this in groups. Even if the activities are carried out in physical environments, they are announced and have implications on the virtual world. Videos watched, theatrical performances, movies and other visual applications make this realm even more real in the eyes of the people.

Compared to real life, the virtual world is more personal and private. It is a more isolated place in daily life. When asked about their opinions, the users state that they are free during the time they spend in the virtual world and that moral, cultural, social, and technological inequalities that can prevent them in their daily lives are not present in this environment. It is observed that, through this environment, they show more interest in daily political, economic, and social issues, learn more and become more involved in events. On the other hand, social media and the virtual world create an informal atmosphere for users. In these environments, without any authority, the individual feels quite free and performs many actions that one cannot normally perform in their daily life, and even intervenes in the privacy of other individuals. In this quite free environment, people who cannot meet in urban squares come together, and thoughts that cannot be expressed are expressed with subsequent comments.

Different city groups can express themselves, disseminate their thoughts, and share their complaints in forums. Thus, this environment shared by millions of people simultaneously has the effect that urban spaces with physical boundaries do not have and can affect millions at once. Communities that share their views are organised by sharing the meetings they will hold in urban spaces in this environment. Feedback, criticism, comments, and recommendations are provided more efficiently through this environment. In addition, people do not refrain from participating in any kinds of activities in such environments since they usually hide their identities. Of course, as technology develops, security forces are also carrying out security activities in these environments. Still, today, the citizens of the city experience the freedom, which they cannot have in their daily lives, in this environment. The virtual world is not an environment that only serves individuals. Family groups and even friend groups can easily carry out their activities here. Thanks to the technological advantages offered by the virtual world, even individuals sharing the same house have started to communicate and chat with each other through this environment. These crowds, who cannot chat even though they are in the same environment, have started to communicate with each other by using their mobile phones and other mobile devices. They are informed of each other, their lives, their sorrows and happiness through social media, and they maintain their daily relations through this environment. Social media has growing mobility as a living space. In addition, thanks to its ability to adapt to new environments, it has a steadily growing public character.

Urbanisation is located somewhere in this area and is directly involved in this process. When scrutinised, we can witness that the urban environments have moved to this realm and that there is a linear connection. Urban spaces develop and change their physical environments and services by advertising on their pages in the virtual world. Social media has become one of the classic nodal points where citizens meet. And this space has increasingly become the urban centre for shopping, recreation, meeting point and entertainment, and this is true both on a global scale and on a local scale. Social media and applications of the virtual world have turned into a market machine selling products, becoming a recreational area and a hospitable place for the citizens of the city. The attractiveness of social media is mainly because the environment is socially open and accessible to everyone, where citizens of all backgrounds and cultures can come together without economic worries, discuss their thoughts, and spend their rest and relaxation times together.

Squares, airports, terminals, and other *urban hubs* are increasingly becoming high-density products, developed for various uses and accompanied by urban concentrations. A high concentration of people from diverse backgrounds is concentrated in these places, and this development is not only valid for those who visit the places temporarily but also for the residents of the region who come together for social contact for shopping, entertainment, and work. As a result of this scale, the intervention of official agencies and the division of functions, urbanism evolves and influences the development of specific forms of urban activities. Of course, this interaction is also reflected in the spaces. As the cities compete among themselves and continue this competition not only economically but also culturally, socially, technologically, and politically, the issue of how and in which spaces the citizens of the city continue to live has gained importance. Of course, urban problems cause a reaction from certain groups and create liveliness in the cities. Still, the positive results obtained affect the hierarchy between the cities and bring certain cities to the forefront within the union among the cities.

For this reason, the existence and abundance of urban spaces that will make the mobility within the cities convenient and efficient are also crucial for the city. Therefore, the level of cultural and social development is high in certain parts of the cities, and these parts are symbolised as *quarters*. Cultural, economic, social and political wealth is dominant in these areas. This diversity and heterogeneous structure affect and develop cultural, political and social productions. In particular, the cultural richness and the fact that the artists produce works locally and internationally lead to the creation of new products by influencing the current understanding of innovation in the city. Thanks to the innovations added to the traditional sense of art, the city's symbols are changing and developing. The artistic activities that occur, particularly in the historical areas in the centre of the cities, or in the neighbourhoods close to these areas, develop the city's culture and change this city's public space. The changing public sphere affects the spaces, which in turn revives the urban movements, and economic and political growth occurs due to the revitalised urban relations. Therefore, urban movements can contribute to the city's development by changing these political, cultural or social urban spaces. The urban spaces that have changed revive urban movements, causing the citizens to mobilise and, thus, the city to gain vitality. In this case, the process of change that includes the citizens, urban groups and urban spaces is an expression of development for cities.

2   City, Space, and Citizen

The rise in the use of the word space in social sciences texts of today is remarkable. Defending that social values are shaped spatially and that spatial characteristics have a social foundation is no longer an ungrounded opinion. In fact, rather than using the concept of space with a conceptual network whose demonstrativeness is proven and with sociological attributes, it is more common to use it with material content isolated from the former. For this reason, it would be beneficial to mention the spatial research question in today's studies.

In the works of such respected geographers as David Harvey, the said research question lies at the centre of these studies. It gained currency along with such thinkers as H. Lefebvre and M. Castells, parallel to the rise in philosophical awareness of the political significance of urban spaces and public arenas upon the 1968 social movements. References towards this term have turned the 'spatial question' into an almost mysterious category for some of today's social scientists. However, within the sociological context of the spatial question framework and the unique value of local knowledge, it is necessary to remember that Chicagoan sociologists studied it as a form of social union. We may even be able to say that this question may have come out in previous centuries. As noted in this book, one can establish a direct correlation between the spatial question and the rise and development of the city.

In our age, the city individually means more than the piles of people and the convenience of social conditions. The city is much more than just the buildings, street lamps, underground transportation technologies, and even urban air transport lines that may emerge in the near future. Besides, it is also much more than a group established merely by institutions and executive organs such as courthouses, hospitals, schools, and professional chambers. When examined, we observe that the city instead refers to a state of mind, certain traditions and customs, and organised behaviours and sensibilities at the heart of such customs. In other words, a city is not just a physical organism or a subsequently produced set of structures. It also contains the daily life process experienced by the city's people. The city is a product of nature, specifically human nature. The city draws all the attention to the culture it produces in the global age. What the house means for the rural area is the same as the city for modern life. The city has been analysed based on urban ecology via its own geography in recent years.

Some factors process their own population and institutions within the borders of urban societies, that is, the borders of every natural space that people inhabit, intending to transform into organised and unique groups. However, the formation of these factors or the beginning of such formation does not mean that the city consists of a geographical and ecological unit in itself. It is also an economic and political unit. The economic organisation of the city relies on the division of labour. The rise in the number of occupations and fields of expertise within the urban borders is among the most striking and least understood dimensions. The said economic structure divides the city into its so-called archipelagos, and political ideas and movements emerge based on inequalities in space and urbanity depending on the development of such archipelagos. Lastly, the city is the natural habitat of civil humans. For this reason, it also becomes the only geography where the policies emerging for the purpose of development are shaped, and the struggle being exhibited based on equality (Park and Burgess, 2016: p. 37)

When examining the urban plans, they establish the boundary lines that broadly assign the location and characteristics of urban structures and stipulate an orderly positioning of buildings constructed by private contractors as much as public authorities in the city. However, the inevitable functioning of human nature stuck in the middle of foreseen restriction begins to attribute a character to this region and buildings that would be controlled less. The residence preference of the population concentrated in certain urban regions in line with the concept of individual ownership did not follow a planned course. Unfortunately, the city cannot determine the values of plots located within its borders. For this reason, determining the value and location of settlement and industrial zones is mainly left to private enterprises. Entrepreneurs, tastes, various occupations, and financial interests tend to segregate and classify the population within larger cities without an error of margin. Due to this style of politics, the city would attain neither a designed nor a supervised population organisation. Urban geography determines the advantages and disadvantages resulting from it as well as the general outlines of urban plans. Such deeply infused elements as sympathy, competition, and financial conflicts occurring between various communities that make up the urban culture verge on controlling the distribution of population as the city grows. Business and industry look for advantageous regions and attracts a portion of the population to such zones. While the rising plot values and prestige increase the demand of urbanites to these areas, notwithstanding, more economically disadvantageous classes are forced to live in the periphery of the city. In time, every region and quarter of the city takes something in from their inhabitants' characteristics and features. Inevitably, every single piece of the city is adorned with sensitivities unique to the population it harbours. The effect of this is that what is at first a mere geographical representation turns into a neighbourhood, in other words, into a place with unique sensitivities, traditions, and history. Within such neighbourhoods, the continuity of historical processes is preserved in one way or another. The past wields its influence on the present, and life everywhere continues to exist with its own motion, more or less independently from the broader cycle of things related to life itself (Park and Burgess, 2016: pp. 41–2).

The city facilitates the movement of individuals not just by increasing transportation and communication networks but also by segregating the urban population from each other. Segregation processes establish moral distances within the city that becomes a mosaic made up of small worlds brushing each other but not enlacing. This ensures the movement of people from one moral zone to the other faster and also encourages a dazzling but dangerous experience of living in adjacent but completely opposite worlds. All these give the city a superficial and adventurous character while complicating social relations and tend to create dissonant types. They also shape urban life for young and fresh nerves with a unique appeal by adding the elements of luck and adventure to the stimulants of urban life. The person closest to success in a small community is the ordinary individual that does not manifest oddity and genius. City, on the other hand, awards them. Neither the criminal nor the detective nor the genius can find an opportunity to improve the unique characteristics they may find in the city in a town (Park and Burgess, 2016: pp. 79–80).

Every quarter with a tendency to separate and segregate the urban population gains a moral quality. Most cities have a zone that fell into disrepute or have high prestige. We would need to talk about the secret impulses of people to understand the reasons behind the efforts to create neighbourhoods in which segregated, repressed impulses, passions, and ideals are declared independence from the dominant moral order dominant by vagrants of all large cities. The urbanites seem to have difficulties keeping all their passions, impulses, and pleasures under control. The main reason behind this is the marginal benefit of the variety clustered around assorted regions formed within the city. The city is flushed with earthly experiences that may appear abnormal to many but also that urbanites cannot pull away from experiencing them. While wanting to suppress such wild and natural characteristics in the interests of common well-being, civilisation also demands them to be kept under control, considering certain cities. At this point comes sports and art. They allow the individual to purify themselves from these wild and suppressed impulses through their symbolic expressions. Specifically, due to the opportunities, it provides the non-normal and exceptional human types, the metropolitan city manifests the human character and qualities otherwise covered and suppressed in smaller communities in such magnificence. In short, the city shows the good and the bad inherent in human nature with their extremism. Perhaps, this is the concept that legitimises the opinion that sees the city clinically in which human nature and social processes may be analysed with ease and efficiency. Unquestionably, the city pushes this environment to the forefront with outbursts that create it. In epicritic times, it may be noted that urban movements are correlated with strikes, elections, religious awakenings, and many other social concepts. Subconscious tensions resulting from this correlation allow reading of social and economic struggles of various groups arising in cities via space. Spaces formed by social relations and the social relations shaped by spaces make the cities more prominent, like the fertile land in which movements burgeon and spike (Park and Burgess, 2016: pp. 82–3).

Urban movement is not proof of transformation or improvement on its own. As is the case in every non-city-oriented movement, it may also be the unchanging and constant order of an implementation designed to control a situation containing continuity. As seen from its name, mobility contains a change, a new experience, and stimulation. The stimulation triggers the individual's response to the objects around them that bear the promise that they can accomplish whatever they wish. As is the case in natural organisms, stimulation is essential to growth for the individual. The society comprises individuals that are spatially separated, regionally distributed, and possess the ability to change location. These spatial relations of people are the products of competition and selection, and new factors are subject to constant change since they spoil the relations of competition or facilitate mobility. Physical foundations of social relations change when spatial relations shift, and correspondingly, social and political issues arise (Park and Burgess, 2016: p. 59).

Urban movements are protests in cities due to urban crises, issues, riots, riots, reactions, and conflicts. Social outbreaks emerged in every era in history; however, the urbanisation process that began in the 16th century generated a new phenomenon. Urban movements that emerged towards the end of the century were the first signs that we now stepped into a new era. And these uprisings gather people from different social groups and cultures. There is no separation.

> Therefore, there would be people in uprisings from all social layers; however, only the proletariat was believed to be in them. The liberal bourgeoisie of 1848 is truly right in the middle. They would oppose the remnants of the ancient regime; they would side with constitutional government, development of industry, and reform. However, they would also have their backs to the wall. They are both a rebellion and at the target of the uprising. They side with a new order, but they support it just for the sake of having one. Revolutions warp time. In the minds of those that experienced the revolution lies the thought that major changes in social structure can be done in just one night.
>
> SENNETT, 2013: p. 294

Behaviours and habits that defy the ages in cities are the natural mixture of urban culture. It is almost impossible in today's cities to judge these values and understand whether the differences that occur in daily life are extraordinary changes or ordinary things that will make no sense the next day. "Contrarily, those that participate in uprisings may start seeing the events through the eyes of their superiors at the time of social uprising, and such look may prevent them from understanding themselves" (Sennett, 2013: p. 294).

So, how urban are these movements? These reactions that begin occurring in the city are attributed to the city by having its identity. The state of conflict brought by radical policies transformed various institutional or ideological issues of communities that live divided in the city into psychological ones. When masks worn by people in a state of upheaval or those in leadership positions were seen as the revelation of their personalities, these issues would instantly transform into a legitimation of the actual role of the individual. An individual laying claim to an issue has become an issue of legitimation of themselves. Unfortunately, such endeavour confused common causes and beliefs with the common self. These political communities are not urban because their political quarrels or revolutionary struggles are only seen in the metropolis and not in any other place. These political communities are urban in the sense that it influences the general political language by also containing the moments in which the first steps for movements are taken in terms of interpreting different appearances that come out among minorities in the city. The term politics is urban both in terms of its meaning in ancient Greek civilisation and the shaping of the developments today. That is, it is a style of cognition that surfaces in the metropolis first and then takes off society-wide, and urbanites begin seeing urban life through the eyes of movement leaders that originate from a special philosophy with a geographical factor being out of question (Sennett, 2013: p. 311).

Therefore, what is the urban revolution, and where does it begin? What will begin in the city? Where will it come to an end? None of these descriptive terms considers the historical process as a whole. Implosion-explosion (metaphor loaned from nuclear physics), in other words, excessive concentration within the urban reality (excessive concentration of people, activities, wealth, things and objects, vehicles, vehicles of thought); excessive disintegration and the projection of numerous derailed pieces (peripheries, suburbs, second homes, satellites, etc.) (Lefebvre, 2017: p. 19). Therefore, movement occurs as a result of numerous explosions and concentrations. So where is space?

> Streets are not only places of transit and circulation. Automobiles invading the streets and the pressure from this industry, that is, the car lobby transformed old cars into pilot objects, parking into an obsession, and circulation into a primary target, and destroyed social and urban life as a whole. These prestigious spaces animate the streets and benefit from this animation. Otherwise, they cannot exist. I become a performance and audience, and sometimes an actor in the street that is a spontaneous

theatre. This is where movement and coalescence occur. Without them, what would come out would not be urban life but a division, a dull disjunction, and a split in society.

LEFEBVRE, 2017: p. 22

All the elements of urban life that are static elsewhere and frozen inside a self-renewing order are liberalised in the streets and flow into the centre. These elements come across each other while retreating to their shelters. This disorderliness is a living one. It informs. It astounds. This disorder, in a way, means a higher order.

As for the revolutionist action, it also occurs in the street. Does this not show that the disorderliness of the street also leads to another order? Is the urban space of the street not where the words are spoken or where words, signs, and things are exchanged? Is where the word is written not a privileged place? Where else can words become wild and written on walls while escaping the law and institutions?

LEFEBVRE, 2017: p. 22

So, what makes the movements in the city in addition to crowds gathering in the streets? What accumulates in the city?

There was also an accumulation process with relative constancy: Accumulation of knowledge, techniques, things, people, wealth, money, and lastly, the capital. The city has become the space for this accumulation. This is the case even though the capital is the product of wealth from the rural areas, and the rural areas directed the industrial investment in the city's favour.

LEFEBVRE, 2017: p. 28

As a result of accumulation, a centrality issue comes out. Movements coming against the centre and sometimes siding with it are a consequence of this.

It would be difficult for the urban society defenders in formation to avoid all sorts of ambiguity and pave a way that is free from deviations. Let us tackle the centre and centrality issues. Without a centre, there would not be a city or urban reality. That being the case, there comes a risk to defend centres where decision structures, centres of power, wealth, and power elements concentrate until they acquire a colossal density in bulk.

Without a centre, there is no place for leisurely activities, celebrations, knowledge, verbal or written communication, invention, and creation. However, until certain production and property relations change, centrality will be handed over to those who use them and benefit from them. At best, it becomes a place belonging to the elite, or at worst, it turns into a military or police zone. Acceptance of the situation does not mean approving the dictatorship of centres of power and authoritarian planning. It is beyond that. In fact, it is exactly the opposite.

LEFEBVRE, 2017: p. 92

City summons everything born elsewhere belonging to nature and labour. So, what does it create? Nothing. It centralises creations. On the other hand, it creates everything. Without exchange, convergence, and rapprochement, that is, without relations, nothing can exist. The city creates a situation. A city situation where different things generate each other, presence their differences, but not come into being separate from each other.

LEFEBVRE, 2017: p. 113

Therefore, the city is a composition. It is closer to being a work of art than a simple material product. While there exists the production of the city and the production of social relations within the city, rather than being a mere production, it is the production and reproduction of individuals by individuals. The city has a history. It is a work of quite particular people and groups that create the said work in history.

LEFEBVRE, 2016: p. 64

While it is possible to mention the interaction between urban structures and their activities as well as forms, it is also a fact that they transform each other. Every urban formation has lived through a rise, ascension to the peak, and collapse. Ruins of declined cities acted as saplings to other settlements. Throughout the process of reflection of the city on a certain level, the general code of the society transforms. The unique code of the city is a modulation, a version of this. It is an incomprehensible translation without its unique initial form. However, the city had an unmatched capacity to voice all interpretations and capture them to write down. In addition, these interpretations also comprised those from rural areas, immediate life, religion, and political ideology. During each crisis period, an urban period of waiting when the expansion and growth of the city are stalled, and urban culture that is guided and determined by social relations dominant till then became static. Rather than a constantly rising rationality or internal harmony, this waiting and crisis that are the symptoms of transformation put projects on development or collapse in the same boat. Confusing this concern with rationality and organisation is to preserve and sustain the previously generated ideology. Since the city is developed as a network of culture and existence, the resulting ideology is the only condition of such culture and order of existence. The global city that becomes the centre of decision, or rather, that groups centres of decision, popularises by organising the exploitation of the entire society today. So, the global city is not a passive place where production or capital is concentrated. In its current condition, the city intervenes the production and who the production owners would be (Lefebvre, 2016: p. 72).

> However, social space is not a thing among things or a product among other products. It contains their relations within the commonwealth and simultaneity, that is, the (relative) order and/or (relative) disorder. As a result of past actions, it allows for new actions and suggests or prevents them. Among these actions, while some produce, others consume; that is, they reap the fruits. Social space contains vast knowledge. Therefore, what is the status of social space? What relation does it have with production?
>
> LEFEBVRE, 2014: p. 99

State and each institution that makes it postulate a space and organises it based on its own needs. Thus, space is nothing but an a priori condition of the institutions and state lying atop these institutions. Is it a social relation? Absolutely may be claimed as yes.

However, social space that is internal to property relations, and on the other hand, based on producer powers, exhibits its utmost value, its reality, both formal and material.

> Space that is used and consumed is also a means of production. Networks of exchange, raw material, and flow of energy both shape the space and are determined by space. This means of production generated this way can neither be separated from producing powers, technique, and information, nor from social division of labour, nature, state, and superstructure.
>
> LEFEBVRE, 2014: p. 110

Counter-space can overcome the contradiction that seems to be imposed between reform and revolution. Every suggestion towards creating counter-space, seemingly even the most insignificant one, may unsettle the available space, its strategies, and such targets as homogeneity, power, and transparency against the established system through and through. The silence of the user can be explained this way: They feel that their slightest movement would have unlimited consequences and that they would ditch the order (production style) that falls in on them with all its weight as soon as they make a move.

LEFEBVRE, 2014: p. 383

The material foundation of the differentiation of physical and social space is the second nature that comes from the primary nature. In practice, society should have been separated from nature before a complete differentiation of social space from physical space. This absolute physical space started to be associated with the given, natural space of nature. At this point, physical and natural spaces are indistinguishable. On the other hand, the concept of social space has gradually been abstracted from natural space. While the philosophy of nature was developed as a special field of expertise under philosophy, nature economics took an opposite course in the direction of the classic political economics by Adam Smith et al. However, even though it is possible to track the difference between natural and social space all the way back to Kant and that it represented the first recognition of social space whose classic political economics was built properly since the beginning of the 18th century, the concept of social space had not been clarified until towards the of the 19th century. The honour of inventing the term social space is generally attributed to Emile Durkheim. Wrote in the 1890s, Emile Durkheim insistently expressed that social space is quite different and separate from the actual space he used with the meaning of physical space. This way, social space appears to be spatial only metaphorically. Just like mathematical space beginning to represent the abstract field of natural phenomena formed by human beings, social space is the abstract field of social phenomenon also formed by people and can be defined in several ways. An object or a relation may be sufficiently real; however, identifying them in the social space as certain points does not actually tell much about their places in physical or natural space (Smith, 2017: p. 120).

Well, then, what do movements gain by producing social space within the city? What kind of developments does social space foreshadow?

The significance of the city problem discussed on a level of social and political dynamics is not restricted only to election periods and the control of government agencies. In other words, protest movements concentrating on urban and ecological issues organise and mobilise crowds, transform power relations between classes, generate new cultural models, and form

one of the most important axes of social change. Effects of these movements in the public eye and in creating an urban policy on a general level
have more significance on the direct effects on urban structures. Social
visibility and ideological legitimacy of them increase day after day.

CASTELLS, 2017: p. 14

The question of the city is fundamentally related to the organisation of
common means of consumption found underlying the daily life: housing,
education, health, culture, trade, etc. In developed capitalism, this states the
increasing socialisation of consumption (as a result of the concentration of
capital and means of production) on the one hand and the other, the fundamental conflict of capitalist logic formed between the production of the
means of consumption and their allocation. While public protests that emerge
as a result demand the betterment of the common material conditions of daily
existence, they also cause a crisis that deepens in this field. To solve this contrast and the following dilemmas, the state increasingly intervenes in the city.
However, as a result of class society, the state acts based on power relations
between social groups, in general, in favour of the most dominant section of
ruling classes. Therefore, these defined issues become globalised, and urban
issue makes the state increasingly involved with daily life and causes political
crises (Castells, 2017: p. 16). "In fact, the urban crisis is a more specific form of a
more general crisis underlying the ecology issue and related to the contradiction between producing powers and production relations" (Castells, 2017: p. 18).

Therefore, dominant social logic indivisibly affects all the public classes
through urban conflicts. Those inhabiting cities and commuting daily show
their reactions through various protest activities, which emerge in the form of
certain urban unionism. Specifically, the significant participation of the new
petite bourgeoisie having a weak fighting and organising tradition in work life
to these actions is remarkable.

Urban struggles have become a vehicle for this social stratum that has
traditionally been distant from the tendency and organisation of the proletarian movement previously to come to the realisation of the objective
opposition to state implementations determined by monopolist capital's hegemony. Therefore, the formation of common consumption units
leads to the common protest organisations of all classes under these conditions, and the interventions by state politicise these protests from time
to time.

CASTELLS, 2017: p. 261

3   Riotous Cities

Taking the working class into consideration as the focal point of revolutionary change, it becomes clear that the revolutionary working class does not only concern the groups working in the factories but the whole city. But when we look at the class organisation, a wide variety of characteristics are observed. In fact, it is fragmented, divided, and multiplied in numbers rather than being an organisation of solidarity. It is temporary in its purposes and needs, devoid of organisation, and has a flowing structure. Day by day, it loses its revolutionary character and transforms into urban movements that take on a reformist structure. Therefore, the working class is neither a revolutionary nor a class movement due to its identity as groups focused on more specific issues. In our age, factories have either disappeared in the capitalist world or have lost their classic industrial working-class identity. Due to the part-time, unorganised and low-paid workforce and the ranks of the unemployed, the new workforce that continues the urban life, i.e. the proletariat, has turned into citizens who have to live in and out of deplorable, high-risk work conditions that harm mental and physical health. Considering the return from the concept of 'proletariat' to the concept of 'precariat', we see that the groups living and working in the city do not have a goal such as unification and that the operating conditions necessary for integrity do not exist. The individuals also do not seem close to this kind of unification. Instead, we observe the emergence of groups based on more specific preferences and urban problems (Lefebvre, 2014: p. 45).

We live in an era when ideals of human rights have moved centre stage both politically and ethically. A lot of political energy is put into promoting, protecting and articulating their significance in constructing a better world. The main centres of these activities are cities. It is at the heart of society's passion for making cities more liveable. So much so that, over time, the community that prospered the city became the community shaped by the city it had built. In our age, the right to the city has come to the forefront and has undergone fundamental and radical changes during the urbanisation process. During the construction and reconstruction of the city, the communities changed, and the change itself continued to transform the community. Rather than being distributed among the whole city, the surplus value created in this process of change remained in the hands of very few people, and inequality occurred. It continued to produce surplus value and deeply affected the urbanisation process. Urbanisation has given birth to its own capitalist and authoritarian system in the process, and different identities and cultures have emerged within the city. The age of urbanisation that the world has come to has caused the problems to become different from the problems that have occurred in the past years, and the people to live more city oriented. Urbanisation, which increased inequality, also caused groups with a culture of unification and solidarity in the past to disband and express their opinions on different issues. While the share of the upper segment from the surplus value increased, the economic struggle of the lower segments transformed into various issues due to growing urban problems, and the struggle has become more personal and about preference issues. Due to the scarcity about finding jobs and the jobs found paying low salaries, people have limited their fields of activity for fear of losing their jobs. In addition, the advantages of living in the city and the disadvantages that arise are converging on issues where people can continue their lives in the city, rather than in such organisations. In addition, although the people living in the city are getting accustomed to living alone day by day, they can use their share of the existing savings, albeit limited, among the rich urban resources.

The cultural life and social resources obtained and the gains obtained in issues for which the citizens of the city struggled before preventing the unification of groups, namely communities. Instead, they bring up the problems they experience due to their personal preferences and deal with the city's problems. The newly established system is intertwined with the transformation of the urban structure. Still, it caused the construction of a new urban life and a new urban identity. The increase in consumption opportunities and improvements in purchasing power makes people focus on cultural codes rather than economic issues. The increase in urban transportation and the intensification of inter-city tourism allows people to spend their rest properly. Although the increase in such social activities gives the impression that thoughts about inequalities will peak and solidarity will increase, citizens mostly share their opinions about their personal preferences, cultural orientations, identity problems and, to a lesser extent, economic inequalities. The unions and union organisations in this urban world losing their power causes the emergence of a more autonomous egalitarian personality. In fact, individuals who stand for a more egalitarian structure choose to participate in urban activities rather than becoming united. They participate in uprisings and organise demonstrations rather than engaging in revolutionary movements (Harvey, 2012a: pp. 3–8).

In the last two decades, more than 100 cities have passed the population threshold of 1 million. This development caused the industrial facilities located in the city to move out of the city and the worker community located in the city to spread out the city. The city is increasingly becoming the place of people who get their share of surplus value as well as the creative and innovative workforce in the service sector. The new owners of the spaces, who are open to every individual on a massive scale, are actually the crowds within the city that have obtained their positive share from urbanisation. While these developments were taking place, of course, there were spaces and areas in the city that retained their public character, as was the case in the past. However, it has become difficult for people to come together due to issues related to time and money, and convergence has gradually started to take place in virtual spaces. In particular, the cities that give importance to their places in the national city network and the global city union have gradually turned their city centres into places of entertainment, tourism, and consumption culture. Those located on the periphery of the city visit these areas only on certain days of the week and enter these areas under challenging conditions. Daily relationships that take their place in virtual networks are evolving in a crucible increasingly filled with popular topics, and people are becoming more and more captive of popular culture. Since it is cheaper and easier to reach and spend time in virtual spaces than in physical spaces, people are increasingly moving away from the spirit of togetherness, the purpose of acting together, and the common goal. The individual, caught between entertainment and popular culture, has obtained certain gains but renounced their share of the city economy, engaging in political polemics, and is now isolated as an individual.

Cities receiving immigration flows have produced new urban identities, and cultural factors increasingly shape these identities. There are, of course, increasing complaints. However, these are generally related to the services and general city services that urbanising cities cannot offer to the population. The isolated individual tends to unite only in terms of urban problems, cultural issues, and an increasingly oppressive global agenda. From this point of view, the transformation in the city shows itself in the changes that occur in the lifestyles. Divisions of work that replace factories offer different conditions to employees and bring them together in different environments. Although segments with different economic incomes receive a share of surplus value in a certain amount and at certain rates, they seem to have lost their class consciousness. While the groups living in certain parts of the city were on the verge of disappearing into the crime network, certain groups created their own unique neighbourhoods by being grateful for their share. Those who reap the economic and social benefits of the city have customised their spaces more than ever before. However, since the transition between the spaces is materially possible, these differences do not bother anyone as much as they used to. Although certain meeting places formed in the centre of the city host movements against such inequalities and discriminations, the city is no longer a revolutionary leader; on the contrary, it has become a living centre that has been improved with reforms. In particular, the environments where different segments of the society come together to become a home for the right holders of the issues that constitute the agenda and voice their complaints.

The city is no longer a small settlement. It serves a huge crowd with a massive size. Interaction and communication between classes have changed, and social and cultural preferences have started to shape the agenda at a higher rate. Inequalities and environmental issues in city services have now become a buzzword for people, and the city has become the centre of complaints alone. The masses, who are unable to get a share of the surplus value within the understanding of the market and can barely make a living, are now struggling to reach the point of cultural saturation. Still, they cannot find the means to announce their economic complaints or gradually forget their focal points. Of course, economic issues and inequalities are not completely irrelevant, but they are not discussed as much as they used to be. The city is now home to the masses who make a living in the city economy but do not want more. Instead, they try to come to the forefront in social terms. For this reason, urban movements have changed the landscape compared to the past. The spirit of unity and the principles of togetherness have changed, and they are becoming the resources fed by the city rather than the resources that feed the city. The city's streets are now meeting places, and the gathering areas are now turning into sightseeing areas. Although the squares preserve their cultural values, they seem to have lost their political significance. This causes urban movements to develop in a more culture-oriented manner. In our age, where personal preferences gain importance, complaints and reactions are also individual, as it turns out. However, political demands certainly preserve their importance, but they do not occupy the agenda as much as they did in the past. But these reactions and demands can sometimes come together. Groups that do not often gather and vent their energy tend to support the events that erupt suddenly. Even if these events are about an issue that they do not demand, they are not ashamed to go out on the city's streets if they have their own complaints. However, since such actions are deprived of a specific goal and organisation, they can quickly turn into acts of violence and damage the places where the movements were born and grew up (Harvey, 2012b: pp. 11–6).

In the 21st century, urban movements appear as global movements that question the place and importance of the individual in urban space, bringing the urban rights and inner-city problems, which have become compatible with the problems of the cities, to the agenda. Urban innovations, environmental problems, cultural connotations, identity crises, immigration and immigrant movements, urban design and transformation stories, housing and transportation problems are the starting points of urban movements. If you pay attention, all of these titles are related to the production and establishment of the city. The bonds and relations of the elements that produce and consume the city with the citizens of the city lead to the formation and spread of urban movements. The creative elements that renovate and rebuild the city enter the domain of the rights of the citizens and create new inequalities among the citizens. Both the weakening of economic and class conflicts with vested rights and the transformation of the new workforce and economic order in the 21st century are also changing the forms and reasons of organisation among the citizens. Joint actions are now formed around social and cultural ideals rather than political ideals. The individual is often bottlenecked not only by economic ties but also by technological, social and cultural ties. As a result of some progress that has become widespread in the city, economic topics are gradually losing their effect on the citizens. Still, cultural, and social issues are gaining importance. When the reaction created by creative ideas and advances in society also conflicts with environmental demands, conflict arises, and global balances come into play. Now, the globalised urban capital gradually decreases the economic value of the masses by acting independently from the local powers. Still, it has only just begun to mention the cultural and social issues that remain in the hands of the masses.

Individuals who have achieved their economic independence but have not yet attained mass freedom have become only reactive when it comes to their personal lives and have gained the authority to engage in joint activities. Contrary to those who benefit from economic surplus production, the deprivations and lack of trust in the organisational structure of those who cannot benefit from it take away the right of individuals to claim their earnings. Diversifying business lines and the lack of the same diversification in the form of organisation limit the citizens' right to assembly. Due to the political life enriched due to the political rights gained in the past, individuals with different aspects and ideas move away from organisations on the borderline of certain ideologies. As the mass parties lost their importance, but the parties kept their place, the society conflicted in this way first came under the hegemony of different organisations within the environment of polarisation. However, the divided organisations lost the balance of power, and the belief in groups that would protect the economic status of the business owners decreased as a result of the exclusion of the communities that do not see eye to eye on political issues. With the memberships being lost gradually and the extinction that came as a result, the masses who were divided into different business lines and working in different city environments could not protect their rights.

In fact, even though progress has been made based on rights, the demands expressed in the direction of expectations have been postponed by the elements dominant in the power landscape. The changing business life in terms of wages and working conditions, unfortunately, prevents the integration of employees. Instead, meetings on social, cultural, and urban topics have emerged in which people become similarised more easily. And the city is home to the construction and reconstruction of these similarities. While the personal preferences of individuals take their place in urban life, they are not legally recognised or marginalised by the dominant elements. While individuals whose lives are blocked can easily reach non-governmental organisations that will guide them in such topics, they are unfortunately far from guidance in other matters, especially in economic matters. While the environmental issues that occur in the areas where the houses are located are attracting more attention globally, issues such as the existing housing problem in the city, rent fees, and the number of affordable housings, unfortunately, cannot organise the masses. The inequalities created by the capital union, which draws attention as an urban growth machine while rebuilding the city, are not questioned, except for the services of the city administrators. The masses, who cannot get the share they deserve from the urban value that emerges in the city, unfortunately, cannot express their reactions, but they can come to terms due to the gap in urban services that occurs afterwards. The main reason for this is political. Organisations that politically distance themselves from the individual cannot attract individuals to their side. Political parties with different policies, and the distrust in them, greatly escalates the polarisation between individuals. What remains are the individual preferences of people and the difficulties they encounter in their daily lives. Where these problems are similar, people can easily come together and create pressure. However, the concerns about economic inequality, which is the main cause of the issue, unfortunately, atrophied due to the different ideals and interests of those concerned. One of the reasons for this is that political persons and organisations cannot keep up with the cultural and social changes that occur in the city.

Political organisations that bring the problems and changes that exist only in certain places of the city to the agenda cannot reach the whole city. However, the city is an area of movement where all these elements intersect. The fact that immigrants and low-income groups attain economic independence that will improve their conditions in the city due to their living and business conditions is a reason for action. Due to the very low level of economic credit, people are often deprived of steps to advance their lives. In the absence of these elements, the urban creative power prefers to marginalise the citizens rather than improve their living conditions. Development projects performed in areas close to the city centre generally push the poor income groups out of the city. The new living spaces created are built not only for the city's upper echelon but also for the demand at the national and global levels. As a result,

the new centres created for the displaced citizens are unfortunately unquali-
fied in terms of living conditions. People who have already moved away from
the city are also pushed away from urban services. The city creates problems
in itself because there are no quality transportation, health, education and
accommodation conditions. On the other hand, the houses built in new areas
are designed for individuals without a home to be tenants rather than home-
owners. This raises another issue. Individuals who are economically weak in
terms of rent move away from the fruits of social life. And they become more
and more radicalised. During this transformation, they create new subcultures
and identities by individuals similar to themselves. However, the dominant
elements of the city do not welcome this.

   In this respect, while marginalised individuals unite to protect their cultural
rights, they move away from the economic reasons that are the source of the
main problem. While the city becomes the place of this cultural freedom, it
gradually becomes the epicentre of profit areas, where new conflicts will arise.
While those who cannot benefit from city services become increasingly hostile
to the city administration, they are far from the factors that brought them to
this situation. In fact, the administrators who create the city policies are guilty
of taking the wrong steps at the beginning of this process, but they are blamed
for the services they could not perform or failed to fulfil rather than the first
mistakes they made. This continues with the inability of individuals to maintain their positions, or the progress made in areas being limited. However, the
source of the problem is forgotten and remains unanswered. Following this
process, in which economic surplus value is generated but only benefits certain segments, social and cultural reproduction is carried out, and in the 21st
century, urban dwellers only question the source of the next process. Social
and cultural reproduction occurs around the dominant popular culture and in
the form of a response. Each district is concentrated with a different culture.
The newly generated identities cause new agglomerations to form in the city
so that the already polarised society continues to live in a new separation. Of
course, as a result, similarities occur as well, but the dominant elements are
not very tolerant in accepting them. This poses an urban problem and gives
way to urban movements.

   The reproduction of capital takes place through the urbanisation process
in various ways. But the urbanisation of capital is based on how the power
of the capitalist class dominates the urban process. The dominance of the
capitalist class affects not only the state supplies that manage the social and
infrastructural conditions but also the entire population. It changes the way of
life, workforce, cultural and political values of the citizens and the mental and
spiritual understanding of the world. This control, authority, and inspection,

of course, was not achieved easily. The effect that produced this urbanisation process became the main area of political, social and class struggles. While the previous struggles only dealt with the capital and formation of the case, urban movements now give importance to the issues related to the urbanisation process. Cities are places where all kinds of people and classes come together voluntarily or through struggle. However, this volunteering and struggle now concern the representation of the city. Cities are revived if the citizens contribute to the activities and development of the city by being satisfied with their living conditions. However, it seems that it is a tradition to gain a place in the city through struggle. And urban movements are the only way for citizens to benefit from the urbanisation process. Because in today's representative democracy, representatives generally do not act without finding a response in the society.

The hierarchical order that occurs in representation takes away the opportunity of individuals to express themselves. Especially in cultural and social issues, individuals have difficulty reaching the channels where they can make their voices heard. Political issues can often be conveyed to politicians through organisations of different types. Still, the space in which communities active in environmental, cultural and social problems can express themselves is limited. It is only possible for the communities formed by non-governmental organisations to reach politicians by creating public opinion, and at this stage, urban movements come into play. The hierarchy and the failure of the representatives to consolidate their place in the society reduces the trust and beliefs of the masses. Therefore, areas of complaint and protest spaces are formed in the city. In this respect, urban movements that hope to find authorities who can reach them on a local scale, share their problems, listen to their complaints, and produce solutions as a result, herald a world that is increasingly globalised but at the same time localised. And this globalisation and localisation are best observed in cities. Citizens living in towns and neighbourhoods in the city bring up local issues as well as issues concerning the central government. In fact, most of the problems concerning the central government and legislation are local interventions. So, we can say that urban movements are a set of actions based on localisation and making it a target.

Cultural partnerships are a dynamic process as well as a process involved in the production of the workforce and future productions. This partnership develops through the language we share, the social practices we create, the socialisation we establish and the network of relationships we define, rather than just the world that hosts us. As these partnerships have been built over time, they are open to everyone in principle. The individual nature of the cities has a closed, socially controlled and appropriated structure inherent in the private and public interests. These features affect all the partnerships that the spaces within the city have in practice. There is no doubt that there is an important distinction between the public sphere and the public good. The public sphere and the public good in the city are generally and indeed always a matter of state power and public administration, but this sphere does not necessarily create partnerships. Sanitation, public health, education and the like are the productions of public spaces and public policies throughout the history of urbanisation. Cities are areas where different groups and classes come together, and therefore conflicts and struggles occur. For this reason, the city administration has generally been skilled in preserving and serving public benefits such as sanitation, affordable social housing, health, education, street construction with ready infrastructure and superstructure, and waterworks for the urbanised working class. While these public spaces and public good depend on the quality of partnerships, they also depend on each citizen's acceptance and appropriateness of political actions. Education is common for all, as long as it is given to all equally.

Squares are common as long as they are evaluated equally and shared by the citizens. While the streets are often home to revolutionary movements, they are common as long as they serve each urban community. Then, the result we encounter in the city is openness and equality in access to these public spaces and the public good. Struggles are being waged in cities to access these areas and benefits. But another point is to protect and preserve the quality of these public spaces and the public good. In particular, neoliberal policies oppose financing these areas and the benefits and gradually lead to the loss of partnerships. The partnership has not been studied and interpreted; therefore, it is an intricate way of life that emerges as a result of unstable and malleable social relations established between the social communities, which are unique as a special kind of thing, value or social process, or the existing or created social and physical environment. As an effect of this, the partnership has a social practice. Together with this practical partner, it produces or establishes social relations, provided it is open to some or all social communities. The practice of partnership in principle relates to the exposure of social groups to the environment within the established market exchange and market value. At this point, we must distinguish between public good interpreted as productive state expenditures and partnerships established in a completely different way and under completely different purposes, which indirectly increase the income and wealth of certain social groups. A community garden can thus be viewed as a good thing in itself, no matter what food may be produced there. This does not prevent some of the food from being sold. The common, even and particularly when it cannot be enclosed, can always be traded upon even though it is not in itself a commodity. The ambience and attractiveness of a city, for example, is a collective product of its citizens. Still, the tourist trade commercially capitalises upon that common to extract monopoly rents. Individuals and social groups create the city's social world through their daily activities and struggles, thereby creating something common as a framework within which all can dwell. While this culturally creative common cannot be destroyed through use, it can be degraded and banalized through excessive abuse.

Streets that get clogged with traffic make that particular public space almost unusable, even for drivers. However, with the levying of congestion and access charges in an attempt to restrict use, it can function more efficiently. This kind of street is not a common. Before the car came along, however, streets were often a common; but that kind of common was destroyed and turned into a public space dominated by the advent of the automobile. But such attempts to create new kinds of urban commons can all too easily be capitalised upon. While sidewalks, bicycle paths, gardens and playgrounds, as well as coffee shops, cafes and restaurants on the side of the streets used to be common areas, cities have put an end to this partnership due to the increasing number of vehicle roads and parking areas, for example, and a new partnership has been formed (Harvey, 2012a: pp. 70–4).

Capitalist urbanisation perpetually tends to destroy the city as a social, political, and liveable commons. When the concept of the urban commons is examined, what we find interesting is that it poses all of the political contradictions of the commons in a highly concentrated form. When we look at it, we no longer start to deal with a local neighbourhood or political organisation but rather the city as a whole. When common values are considered, the city is considered a whole, and therefore the regional planning and city planning of the state come to the fore. However, the functionally efficient use of common resources for the city's population should be recognised. These common resources are water supply, transportation, sewerage, waste management, open spaces and recreation areas. However, what is essential for the efficient use of common resources is the steps taken at more local and micro levels rather than central planning. Of course, the central government can intervene, but each locality (that is, each city or even different regions within the city) may have different needs and efficiency principles. So how can decentralisation be built? How can high-order hierarchical authority become more localised, and cities can take over the administration by expanding authority? Based on the dispersion of not the control but the administrative powers to the cities in a decentralised way, it may lead to the advancement of urban services and the sharing of urban profits by the citizens of the city.

The state can retain its control and administrative power over the cities with the central government (i.e. the government and the legislature). Still, the city administration can also transform into a more decentralised form of administration. In this way, the common public space and public good can thrive and develop with the intervention of social communities organised in local areas. In this way, the organisation of politically, culturally, and socially divided groups becomes easier, and the sensitivity of these groups to the problems that arise in terms of urban services and urbanisation increases. Each city has its unique history and conditions. For this reason, the similarities are more obvious and at a higher level in the city. Communities that cannot unite at the national level can mobilise more easily on a local scale and find more effective, efficient, and faster solutions to emerging problems. In this way, urban development penetrates more layers, and urbanisation without a city is prevented. In this way, we do not reach two-headed management; on the contrary, we are faced with more efficient implementation and more experienced control and execution. Cities that have managed to organise themselves can determine their own common good and common goals. It is possible with this localisation to balance production and consumption, increase local entrepreneurship, resolve environmental issues with local participation, spread the spirit of unity throughout the country with the development of cities, and increase the number of stakeholders for public targets. Since these developments do not exist, democratic urban movements have to face the problems created by these due to the lack of production, protection, public good and use of urban commons in the cities. The role of commons in urban form and urban policy is now gaining function and experience. This is increasingly becoming a practice around the world. When the role of these commons is underestimated or disregarded, urban movements come into play and direct the city's energy to such activities. It can be seen that the participation of those working in cultural activities and production, namely those working in the service sector and workers, has increased in recent decades. And this trend is increasing rapidly, reaching more and more numbers. While this cultural mass creates the creative core, it causes the emergence of different identities and elements within the urban culture. Increasing political commitment through socialisation strategy and reshaped and revitalised institutions cause political and cultural upheavals to be channelled in the city more efficiently and with the right energy and culture-oriented actions to come to the fore more. However, the market and commercial activities also impact cultural activities.

Under the influence of popular culture, citizens change their cultural values. This development not only reveals similarities across the country and even on a global scale but also causes localised cultures to remain in the background.

Events that develop in this way cause the citizens to become alienated from their own city and channel their sensitivity to other issues. However, cultural partners result in the expression of reproduction and entertainment by the excited citizens and the repetition of the production with this excitement. This form of culture has become the common and has caused the citizens to adopt it as a common value. In addition to these, common culture among the citizens returns common memories, architecture, effective communities and cultural products. While the citizens can experience the elements of their own culture in the places belonging to their own region, they also create a unique production. Individuals caught between popular culture, global culture, local culture and alternative culture create their own subcultures, and these similarities create a recovery among the citizens. The citizen, who transforms the cultural elements they have acquired into an identity, finds a new way to face urban problems and fights for the right of expression (Castells, 2017: pp. 84–9).

The history of urban-based class struggles is exceptional. The events of 1789, 1830, 1848 and 1871 in Paris are the most prominent examples from the 19th century. The events that took place in 1789 differ from those in the city until that day. It is a series of events initiated by completely city-oriented groups, where different social segments seek their rights. Later, the events in Petrograd came into existence, followed by the events of 1927 in Shanghai. In Shanghai, these events were repeated in 1967. The events in Seattle in 1919 were followed by events in Barcelona. The civil rights movement that emerged in the United States in the 1960s swept through cities. The events related to students that started in Paris in 1968 spread to the cities of the world in a short time. Chicago, Mexico City, Madrid, Bangkok and Prague Spring are the best examples of this. More recently, the events in Seattle in 1999 are significant. Tahrir Square, Occupy Wall Street, the Plazas del Sol, Madrid, Oaxaca, Mexico, El Alto, Bolivia and Syntagma Square, Greece: all these centres are the most important examples of urban movements today. As can be seen in these cities, several different protest events spread prominently within the urban network. For instance, after the events in Paris in 1848, it spread to Vienna, Berlin, Milan, Budapest, Frankfurt and other European cities. The revolution in Russia soon spread to Berlin, Vienna, Warsaw, Riga, Munich and Turin. The events in 1968 were observed in Paris, Berlin, London, Mexico City, Bangkok, Chicago and many other cities. The events of the 1960s spread throughout the United States and became an urban symphony. In 2003, anti-war demonstrations affected Madrid, London, Barcelona, Berlin, Athens, New York, Melbourne, nearly 200 Asian cities, African cities, and South American cities. When we look at the spread of these movements, we cannot ignore the urban network that has faced similar problems. Of course, global policies can be the reason for the start and aftermath of these events, but we should not forget the complaints of people who are deprived of their rights in the city. The reflections of these waves are observed in Tahrir Square, Rabia Square and Occupy Wall Street movements. Communities deprived of political and economic representation suddenly emerged and voiced urban problems. These actions, which are planned against the city administration and the existing policies in the city's network, are, of course, the most important examples of the urban struggle. Of course, there have been gains due to these movements, but another point of view has also settled.

According to this view, political institutions should take control of cities and constantly monitor the potential centres of action. It is considered that where the groups that are likely to be organised are kept under control, the extent of movements will decrease. The second major point is that political urban movements and protests frequently gauge their effectiveness and capabilities in terms of their ability to target urban economies. Immigrant actions that took place in the United States of America in 2006 are movements of immigrants that seek their rights but who actually demand their economic freedom. Most immigrants participating in these movements appear to have entered the country only a few years ago. The migrant worker movements, which started in cities such as Los Angeles and Chicago, spread to all cities in a short time. The complaints, which were only initially concerned with immigrant rights, suddenly began to question the country's economic conditions. When the conditions arising from the different structures of the cities are taken into account, it becomes apparent that the citizens now inhabit the cities, and if their rights are not given, they will resist the invaders. Cities have allowed protest movements in which people exercised their right to complain against national and global powers who tried to destroy them. Particularly, the anti- or alternative globalisation movements that started after the 1990s brought together different urban groups within the cities. In response to organisations such as the World Bank, IMF, G8 and G20, the mobilisations in the cities began to group. These international meetings show us another face of cities. They seek to form unity against not only their own issues but also the problems that they will have difficulty coping with. Issues such as climate change, racism, women's rights and equality are slowly causing the cities to react together. These events, which we can refer to as urban movements occurring in cities, are the reactions of cities to global problems, and, once again, the city is at the centre of these movements (Harvey, 2012b: pp. 115–9).

Can urban movements be considered a set of events that strive and struggle for a better quality of urban life? Of course, but not every action is alike in its quality and effect. Although urban movements that are handled on a global scale mostly deal with the global problems of the residents, local improvements are not ignored either. However, the organisation is different in purpose and task. Well, does it distinguish or separate from the cities? Of course not. Again, it is an action produced by the city. The existence of the same organisation in different cities and engaging the same in similar actions do not expand it beyond the cities. Again, they are urban movements because they are carried out by the elements that originate from the city and are fed by the city. In addition, such movements have impacts and reactions on a local scale. Communities that complain about the global economy question the existing economic structure in society. This is not necessarily a separate action of current collaborators in their own cities, but it can be an extension. Culture and identity problems, which are more common today and form the core of new urban movements, should be handled similarly. Global culture does not remain the same when combined with the local (i.e. the city) culture. Although it follows the same pattern, it is a derivative of the latter. Many branches derived from it take their place in urban culture. This causes the emergence of different identities, and in this identity crisis, personal rights come to the fore, and cities are central to these demands. Particularly, the masses that unite at the local level can bring urban movements to the agenda with their own methods. For example, some groups can take action against the global economic order by designing a production and consumption mechanism on a neighbourhood scale. This activity can develop entirely in a town or on a larger urban scale.

A more autonomous production and reproduction can turn into action for the economic complaints of the masses. The second-hand market or its conversion can be another example. The goods exchanged with charter agreements are a reaction to the financial system and consumption habits, and this reaction can only come to life in the cities. Or they can set up their own organisations by founding establishments or associations. In the structure of this organisation, they can engage in an activity in the form of democracy and the management of partners by providing a horizontal managerial form, that is, non-hierarchical integrity. These small organisations can expand beyond the local dimension and reach an urban scale. This can allow the administrations that oppose the decentralisation structure to take a lesson, and the source of these changes is always the city. However, the city requires more involvement to be effective in surplus production and sharing its values.

The masses who do not play by the rules valued by the market are unfortunately excluded from the agenda. In fact, many citizens cannot even enter the game and are left out of the market. This creates a crowd in these cities, dissatisfied with their lives. This production and value, therefore, emerge in the city. The class relations, power relations and relations between the rich and poor observed reach their peak in the city. Each city is unique in terms of the number of citizens who can find the room to breathe and who are under pressure in the established economic, social, and cultural environment. For this reason, urban movements play a constructive role in these matters. It is now the scene of conflicts not only between economic classes but also cultural, social and identity classes. There are cultural surplus values as well as economic surplus values, and there are numerous identities derived from these values. Even if the culturally excluded or marginalised groups find a place in the city's culture, they have difficulties finding a place to express and maintain these cultures. And that causes a reaction. This is a struggle for life. The same goes for identities. Identities that are not similar, despite not being contrary to the dominant identity of the city, are excluded by the city. Of course, exposed to this situation, the citizens lose their living space, and their lives turn into a struggle. They search for areas in the city where their preferences are not judged, and they can easily put their preferences into practice, and they demand that these areas be public spaces. This is how urban movements develop.

Cities are home to urban movements. Urban movements both feed the city and are fed by the city. Every different view that comes to life in the city has the freedom to express itself. The city is built for this. The economic, political, cultural and technological order established in the city, of course, has to change over time. New understandings, identities and problems that emerged over time reveal the necessity of the citizens to create new movements. However, not every move may have the same effect on the city. Actions seen in cities may spread to other cities, and activities may spread within the city's networks. However, it should not be forgotten that urban movements exist for change. Crowds who voice their reactions, problems, complaints, and expectations struggle for change. The city gives them a chance to express themselves, i.e. to build their own values. That is, they are born in the city. So, they should not destroy the city. In other words, they should not harm the city and the citizen. Movements struggling for change should stay away from acts of violence. Participants and activists in the movement should pay particular attention to the locations that host the movements. Destroying these locations will not bring anything to the movement but will harm the cities that are the starting point of the movement. So, violence must be avoided. No matter what side the violence comes from, it harms the city and its inhabitants, bringing no gain. Urban movements are fireflies, not flames of fire. The city is an incubation, not a skin that must be shed.

4   Dwellers of the Dream Streets

The most valuable asset that the streets offer us is the space that forms the centre of our living space. The space offered to us by the street helps develop our memory by combining the past with the present and unites the people with the space. By creating possibilities and focusing on these possibilities, urban cities enable different citizens and groups to communicate with each other (Hall, 2012: p. 6). In the context of multicultural streets in cities that are the source of diversity, space and time dimensions help understand participation, unity, and belonging. The human relations that lead to the formation of the streets and the spaces that develop in this context gradually change their roles in daily life, and the spaces gradually lead to the emergence of human relations. In this context, public and private, secular or divine and microcosmic and earthly spaces help the streets develop within the relationships that define these spaces. Within this diversity, the users of the streets decide which streets and which places they will use on these streets while also shaping when they will prefer to do so. Even in a very short time, it is possible to see how the citizens of the city are organised in different streets and how they differ from each other. When we look at the neighbouring streets that have their own spaces and, therefore their users, we see that there are areas open to the use of a wide variety of citizens and suitable for them to become organised. Consequently, we must learn when the layers of space and time are intertwined and how they still remain different. We also have to learn the patterns of the citizens' meetings and how there are transitions between the layers (Hall, 2012: p. 30).

City streets are lines, but also labyrinths. Streets, which are the areas that connect the citizens and the spaces, are the meeting points where the urban areas are shaped from the front to the end, and the background world and the lower worlds meet. The first visible features of cities are citizens making themselves visible and expanding their scope by establishing relationships due to entrepreneurial and cultural motivations. For this reason, although the language of some of the streets, which are shaped inside the city and shaped the city itself, is singular and their activities are unidirectional, the common language of the majority of them is people, and their activities are diverse. Citizens with different ethnic, cultural and identity structures make their existence visible by reviving these streets. Citizens changing within the ongoing street culture are changing the language of the street. The balance of power may shift, and conflict may escalate. However, the streets do not give up on hosting the citizens of all identities. Diversity has become the language of the streets. In this context, the streets have become the meeting point of the traditional past, the changing future, and associations that have become a net-work of global and local relations.

The streets are open to everyone. People from all identities and cultures are busy changing their lives by travelling back and forth on the streets. However, diversity, which is the language of the streets, can become monotonous and isolate itself from the city, unfortunately, when it restricts the types of users that make up the spaces forming the streets. However, even this obstacle could not prevent the streets, which shaped the spaces in question, from being home to various types of citizens. Such initiatives that interrupt the cultural vitality of the cities also destroy the history of the streets. However, the streets have been examples of social inclusion and exclusion throughout history. In the past, only people whose economic and cultural characteristics matched a spe-cific place could enter certain streets of particular regions. While these may be very luxurious areas in the centre of this city, they may also be back streets on the city's outskirts. Today, the most influential factor limiting the partici-pation of the citizens is innovation. Since specific segments of the society can only meet the technological and innovation culture requirements, innovation changes the language of the streets. The existence of streets that limit the user materially and morally with their changing design and architectural structure increases the visibility of the streets where the corresponding traditional sense of belonging is established. While traditional streets are developing with a structure ready for their history, they are in search of different types of innova-tions as it is triggered by the innovation that spreads to the city to respond to such innovation. Therefore, innovation not only changes the language of the streets but also causes them to diversify (Hall, 2012: p. 50).

The cosmopolitan structure of the cities also affects the streets. The unity realised by recognising the diversity can be accepted not as a uniformness but as a result of a relationship that seeks common points as they interact. Social cohesion may become more visible in the streets. Still, it is not a situation that arises from the crowds gathering on the streets, ethnically or culturally the same. Of course, each street has its own function and concentration of space. Its users often have similar characteristics. However, it would not be beneficial to define an experience that every citizen can breathe with a singular relation-ship because the streets are the meeting point of different business lines and, therefore, the citizens of different social and economic cultures.

At the point of socialisation, the streets are the exclusive places for society. Streets are places where people from different cities interact with those closest to them. They are also places where they notice innovation and try to keep up with it. Innovation emerges when new types of practices, functions, relation-ships and cultures that emerge on the streets, which preserve their historical heritage, begin to occupy the streets. Urban change, therefore, starts in the streets. New users appearing among the ordinary users try to add new traditions to the traditional street culture in the coming years, bringing a change in places and citizens. Although social skills exist in conventional relationships, the new generation, new culture and the understanding of the changing city require the users of the streets to adopt new social skills. The unique culture that emerges as specific groups, who live in the backstreets with their traditions, mix into the streets can also change the language of the streets as new cultures emerge that are entirely unrelated to the city. In the streets where global changes are rapidly becoming visible, the availability of places that allow local cultures to be experienced proves that the streets are actually the home of diversity. Therefore, streets where different cultures come together have a distinguishable understanding of solidarity.

The dimensions of familiarity, sincerity and sensitivity encapsulate the streets and allow the development and change of the citizens. Of course, this process is not a factor in the deterioration of the traditions of the streets. Streets transform change into development by preserving the spaces that will conserve their history in this change. Local cultures clustered around the streets may be more sensitive and less active in the public sphere. However, the streets, which are common areas around this cluster of young, old, poor and newcomers, are the structural basis of coexistence. Like the body's backbone, it enables different groups and citizens to live on the streets in cooperation and solidarity. This is why the streets, where local cultures are more influential, actually become living spaces for groups that transform within this culture. The tolerance of the citizens, who see the streets as their domestic spaces, to the emerging new identities, as well as their satisfaction with the availability of spaces belonging to them, cause these streets to host more participants in the city. And this interaction and participation keep these streets alive (Hall, 2012: p. 108).

Familiarity is the main element of solidarity in the streets. Although they are different from each other, the groups from certain parts of the city and clustered around the streets feel close because they share the common area, causing the streets to become a place of resistance. The fact that intertwined relations come together for a common purpose, namely life, ensures that there is a struggle against the negative changes that occur in the city and the reflection of these changes on the neighbourhoods clustered around the streets. Of course, neighbourhoods clustered around the street bring different social structures and economic contexts to the street. Increasing cultural changes and the identities produced by the city increase the number of citizens hosted on the streets. Among these groups, even those that can be described as marginal can find a place for themselves in the familiarity of the street. These streets are the cocoons of struggle, resistance and innovations that will ensure the city's development. However, there are also more conservative streets in the city. This conservatism is not only seen in high-income areas of the city but also other parts of the city. The streets of the neighbourhoods that do not want different groups to be hosted in their living spaces are also more secluded and monotonous. This is also true in high-income neighbourhoods as well as in low-income neighbourhoods. The difference is that since certain sections of the city obtain the highest share from the innovations and surplus value produced by the city, the streets belonging to these sections are closed to the use of every citizen by invisible obstacles due to both physical and material factors. On the other hand, the streets surrounded by low-income neighbour-hoods turn away from the city by closing themselves to new users due to both cultural and moral general rules.

In fact, the areas that open their doors to everyone, which we see as fit for the definition of a street, are determined to move the city further by rebelling against the existence of these two types of streets. For this reason, the places where the struggle started, spread, grew and gained prestige are located on such streets. These streets, nurtured by the diversity of the neighbourhoods around them and, being discontent, spread to the whole city, are the cocoon, home and future of urban movements (Hall, 2012: p. 129). He saw the streets as a place where the citizens gained their individual identities and, where the places they lived could introduce themselves to other identities. Therefore, the streets became the home of integrating all kinds of local or global focal points. Social interaction emerges as the language of the streets, which is the only place where the relationship between space and society is experienced. Streets, which are diversified by the presence of local and global features, where opportunities and problems arise, are areas where structural per-spectives coexist equally. Therefore, streets are spaces where differences and associations meet, come together, interact, and take shape. Creativity and communication are thus seen on the streets. The existence of different spaces that serve the neighbourhoods surrounding the streets nourishes and keeps the society alive, just as the blood circulating the body does. Within this order, of course, some spaces are shaped according to the personal preferences of identities, groups, and citizens. However, the design and placement of these spaces in a way that allows everyone to live as neighbours causes the street to become open to all kinds of ideas and changes. For this reason, it is usual for groups affected by different initiatives first to express their reactions in these streets (Hall, 2012: p. 130).

The existence of physical and perceptual boundaries means that the people living in the city are deprived of the time and space they will share. Such areas in the city prevent the city from maintaining a vibrant and prosperous life. Social and spatial distinctions make the city unliveable because the concept of belonging directs the citizens to other residents with a negative point of view. Social and spatial limitations based on race, culture and class differences affect the streets, the cities' establishment networks. The streets of the areas where this perception is intensely present are becoming stagnant areas, which are far from all kinds of development and gradually lose their users. Urban edges, which also include the areas where luxury spaces are located in the centre of the city, host the initiatives and events that lead to the formation of urban movements. At the same time, the streets, which are lively and diverse, become the capitals of resistance against this development. Compared to the streets of the urban edges, which are assumed to be more homogeneous, the streets, which are home to liveliness and diversity, create a unique solidarity thanks to their friendliness and familiarity, and form a unification against the edge areas. The shared common vision and understanding compel the citizens of the street, who are the owners of the street, to react with the spirit of mobilisation against all kinds of policies and initiatives developed against them. As a result of the interaction created, the shared action spreads from the lively streets to every part of the city. Because such streets serve not only in the neighbourhoods clustered around them but also in the city.

The daily life prevailing in the city's peripheries reflects the limiting daily life of the local world with certain conversations, meetings and shopping opportunities. Yet this hierarchical and routine way of life reduces the fragility and resilience of local worlds. The street life that spreads around the symbolic spaces seems to have been created for certain masses, not the city citizens, to spend their lives. In fact, such places and the streets where they are located can be found in every city. And to a certain extent, they are essential for the city's health. However, the spread of such streets in the city and the expansion of the physical and perceptual boundaries for such streets create a negative atmosphere for the citizens and reduce their motivation. Urban dwellers become disconnected and begin to distance themselves from each other. The solidarity that exists at the local level actually moves away from being organised in a way to react in a time of crisis. Loss of common values, lack of institutionalisation, and organisational flexibility cause individuals and groups to become lost in their local lives and erode social and political symbols and values (Hall, 2012: p. 132). Therefore, contemporary city streets are complex spaces, and it can be easily read from the streets that the textures that make up the social and cultural whole of local environments change easily under global influences.

The city's streets are becoming parts of global change together with local col-laborators. Such streets, which are the global marketplaces, live in conflict with the existence of diverse streets which are affected by global developments and considered, at least, to be markets. To try to destroy either of these two types of streets is essentially to destroy both. However, it is necessary to keep the balance of the scale in place.

If the urban policies and initiatives necessary to enable the citizens to adopt these two types of streets are not implemented, these two types will compete against each other in conflict. This conflict embodies the existence of urban movements. For this reason, from past to present, urban movements are the voice of the streets (Hall, 2012: p. 134). Face-to-face relations established on the streets make solidarity stronger and more sincere. In addition, conflict and joint action between different groups that see each other on the streets are more effective. The rulers of different streets experience, challenge and strug-gle with each other through their streets. The rapid change that develops on an urban basis shape the network that the streets establish with each other. The resulting inequalities, exclusion and unfair practices increase the tension between the streets and create the gas clouds necessary to form urban move-ments. Social and cultural life embodied around the spaces creates a culture of struggle by making the masses hostile to each other due to the privileges and unbalanced development in the city. For this reason, incidents amounting to attacks occur between the masses. In fact, the city creates the common streets for both groups with natural methods, and the real struggle takes place for these areas. While urban renovations or other urban policies are being devel-oped for these streets, activities for and on these streets are observed against these developments. And these streets are not just areas of local, urban and national struggle. At the same time, they become arenas of struggle for global issues (Hall, 2012: p. 136).

Speaking of the symbolic streets where selected spaces are located in the city, we should emphasise that these areas are also the target of urban terror-ism. Since such areas are famous both within the city and globally. With the violence that erupts due to urban conflict, the global terrorist organisations operating on a global scale attempt to multiply the effects of their actions by choosing such areas as targets for themselves. The streets we mentioned are the most densely populated centres of the city. They are also the areas with the highest traffic of vehicles. These are hubs for business. In fact, they are critical centres not only for business but also for finance, politics, religion and the media. The streets we are talking about have symbolic and strategic values. There are many buildings and squares around these streets that are the meet-ing points of society. The area formed by the streets hosts the very spaces that are economically vital and lie at the heart of local democracy. The struggle for these areas can easily turn into violence with false news. The high-tensioned struggle of groups aiming to share all kinds of values produced by the city and those who want to enjoy the privileges of these benefits may seek to occupy these areas. These dynamic and lively areas can suddenly turn into dead zones. By choosing the streets surrounded by these dynamic and lively areas as their target, terrorist acts attempt to draw attention to their actions worldwide and bring results for their causes to the extent possible (Savitch, 2008: p. 15).

Three factors are essential for urban terrorism. They are territory, space, and logistics. Urban terror seeks to reach its potential logistics targets by attacking small spaces and critical areas in the territory to decontrol large swatches of territory. For this reason, they attack the most dynamic and lively streets of the city with a high symbolic value. Since these areas are the home of all kinds of citizens, they want to weaken their opponents (i.e. foes) by carrying over their struggles to these areas by intimidating them. Urban terrorism is common in cities where urban movements do not evolve properly. In the administrative systems where local and national democracy is not the dominant element, large urban movements that erupt instantaneously cause many actions involving the element of violence, and urban terror comes into play and takes control even in places where such activities are not possible, or in cities where more marginal groups emerge (Savitch, 2008: p. 25). Space is the oxygen of the city. The existence and diversity of spaces are necessary for society to breathe. However, another necessity for living is the street itself. The streets that give way to and shape spaces are essential for the citizens of the city. Streets are areas of the city where relationships are established, happiness and sadness are shared, solidarity is made visible and shared values are created. Therefore, urban movements are born, grown and developed around these streets. It is not surprising that violence also targets these areas in this respect. Some measures are taken to prevent violence and terrorist acts from occurring in the city and occupying these areas. These measures, unfortunately, can sometimes be the target of designs developed by those in power to protect their authority. Of course, security measures must be taken, and the streets must be protected from violence and terrorism. However, in terms of the peaceful struggle of urban movements as well as the balanced development and progress of cities, it is also essential for the streets to be open to the citizens and to host demonstrations for the continuation of the current liveliness and the sustainability of the mobility (Savitch, 2008: p. 134).

When we look at the spread of urban movements in Europe, it is observed that the liveliness of the streets and the issues voiced in the streets are transformed into lobbying activities by certain groups and organisations. Urban

movements have specific networks and coalitions thanks to the liveliness of
the street. As a result of these connections and relations, the mobility of the
streets is brought to life. Although lobbying activities are mostly seen as carried out by the multi-national companies and some NGOs, today, the owners
of urban movements can direct their requests to the relevant people thanks to
the developing communication tools. It is observed that a different window of
opportunity has been opened to the citizens of the city today, as the demands
and targets reach the city's administrators and holders of power through the
organisations that are already established or will be established after the
action. This new window, which we can consider a digital space, hosts activities that are the function of streets. Today, the streets where the reactions are
concentrated, organised and exploded are replaced by digital spaces. To speak
for now, digital space and street substitute and feed each other. However, it is
not yet entirely possible to say what the new age will bring to cities in terms of
the development of urban movements. So, the digital space, which has come
to the fore as of the end of the past era and which will embrace the current
era, and its meaning for urban movements should be examined (della Porta,
2009: p. 85).

5   Reflection of Digital Space

The bright future promised by information technologies expands the limits of
creativity and communication far into the horizon, invites us to the days when
experience will develop in a new process, and heralds the structural changes
that challenge our society, both internally and externally (Castells, 1991: p. 1).
Information technologies that have changed the face of cities create new *electronic cottages* in the city. In the age of information, citizens can venture into
the universe from their homes and engage in all the images, sounds, communication networks and flows, information transfer and political activities of
the world, and by remaining potentially interactive, they bid farewell to the
monotonous relations of the past and become active participants of the new
age that cities need. Thanks to the information technologies, citizens can
directly participate in activities regardless of which parts of the city they are
in (Castells, 1991: p. 1). We can easily include the clustering observed on the
city's periphery in this. New information technologies bring radical changes
in society and affect numerous changes in regions and, more importantly, the
cities. But these effects are increasing and getting stronger day by day. The
interaction with economic, social, political, and cultural processes shapes the
use and production of new technologies (Castells, 1991: p. 2). To better evaluate

the effects of new technologies on society, the region and, more precisely, the city, it is necessary to look at the broader context of the transformation of the relations between production, society, and space, of which new technologies are the main instrument (Castells, 1991: p. 2).

New information technologies are not the source of the organisational logic behind the transformation of the social meaning of space. However, in line with the historical perspective of this logic, they are instrumental in discovering new horizons. Fundamentally, information technologies have been and will be used in pursuit of different social and functional goals, thanks to their flexibility. However, it should not be forgotten that today capitalism is progressing in a direction determined by the process of socio-economic structuralism (Castells, 1991: p. 348). However, it is a matter of curiosity when it is used and will be used by the anti-capitalist masses or by the masses affected by the negative consequences of capitalism in the city, and how its progress will continue. Therefore, societies do not remain passive change elements; they are included in the process with formations concentrated in cities. The meaninglessness of spaces and the weakness of political institutions become the elements of resistance, thanks to social actors at varying scales, individually and collectively. Within the new historical landscape, the citizens protect, spread, and construct their own cultural identities. They struggle to achieve their wishes for their own culture, regardless of any region of the city, and try to preserve the meanings of the spaces they own. We see that groups have emerged that spread their struggles across the city at a level that will also affect different communities by organising against the negative changes in their cities and neighbourhoods.

The diversity that occurs in the geometry of the space of the information flow makes the underlying mobilisation more defensive, preventive, regionally based and culturally specific. The separation into groups following the individual acquisition of identities, and the communication required by group organisation, have changed the codes of definition for the individual identity and triggered the formation of a socially recognisable and easily accessible citizen. Although the increase occurring in individual identities and the groups becoming more organised due to new communication techniques raise the assumption that spaces seem meaningless, in fact, urban spaces are gifted to urban culture more strongly by tribal-like groups formed by these individuals. Cities are disappearing as socially meaningless spaces amid non-historical and unsimplified identities of local communities. This disappearance does not apply to the entire existence of the city. Now, the means of communication in terms of the liveliness of the streets, the sound of the squares, and the time and space limits of bilateral relations are disappearing. The actions taken by the communities to maintain their cultural activities and, more importantly, by individuals belonging to emerging new cultures and identities to become a community are changing, which, in turn, also transforms the spaces.

We essentially have started talking about the existence of groups that are incredibly close to and familiar with each other, yet also extremely stranger to each other, in an environment where groups that are fundamentally unfamiliar with each other hardly get to know each other due to limited means of communication. This process limits the citizens from the spaces of the city to the rooms of the houses or the windows of digital devices. However, in this way, they can easily be aware of the existence of different groups. On the other hand, as the urban spaces changed in terms of their common sharing, the citizens of the city started to live as groups that were aware of each other but were strangers to each other. In this process, the sharing of urban spaces took place. The number of places used more frequently varied based on communities. However, common areas still retain their symbolic value and are as valuable as digital spaces for groups. So, as shaped by capitalism, consumers are moving away from the urban space with their lifestyle and shopping in the virtual worlds. However, the common urban spaces that are necessary for the continuation of the potential of this virtual world maintain their importance, and these areas have now made it necessary to adopt not only capitalist production and consumption tools but also groups that have had a share of the harmful results of this effect. So, even though digital space is an open space for everyone and prevents the daily intensive use of urban spaces, it made these spaces more important and diversified (Castells, 1991: p. 349).

The concept of networking and connectivity are not specific to the 21st century. The network emerges as the basic pattern for every area of life. The concept of network is common to all areas of life. Wherever you look in life, you will see networks and connections. When we examine the existing social networks in social life, we see that connection is the source of social interaction and generation of meaning, and communication connections are essential for the vitality of social life. Examining the social structure from the past to the present, the importance and existence of communication, that is, the network, can be seen in every environment where civilisation is located. Even the associations that make up civilisation have been realised because of the concept of network. It is seen that transportation and communication resources are developing day by day thanks to the association of networks. It is understood that there is an acceleration in the progress of development as the number of people connected to the network increases. It is clearly seen that the concept of the network that holds the society together, especially as cities are established and developed, is the only element of progress (Castells, 2005: p. 4).

Therefore, we can argue that communication techniques improve the network society. It should also be noted that the network society is open to strategies and formations that will use its communication resources for all defensive and offensive situations.

With the existence of vertically deployed classes, the elements that can communicate and direct each other are classes with higher economic and social opportunities. Today, with the electronic revolution, there is an increase in the number of masses that can reach communication resources. Still, we see that there are not a lot of obstacles limiting access to communication tools. Of course, it is possible to talk about the masses who have their privileges in using the communication tools, but we live in a communication and information age with the power and speed to prevent these encrypted associations. While it is possible to talk about the hidden pages and networks of capitalism that developed by using the same communication tools, it is also possible to speak of groups that entered into a struggle of opposition using the same tools. In fact, terrorist organisations, which prefer secret connections and communication as much as the capitalist system, carry out their terrible acts with similar means. Therefore, dominance and resistance grow by feeding on the same sources. And for the same reason, hope and fear, as emotions of the same medium, affect and grow networked citizens (Castells, 2005: p. 35).

High-speed, adaptable and flexible new information technologies prevent decentralised and distributed networking forms from overtaking the traditional vertical hierarchy. This relationship can be detected in urban movements more than in any other area. Today, where capitalism and giants fighting for urban power capture an increasingly international network, the more active and widespread group of this type of relationship comes from the associations of struggle that have taken up arms against such giants. The crowds gathered in Seattle against the giants of the world organised in a short time and had no difficulty in spreading their struggle to Prague, Quebec, Genoa, Barcelona, Porta Alegre and the whole world. Associations such as the movement for global equity have quickly created a global network using electronic tools and information technologies. Individuals who came together in this network organised in their own cities carried out actions simultaneously with each city and in their cities from time to time and expanded the scope of their struggles. The citizens included in this network have succeeded in spreading their goals and causes of struggle to their surroundings using electronic (i.e. digital) spaces. The environment where this struggle takes place is called *netwar*.

The common denominator of the parties is the electronic kiosks that will be reflected in the urban space. The electronic fabric of the struggle creates a new area of freedom for every individual in the network, and there is equality also concerning the access. By using the communication tools used by the dominant powers, the relatively weak groups can create an opportunity for themselves to seize the city's power against the former (Castells, 2005: p. 341). For example, in response to the meetings held by powerful companies and countries to increase their dominance over cities, opposing groups formed the World Social Forum in 2001 in Porto Alegre, Brazil and spread it to the world. In addition, the World Economic Forum for global equity has been organised regularly. Hundreds of thousands of people can attend these meetings directly, and the number of participants is even higher thanks to electronic communication tools. Moreover, thanks to the existing electronic networks, the objectives, goals and results of these meetings can be communicated to large masses among the citizens who are in contact. Contrary to the traditional hierarchical political and social order, distributed power and collective togetherness widen the scope of such meetings (Castells, 2005: p. 344). Movements for global equity as well as local movements that take action under their influence develop the actions, which they plan and coordinate with their email lists through their web pages. Each movement has its web pages and email lists. Thanks to the forums they have created on the Internet, they can announce the details they share on their pages and new, more significant developments in these forums. In addition, and perhaps most importantly, participants in the network express their opinions equally and freely in these forums. The unity created by this synergy is also reflected in the actions, causing them to undertake more effective activities day by day (Castells, 2005: p. 348).

Thanks to the developing technology, these computer-oriented communication tools have become even faster and more accessible. In particular, emerging social media applications have further expanded the network of urban movements and made it accessible to almost every citizen. Audiences see and react to the posts simultaneously and at the same speed. Everyone shares opinions and thoughts without any censorship. The associations' goals, wishes, and desires are shared easily in such areas and used as an incentive to reach more participants. With its unmediated and cost-free structure, such digital spaces seem to have been created so that the masses can gather in urban spaces and act together. These spaces, which we can consider a kind of informational utopia, have become essential for the masses to make their voices heard more strongly on the streets.

We see that the developments in electronic communication and information systems allow the increased irregularity in daily life and spatial distances in work, shopping, entertainment, health, education, public services, administration and similar elements. Although it is thought that cities will lose their importance in this process, due to the areas where services are provided and the number of people who want to benefit from these services, cities have not lost their importance; rather, they increased it. The transfer of many services from urban spaces to the digital space, of course, downgrades the function of cities. However, urban services and their beneficiaries have not disrupted the continuity of urban spaces that have transformed; on the contrary, they have triggered their transformation (Castells, 2010a: p. 424). As observed in many cases, urban movements develop their discourse, actors and organisations depending on the practice and structure of the local government. Due to the involvement of local governments in the process, the number of participants in urban movements diversified naturally. The fact that the neighbourhoods and communities keep up with the development causes the alternative social change aimed by the urban movements to come to the fore earlier than expected and to find supporters. Bringing the communication technologies into the use of every citizen allows them to bring up all kinds of complaints, and especially the presence of regions in the city that have difficulties accessing common digital tools causes the complaints to intensify (Castells, 2010b: p. 65). However, it is also claimed that globalisation and informatics enable the network of wealth and the power that transforms our world to become active in the urban environment.

The development of information technologies increases our production capacity, cultural creativity and communication potential. For this reason, as in the past, political representation and social control are being handed over from the central governments to the multinational companies and international organisations that adapt more quickly to this virtual environment. The opposite of this comes from the existence of the network that expands as the groups that are concentrated on a local scale, which originate from the society itself, find their international counterparts. This network, just like the network that distances itself, increasingly sees its existence in the digital space and its future. However, due to the increasing flow of information and the fact that the power, unfortunately, still rests with transnational institutions and companies rather than those of a local scale, the factors that determine the daily lives of the citizens and the policies that affect their future are managed by a minimal group. This and the tools and purposes of the administration are carried out with the arrangements, marketing and designs made in the digital space. Every city citizen is made dependent on elements that destroy them and is exploited and removed from their existence without even getting close to the threshold value. Contrary to popular belief, the dominance of these powerless and gradually weakening crowds, which have surrendered to the new global order, is slipping out of their hands. Of course, in countries where democracy is valid, the administrative power is based on the people as much as possible.

However, local governments are still insignificant and powerless. In addition, groups that are candidates for administrative power still confront the citizens as supporters of global leaders. Worse still, global organisations and companies use communication networks and information technologies that effectively change and shape citizens' views. Undoubtedly, society is struggling to exist in the digital field by taking up the weapons of its rivals in this struggle that hurts itself. However, the views and unity of struggle blooming in the digital field should be reflected in urban spaces (Castells, 2010b: p. 72). Email lists, chat rooms, forums and social media have now become centres of opinion and change, as an agora of the past.

The power groups that wish to maintain the existing power relations here will, of course, do their best not to lose their places to their opponents. However, the clustering of masses and the ideal of unconscious society aimed by capitalism work in reverse and unite the masses, and the right ideals presented to these masses can spread to the digital agora quickly. Locally isolated groups, disenfranchised communities and citizens excluded due to injustices can easily enter into solidarity within the digital agora and create an order of mobilisation. Local associations maximise information sharing and strengthen the organisational logic since access to the new agora can be achieved worldwide. Due to the diversity and knowledge of the participants, the threat at hand is better understood, and the measures and reactions to be taken are implemented more accurately (Castells, 2010b: p. 155). For example, environmentalist urban movements, which are concerned about the future of our world, have succeeded in attracting the new technological paradigm that uses communication tools very effectively to increase the social force they need. They can mobilise on a global scale by transforming their actions, which they designed and implemented using communication tools and information technologies, into a form of underlying reaction. Environmentalist urban movements, which plan their actions by communicating with local partners, can attract the media's attention thanks to their colourful actions and the creativity of their activities. By concentrating on the media tool, they can reach their supporters to the users of this medium. The actions of local partners, which they have built on their private concerns, can even find a place in local media outlets. By ensuring that these actions take place in the digital space, that is, social media, they can reach the masses without commenting directly (Castells, 2010b: p. 186). As soon as the new urban movements that oppose globalisation realise that they cannot be as useful as they wish to be in their activities by participating in political organisations, they carry out their own actions in line with the demands of direct democracy.

In fact, when we look at the scope and diversity of their actions and networks, these movements do not oppose globalisation. Their reaction is against the policies of the current rulers of globalisation that negatively affect the citizens of the city. Although the globalisation policy, which affects the functioning and development of society, sees every citizen as equal, this turns into an illusion show. Their actions to reach every citizen actually form the foundation of the steps that will suffocate every citizen. While exploiting the society, which they approach from a consumer's point of view, they disrupt the living spaces of cities and the natural evolution of the world (Castells, 2010c: p. 165). Touraine's view of the horizontal social hierarchy explains the purposes of this order very well. Considering that the places that attract society's attention are becoming increasingly digital, there is no problem in the relationship between the user and time for the spaces. The new spaces mentioned are the areas that everyone can use at meagre costs. But that does not mean there are not very specific areas. This type of area exists in digital spaces. However, spaces that everyone can use in an unlimited fashion are not only a centre for sharing ideas, but also the main headquarters of the marketing war directed at the citizens in line with globalisation. The sphere of influence is unlimited as the number of users of this new space, where collective reactions and identities are measured, analysed and directed, are counted in the millions. The urban movement struggles to raise awareness and mobilise the citizens by displaying itself in the middle of such unconscious use (Castells, 2010c: p. 74).

New determining factors have helped make the urban movements seen at the beginning of our era successful. Like what happened in Tunisia during the Arab Spring. The most decisive factors of these movements are the support of the internet and the dominant media powers. Again, as in the Tunisian example, the internet plays a dominant role, but the contribution of media powers such as Al Jazeera should not be underestimated. When we look at the urban movements seen at the beginning of our era, we can observe that the protests are aimed at economic, social and political situations. Unemployment, inflation, inequality, poverty, police violence, lack of democracy, censorship, and corruption are the main factors causing citizens' uprisings. In addition to these adverse conditions, many urban deprivations also trigger the emergence of urban events. The fact that these deprivations and injustices are done in plain sight does not incite any reaction in daily life due to the pressure exerted on the masses.

The digital space, where people can hide more easily but speak more openly, freely and liberally, enables especially young citizens to communicate, talk, discuss and organise. The Internet can provide a more equal and freer social network organisation. In the emerging new order, we see that the segment that triggers, organises and expands urban movements consists of bloggers, social network formations and cyber-activism (Castells, 2015: p. 26). Such accessible environments enrich the environment of thought restricted by the media organisations held by the central government and global powers and open it up to society. Of course, there are also media representatives operating in opposition to the major media organisations. For example, during the urban movement that took place in Tunisia, it was seen that a large part of the people followed the Al Jazeera television channel and the website instead of the censored state channels. Due to the existence of mobile phones and making communication faster, the fate of urban movements has changed. In particular, Twitter has revolutionised the development process of urban movements. The participants conveyed the developments to the other participants and the world by sharing them on Twitter. This information network, free from censorship and oppression, expanded the equal and accessible environment that the participants established with each other as much as possible. However, the existence of people who post false information has shown the world that this liberal environment is not free from concerns. The blog posts were also seen as a kind of news and call for the mobilisation and mobilised the masses (Castells, 2015: p. 27). Social media elements such as YouTube and Facebook have taken on important tasks in developing the participant networks and conveying the events that took place during the urban movement to the masses without intermediaries. Interestingly, search engines such as Google reported that the searches performed in the days when the urban movements started also significantly increased. It should be noted that the developments reflected in social media, especially during the Arab Spring, increased the interest of digital space users in urban movements all over the world (Castells, 2015: p. 58). We see that the internet is a safe space for angry and hopeful network users when we look at it. Elements that prevent information sharing in urban spaces are not common in digital space. For this reason, interested users can easily expand their reactions in the digital area and carry the movement to urban spaces as it evolves (Castells, 2015: p. 82). The majority of this mobility seen in digital space consists of the young population between the ages of 16 and 34 years.

It is seen that this part of the population, which is most affected by the adverse conditions of the city and has the responsibility to construct their future, plays a dominant role in urban movements and in the digital space where urban movements are organised. Especially in countries with a young population, the perspective of central powers on digital space is not very optimistic. In particular, sharing information (which triggers the movements and the publication of the events that agitate the masses) on social media without

intermediaries and comments causes the urban spaces to be filled and occupied by reactive crowds. The central government and global powers, who are
disturbed by this situation, depict the social media applications, which are the
agora of the digital space, as the enemies of the society and tend to reduce
their prestige. If this policy does not work and urban movements stir up too
much interaction, some power holders turn off the access to some social media
applications to limit the possibilities of digital space and even go further and
completely shut down the access to the internet (Castells, 2015: p. 223).

6   Evolution of Space

We begin this section with the basic premises. Cities are located within con-
strained regions where different uses are created, mixed and continually
increased. Within these restricted regions, cities allow the production of goods
and the continuation of social life. Human mobility, interaction and information flow are critical factors for maintaining the dynamic structure of the
city. For this reason, the city turns out as a meeting place for members of one
or more committees. Cities are places where unknown spaces gradually gain
meaning and are transformed into spaces, thus turning into memorable landscapes. Civitas, city, agora, neighbourhood, and central business district (CBD)
and skyscrapers increasingly appear as contributions to the dense capacity of
the city, as each individual stitch of a rug embroidered on the city. Because
thanks to this capacity, cities can constantly rediscover their regions and adapt
to challenges (Whyte, 2009: p. 36). Different academicians have discussed
this process from various perspectives. Lewis Mumford called this process *the
crystallisation of the city*. Louis Wirth called it *a mosaic of social worlds*, while
Henri Lefebvre called it *the rhythm of the city*. When we look at these different
perspectives, the movements that cause cities to live, grow and withdraw vary
depending on the developments in other parts of the city. Unfortunately, without this mobility and development, cities are on their way to extinction in a
crippled or paralysed state (Savitch, 2008: p. 94).

   This mobility and development are primarily seen in the slums or suburbs
within the city. When we look at the urbanisation occurring, especially in
the cities of the developing regions, we observe the changes occurring at an
increasing rate. When unequal developments and the new international division of labour begin to shape the geography of cities, we see that millions of
urban residents are starting to live in areas that are highly catastrophic ecolog-
ically and are gradually moving away from the city. When we look at the users
of these catastrophic areas that emerged in the cities, we encounter them as

those that obtain the least share of the city's production and surplus value but are the strongest among the city's communities in terms of social organisation. The inhabitants of these regions differ from other parts of the city in terms of political cohesion due to the structural features of the places where they live and are the centres of the areas where urban movements meet and flourish (Castells, 1983: p. 175).

The fluctuations in the cities and the spatial change and transformation of the enclaves that emerged as a result allowed the birth of different organisations and administrative powers in the city.

> The emergence of cities also necessitates the administrative devices, the police, taxes, etc., in short, the municipal organisation, and therefore politics in general. Here, for the first time, the division of the population into two great classes is clearly seen, and this division is based directly on the division of labour and the means of production. In fact, the city is the gathering of population, means of production, capital, pleasures and needs in one centre. However, the opposite is true for the countryside: isolation and disorganisation.
>
> MARX and ENGELS, 2018: p. 56

The existence of these different enclaves, which started to be observed in the city, became more visible after the industrial revolution. Because with the industrial revolution, factories and production areas gradually began to settle in the centre of cities and occupy the city's central spaces.

> However, with Watt's second and so-called double-acting steam-engine, was a prime motor was invented, that begot its own force by the consumption of coal and water, whose power was entirely under man's control, that was mobile and a means of locomotion, that was urban and not, like the waterwheel, rural, that permitted production to be concentrated in towns instead of, like the water-wheels, being scattered up and down the country, that was of universal technical application, and, relatively speaking, little affected in its choice of residence by local circumstances.
>
> MARX, 2018: p. 363

Not all life is modern; but all modern life is city life. Because modernization of life means that it resembles more to city life (Bauman, 2001: p. 169). Following the city life that has become increasingly modern, changes have also been observed in the lives of the citizens. He thought that the ordinary person in daily life was not passive about being exposed to the effects of the manipulations here; on the contrary, he thought that could change the effect in the way he wanted, not as the capitalists desired.

DE CERTEAU, 2008: p. 43

We are witnessing a regional and spatial differentiation in the city, with characteristics such as the population's size, density, and heterogeneity. These three characteristics of the population create an absolute condition for regional differentiation. A crowded and dense population with some diversity paves the way for the formation of certain regions in the city with the motives of competition and progress.

WIRTH, 2002: p. 89

There are some urban hierarchies between these different regions, as well as some different positions among their inhabitants.

There are certain streets in Paris which are as degraded as a man covered with infamy; also, there are noble streets, streets simply respectable, young streets on the morality of which the public has not yet formed an opinion; also cut-throat streets, streets older than the age of the oldest dowagers, estimable streets, streets always clean, streets always dirty, working, labouring, and mercantile streets.

HARVEY, 2012b: p. 59

Starting with (Louis) Napoleon III, governments have sought ways to intervene in the city to change the social balance in favour of the state. Louis Napoleon focused on urbanisation and relevant security policies to keep in line the strikes, barricades, neighbourhood organisations, civil disobedience and the pursuit of rights that paralyse life in Paris every day. Baron Haussmann, who was given great powers, set the course of a reformation in the city's history by initiating acts of creative destruction in Paris, which will be discussed a lot in the future and explain a phenomenon. In the process that took Haussmann 17 years, monumental buildings, wide boulevards, the famous Opera House and Les Halles emerged. He produced a new style with the borrowing and expropriation model he developed to finance demolitions and later inspired the search for financing for many urban interventions. Thus, the first attempts to include the urban land rents in the circulation of capital began, becoming widespread later. Therefore, different practices have been initiated in developing models in central budgets on security and infrastructure issues. The new road arrangements in Haussmann's planning, considering tidying up the dangerous classes and unhealthy housing and transferring the industry out of the city, will work to suppress the revolutionary disorders easily and enable the security forces to act comfortably when necessary. While this structuring contributes to the aeration of unhealthy neighbourhoods, it will also ensure more functional daylight during the day, and kerosene lamp lighting at night. In this respect, the city should not be left to its natural development and formation but should be guided by those who have power or competence (Sarı and Esgin, 2016: p. 91).

The essential point is to see urban social movements as mediators and militant particularism as a translation from the personal to a broader terrain of politics. Plainly, democratic procedures and governance in general, as well as in urban settings, already do and will continue to rely upon the foreseeable future upon the mediating institutions of local action and the formation of local solidarities. Whether or not such mediating institutions will play a positive or negative role in the democratisation of urban governance remains, of course, to be seen. But the broader political-economic forces ignore this dimension of human action at their peril. Hollowed-out local institutions are even more of a threat than a militant particularism characterised by relative autonomy and a charismatic vitality seeking broader-scale reforms. The dialectics of the grassroots and the powers of militant particularism are vibrant forces in urban life in particular and sociopolitical life in general (Harvey, 2015: p. 259). The domain of spatial practices has, unfortunately, changed in recent years. This makes any firm definition of the urban as a distinctive spatial domain even more problematic. On the one hand, we witness the greater fragmentation of the urban social space into neighbourhoods, communities, and a multitude of street comer societies, while on the other telecommuting and rapid transport make nonsense of some concept of the city as a tightly walled physical unit or even a coherently organised administrative domain.

The 'megalopolis' of the 1960s has suffered even further fragmentation and dispersal, particularly in the US, as urban deconcentration gathers pace to produce a spread city form. Yet the spatial grounding persists in some form with specific meanings and effects. The production of new ecological patterns and structures within a spread city form has significance for how production, exchange, and consumption is organised, how social relationships are established, how financial and political power is exercised, and how the spatial integration of social action is achieved. I hasten to add that presentation of the urban problematic in such ecological terms in no way presumes ecological explanations. It simply insists that ecological patterns are important for social organisation and action. The shift towards entrepreneurialism in urban governance has to be examined, then, at a variety of spatial scales: local neighbourhood and community, central city and suburb, metropolitan region,

region, nation state, and the like (Harvey, 2015: p. 425). If claims to unique-
ness, authenticity, particularity and speciality underlie the ability to capture
monopoly rents, then on what better terrain is it possible to make such claims
than in the field of historically constituted cultural and special environmental
characteristics?

> Many rest upon historical narratives, interpretations and meanings of col-
> lective memories, significations of cultural practices, and the like: there is
> always a strong social and discursive element at work in the construction
> of such claims. Once established, however, such claims can be pressed
> home hard in the cause of extracting monopoly rents since there will
> be, in many people's minds at least, no other place than London, Cairo,
> Barcelona, Milan, Istanbul, San Francisco or wherever, to gain access to
> whatever it is that is supposedly unique to such places.
>
> HARVEY, 2015: p. 490

The most obvious point of reference where this works is in contemporary tourism. For what is at stake is the power of collective symbolic capital, of special
marks of distinction that attach to some place, which have a significant drawing power upon the flows of capital more generally. Bourdieu, unfortunately,
restricts them to individuals that the collective forms might be of even greater
interest.

> The collective symbolic capital which attaches to names and places
> like Paris, Athens, New York, Rio de Janeiro, Berlin and Rome is of great
> import and gives such places great economic advantages relative to, say,
> Baltimore, Liverpool, Essen, Lille and Glasgow. The problem for these lat-
> ter places is to raise their quotient of symbolic capital and to increase
> their marks of distinction to better ground their claims to the unique-
> ness that yields monopoly rent. Given the general loss of other monopoly
> powers through easier transport and communications and the reduction
> of other barriers to trade, the struggle for collective symbolic capital
> becomes even more important as a basis for monopoly rents. How else
> can we explain the splash made by the Guggenheim Museum in Bilbao
> with its signature Gehry architecture? And how else can we explain the
> willingness of major financial institutions, with considerable interna-
> tional interests, to finance such a signature project?
>
> HARVEY, 2015: p. 490

Every great city has one or more slums, where the working-class is crowded together. True, poverty often dwells in hidden alleys close to the palaces of the rich; but, in general, a separate territory has been assigned to it. Here, removed from the sight of the happier classes, a struggle for living takes place. These slums are pretty equally arranged in all the great towns of England: the worst houses in the worst quarters of the towns. Usually one- or two-storied cottages in long rows, perhaps with cellars used as dwellings, are almost always irregularly built. These houses of three or four rooms and a kitchens form, throughout England, some parts of London excepted, the general dwellings of the working-class. The streets are generally unpaved, rough, dirty, filled with vegetable and animal refuse, without sewers or gutters, but supplied with foul, stagnant pools instead. Moreover, ventilation is impeded by the bad, confused method of building of the whole quarter. Since many human beings here live crowded into a small space, the atmosphere that prevails in these working-men's quarters may readily be imagined. Further, the streets serve as drying grounds in fine weather. Lines are stretched across from house to house, and hung with wet clothing.

ENGELS, 2013: p. 64

More recently another different method of building was adopted and has now become general. Working-men's cottages are almost never built singly, but always by the dozen or score. A single contractor builds up one or two streets at a time; these are then arranged as follows: One front is formed of cottages of the best class, so fortunate as to possess a back door and small court. These command the highest rent. In the rear of these cottages runs a narrow alley, the back street. It is built up at both ends, into which either a narrow roadway or a covered passage leads from one side. The cottages which face this back street command least rent and are most neglected. These have their rear walls in common with the third row of cottages, which face a second street and command less rent than the first row and more than the second. By this method of construction, comparatively good ventilation can be obtained for the first row of cottages, and the third row is no worse off than in the former method. The middle row, on the other hand, is at least as badly ventilated as the houses in the courts, and the back street is always in the same filthy, disgusting condition as they. The contractors prefer this method because it saves them space and furnishes the means of fleecing better-paid workers through the higher rents of the cottages in the first and third rows. These three different forms of cottage building are found all over Manchester

and throughout Lancashire and Yorkshire, often mixed up together, but
usually separate enough to indicate the relative age of parts of towns.

ENGELS, 2013: pp. 88–89

People experience space but also think through space and imagine through
space. Therefore, space not only gives form to the existing social world (experienced and understood as a meaningful life condition), but also to possible
social worlds that may inspire action and express collective dreams (Stavrides,
2016: p. 11). It is indeed correct that the demarcation of an area goes hand-in-
hand with its description as a potential site of fighting. Although the act of
marking out an area seems to be an attempt to ward off a fight it necessarily
constitutes a declaration of war (Stavrides, 2016: p. 13). The idea that city-space
does not simply contain or support social life but also expresses social values
necessary for social reproduction is well documented in the social sciences
(Stavrides, 2016: p. 27). Therefore, as a socially meaningful production, space is
defined, or rather embodied, in the process of "temporalisation" through spatial life rhythms. The space is recognised as a familiar place, or is transformed
into a place that is owned, as similarity can be made between the events that
took place there, and the events that took place in the same place before.
Rhythmicality is a way of understanding the present and the future as being
punctuated by defining repetitions (Stavrides, 2016: p. 30).

One of the basic attributes of the partitioned city is that it destroys what
appears to constitute the public character of public space. Public space, as created by the practices that inhabit it,

> is always contestable, precisely because whereas there are criteria that
> control admission to its purview, the right to enact and enforce those
> criteria is always in question. The partitioned city is full of privatised
> public spaces in which public use is carefully controlled and specifically
> motivated. No contestation is tolerated. Users of these spaces must be
> checked and categorised regularly. They must follow specific instructions
> in order to be allowed access to various services and facilities. A shop-
> ping mall or a large department store, for instance, are such quasi-public
> spaces. A company-owned town or an enclosed community, separated
> from the network of public spaces that surround them (streets, squares,
> forests, etc.), controls local space by limiting its use to certified residents.
> Holiday resorts often exhibit former traditional public spaces in theme
> parks featuring rural or village communities.
>
> Public life is reduced to the conspicuous consumption of fantasised
> identities in a sealed-off enclave that mimics a "holiday city". What

defines these spaces as sites of "public life" is not the clashing rhythms of contesting practices (that create the political) but the regulated rhythms of routines under surveillance. The publicly exhibited identities of the users are enacted in accordance with those rhythms that discriminate and canonise them.

HENAFF and STRONG, 2001: p. 4

There is a whole range of contemporary urban spaces where the rules of urban identity formation do not seem to apply. People are always passing through such spaces, yet no one understands them as locations that define their inhabitants. An open and generalised anonymity seems to prevail here. In airports, supermarkets, motorway service stations or hotels, most people are in transit as if their lives were unfolding "in parentheses".

STAVRIDES, 2016: p. 36

We know from anthropology that the social experience of threshold crossing is an experience of change. This change does not have to be collectively created, as in an uprising or any other qualitative leap in terms of social relations. It can be a change affecting specific groups of people in specific periods of their social life.

Anthropologists have provided us with many examples of spaces that periodically host ritualised transitions from one social position or condition to another. Famously, Arnold van Gennep has described "rites of passage" (van Gennep 1960) as those ritual acts connected with spaces that symbolise transitions (for example, from childhood to adolescence, from single to married life, from the status of the adolescent to that of the citizen, warrior or hunter). Ritual acts supervise the passage from one social identity to another, thus ensuring the overall stability of society and the corresponding social relations. In Agamben's threshold, however, there seems to be a kind of circular movement. The state of exception equates "before" and "after," as it is expected to ensure that after this in-between period, order is restored as before. The state of exception renders before and after indistinguishable. they are not different, so they can be interchanged (Stavrides, 2016: p. 42). A potential city of thresholds emerges when public space is occupied and organised by all these different people. Both symbolically and practically, these groups create an open-to-all, porous public urban space. If a new form of governance is tested in the temporary-permanent construction of red zones, a new form of emancipating culture is spontaneously tested in public space. In the migratory and ephemeral practices of social movements oriented towards urban demands, this potentially emancipating culture is ambiguously performed. The more these acts of essentially urban protest spread in the city, the more we can hope for passages to replace metastatic checkpoints. Perhaps instead of the "bourgeois utopia" of completely secure urban enclaves or the fantasy of identity-conferring ghettoes, we can see the emergence of porous public spaces: the heterotopias. An open city is a city of thresholds (Stavrides, 2016: p. 58).

> We can distinguish three basic categories of spatial experience. The first is organic space: it refers to the kind of spatial experience which appears to be genetically transmitted and, hence, biologically determined. Much of the behaviour examined by ethologists fits into this category. The second is perceptual space: it involves the neurological synthesis of all kinds of sense experience – optical, tactual, acoustic, and kinaesthetic.
>
> HARVEY, 2016: p. 32

This synthesis amounts to a spatial experience in which the evidence of various senses is reconciled. An instantaneous schema or impression may be formed, and memory may lead to the retention of that schema over time. When memory and learning are involved, the schema may be subject to addition or subtraction by culturally learned modes of thought. Perceptual space is primarily experienced through the senses, but we do not yet know how far the performance of our senses is affected by cultural conditioning. The third kind of spatial experience is abstract: the symbolic space.

> Here, we are experiencing space vicariously through the interpretation of symbolic representations which have no spatial dimension. I can conjure up an impression of a triangle without seeing one simply by looking at the word "triangle". Mathematics and geometry provide a convenient symbolic language for cussing and learning about spatial form, but it is not the spatial form itself.
>
> HARVEY, 2016: p. 32

In other words, the shaping of space which goes on in architecture and, therefore, in the city is symbolic of our culture, symbolic of the existing social order, symbolic of our aspirations, our needs, and our fears. If, therefore, we are to evaluate the spatial form of the city, we must, somehow or other, understand its creative meaning as well as its mere physical dimensions (Harvey, 2016: p. 35). "Pareto optimum" (a situation in which nobody can become better off from moving without making somebody else worse off) is important in this regard.

To give a simple example: it is clear that there has not been an equal response in the urban population to the potential of mobility associated with the automobile. The time lag is anything from 20 to 40 years between different groups in the population. It would be very surprising indeed if the better educated and more affluent groups had not taken advantage of this time lag to further their own interests and enhance their own income. The allocation of resources then takes place as an adjustment to this new income distribution and a cumulative process of increasing inequality of income distribution gets under way. This is a crude example, but I think it is very general. Certain groups, particularly those with financial resources and education, are able to adapt far more rapidly to a change in the urban system, and these differential abilities to respond to change are a major source in generating inequalities.

HARVEY, 2016: p. 57

Territorial organisation has many functions to perform within the city system. The classical problem of regionalisation is to find a hierarchy of regions which will perform all of these functions reasonably well (see for instance, Boudeville, 1968). Some functions must be performed at the metropolitan level (for instance, the planning of transport systems, parkland facilities) while others can best be operated at the local level (for instance, play areas, childcare centres). The first problem, therefore, is to find a form of organisation capable of dealing with the obvious fact that different facilities have to be provided at different spatial scales. The second problem is to identify a form of organisation which is flexible enough to deal with growth (social and economic), spatial overspill effects, changing spatial relationships, and so on. If the organisation is not flexible, it will act as an automatic constraint upon what Friedmann (1969) calls a general process of polarised development. In other words, any territorial organisation must be designed so as to be reactive to the dynamics of the urban system (Harvey, 2016: p. 89).

What this analysis of the housing market shows us is that a free market cannot give rise to prices conducive to a Pareto optimum and that the housing market, for reasons of its own spatial internal logic, must contain group action if it is to function coherently. This explains, in turn, why the housing market is so peculiarly susceptible to economic and political pressures, since it is only by organising and applying these pressures that individuals can defend or enhance the value of their property rights relative to those of other individuals. In this, as in most things, it is the economically and politically weak who probably suffer most, unless institutional controls exist to rectify a naturally arising but ethically unacceptable situation (Harvey, 2016: p. 67). The high rental value of land in central cities should not necessarily be interpreted as a reflection of differences in marginal productivity of land (as Mills suggests). Absolute and monopoly rents at these locations enter into the costs of production. Differential rents do not. If absolute and monopoly rents are dominant in the determination of land value at central locations, then it is land value which determines use. If differential rents dominate, then it is use which determines land value. In practice, of course, rent arises out of all three circumstances, and it is often difficult to determine what portion of the overall rental value arises out of which circumstance.

It is probable that the structure of the transport system and the nature of production in the new industrial and commercial cities of the nineteenth century, meant that differential rent was a major source of rent during that period (the concept is particularly appealing in late nineteenth century Chicago for example). But it is very likely that in the contemporary metropolitan centres (as well as in older commercial and administrative centres such as London in the eighteenth and nineteenth centuries), the reverse process in which absolute and monopoly rents enter into the costs of production and thereby determine use, is of much greater significance. The problem under these conditions is to discover (or generate) firms with production functions which can readily adjust to absorb these costs. It is not surprising to find, therefore, that the highest rent areas in the city are colonised by commercial activities whose productivity cannot be measured – government offices, banks, insurance companies, stockbrokers, travel agents and various forms of entertainment, are good examples. Hence arises the paradox that some of the most unproductive activity in society is found on land which is supposedly of the greatest marginal productivity by virtue of its location. The solution to this paradox is simple. Land and property rent in central locations does not arise out of the land's marginal productivity but out of the processes which permit absolute and, even more importantly, monopoly rents to be charged (Harvey, 2016: p. 173).

The production of goods (such as automobiles, computers, etc.) that will be renewed in a short time is another necessary tool to maintain the actual demand and is very important in terms of increasing the circulation rate of surplus-value. In the redistributive city, it was the physical life of buildings which mattered, and many buildings were built to last. In the contemporary capitalist city, it is the economic life which matters, and this economic lifespan is contracting as it becomes necessary to increase the rate of circulation of surplus value. Buildings in good condition are torn down to make way for new buildings which will have an even shorter economic life span. It is not a mere cultural passion for newness which leads to the tearing down and building up in metropolitan economies (particularly evident in the USA), it is an economic necessity. Shortening the economic and physical life of products is a typical stratagem for accelerating the circulation of surplus value in all sectors of the economy. It operates most intricately in the housing market: here, the need to realise profits on speculative investment in suburban land and construction as well as in the land-use transition process, stimulates demand for housing and commercial properties in certain locations while cutting off the flow of funds into other sectors (Harvey, 2016: p. 245). Therefore "the rich can command space whereas the poor are trapped in it" (Harvey, 2016: p. 159).

Today, the ideas that call themselves anti-humanist, mystical ecology also adopt the same way of thinking in a different manner. These ecologists, like their opponents, argue that humanity is dominated by nature, either in the form of "laws of nature" or an unspeakably sacred "wisdom of the world" that can guide human behaviour. However, while their opponents speak of the need for nature to "surrender" to a "conqueror", active-aggressive humanity; anti-humanist and mystical ecologists advocate the passive "surrender" of humanity to an "all-conquering" nature. Although these two ideas differ in the discourse they use and the things they respect, domination is fundamental to both; nature is to be either controlled or obeyed – in both cases, nature is a taskmaster who is burdened with duties (Bookchin, 2013: p. 49). Tribal societies, considered to be egalitarian, recognised the existence of such great inequalities and sought to find compensation mechanisms to enforce genuine equality. For example, the principle of the irreducible minimum provided a solid basis for overcoming the economic differences that made those who were formally equal in modern society essentially unequal. Everyone had the right to basic means of life, regardless of status, capacity, or even willingness to contribute financially to the community. No one, who is a member of the community, could be denied of his rights. Special treatment was given to the disabled, elderly and the weak whenever possible, in order to "equalise" their material status and to minimise their feelings of dependency. We have evidence that this care also existed in Neanderthal populations 50,000 years ago. The discovery of a congenitally disabled adult male skeleton that would not have survived without the special care of the community is proof of this fact.

At the level of economic life, the leading principle of justice – the inequality of equals – had not yet emerged, of course. Preliterate societies were guided by another principle, the principle of equality of the unequal, which underpinned the ideal of freedom (Bookchin, 2013: p. 116). The concept of citizenship did not emerge from a vacuum of streets that serve to assert itself, houses that serve as a seclusion for the sovereign, and a large population that promotes personal contact. A surprising feature of Çatalhöyük was the absence of streets. Although there were small squares in this Pueblo-like city, there were no open roads. Streets and wide boulevards, which modernists such as Marshall Berman and Richard Sennett regarded as a structural necessity for the city, were absent in these old cities; the aforementioned boulevards are the places where today's simple ego shows up with a snobby attitude. In order to go from one place to another in Çatalhöyük, one had to jump from roofs, go up and down stairs, pass through hollows in houses and small squares (Bookchin, 2014: p. 67). "But the difference is the price of our existence" (Lösch, 1954: p. 508).

When we look at the transformation of urban space; urban planning, urban design or just planning is sharply questioned. As far as planning is considered, we see that the design is made piece by piece, which prevents the urban design from being considered whole. For example, when designing roads, the environmental impact of the roads and their effect on spatial interactions are ignored. Another misconception that designs that do not address the development of space fall into is that they rely on designs that are distant from society. Camillo Sitte, one of the first pioneers of planning, stated that urban planning is a whole of all arts and cannot be performed by venturing away from the structure of society. Over the years, a more natural approach has emerged against the increasingly abstract production in planning. However, it should not be forgotten that the places where people live are natural growth areas, just like the naturalness of an oyster's bed. However, discussions of natural vs artificial in terms of planning have gradually increased. Participating in the discussions, Christopher Alexander stated that the city is not a tree (Martin and March, 2010: p. 6).

Designing the streets and the enclaves that reveal the regions according to the grid plan causes the spaces that make up the city to be divided under certain planes. Scale and pattern affect the direction of urban space towards change, and completing this development is essential in terms of both artificial and natural design. The pattern formed in the design of the roads according to the grid plan affects the presence of buildings that will emerge on the enclaves and structural change of urban spaces. The fact that artificial designs of cities are seen more primarily in European and American cities compared to organic designs erase some traces of the typology of cities, and also reveal new traces. However, this planned design and development strategy does not require that living spaces continue or be preserved as planned. On the contrary, these similar design patterns create a spatial diversity that resembles each other in shape but differs in lifestyle and standard (Martin and March, 2010: p. 10). So, how did this process in which spatial differentiation and different design techniques and strategies begin? How did the evolution of space start and continue?

In Mesopotamia, the cities that appeared as a whole began to take shape to reflect the power of humanity. Although there are other settlements where spatial differentiation has not been seen before, Mesopotamia is the first region with different uses and diversity. When we look at the cities of this region, it is not difficult to claim that the housing structures have not survived. However, the monumental structures have survived to the present day intact. Especially the abundance and durability of sacred places are a fact that cannot be ignored. So, the beginning of the space and the measure of value first appear in the design and construction of the sacred spaces (Frankfort, 1970: p. 22). Temples and palaces represent the beginning of the evolution of space as the first buildings with aesthetic value at the beginning of history. Cities are formed from the integrity of spaces clustered around adobe buildings as heaps formed of separate elements. It can be said that individual houses are usually shaped by contractors to be located within the determined plots. Houses consist of the irregular form of small rooms placed around a room. However, when we look at the city of Ur, we observe that the houses are more sophisticated. In the houses of this region, we see a large room that serves as a courtyard and a row of rooms wrapped around it. There is also an entrance lobby that serves as a welcome room. As a second floor is accessed from the stairs, a new place was created to watch the surroundings on this floor, and balcony was invented. This building form can still be seen today near Baghdad. Although these houses, designed for individual use, are built by the contractors on the specified plots, the cornerstone of the city design and the layout plan of the houses is the temple and palace belonging to the city. These two structures appear more robust and majestic than houses and marketplaces, and they are outside the classification as space (Frankfort, 1970: p. 110).

In the differentiation of the space, the interior design is as effective as the exterior design and the design of the outer environment. Today, the unambiguous fact is that the walls of public buildings are decorated with paintings and pictures. The contents of these paintings are divided into three different groups according to the structural and functional characteristics of the building. The first is the walls where mythological events and legends are depicted. And it is usually observed in holy places and palaces. The second is the battle scenes. These paintings depicting the victorious soldiers of the war are mostly found in the administration buildings, namely in the palaces. The last one is the paintings with the Altars. These paintings and pictures are located in holy places and temples (Frankfort, 1970: p. 124). The architecture reflects not only spatial diversity but also technological developments. When we look at the development timeline, we see that the first floors of the foundations of palaces and temples gradually started to consist of stone structures. This has caused the temples and spaces to become spaces that offer higher and wider areas (Frankfort, 1970: p. 137). When we look at the development of the space in this period, it is observed that the planners emphasised regularity. When we look at the plans of the spaces as well as the location and design of the squares in the city, we see that symmetry comes to the fore. Since urban planning constitutes a certain order, a more regular and symmetrical design stands out in contrast to the previous form, i.e. the organic structure.

The positions of the gates used to enter and exit the city, the sizes and locations of the palaces and temples and the harmony of the different levels formed by the passages in the city are seen as a construction of the order. In particular, the palace and the temple are located in the city's centre, which is the most sheltered area. As certain walls surround them, sometimes small market areas accompany these structures. At the same time, these market areas must have been intended to be urban open spaces. Afterwards, there is the second district in the city, where the residences and more diverse market areas are located. The important thing for this area is the direction of pedestrian and vehicle traffic and its harmony with the sheltered area, which is the city's centre. So, in the periods when cities first emerged, religious relations came to the fore as an urban movement. The more valuable structures as well as the spaces designed around them, intended to manage this mobility, form the temples. In addition to these places, we see that palaces gained importance in the city and new space formations emerged to manage the various movements that appeared in the increasing population and manage the essential elements of life. Therefore, as the first urban movements, religious movements caused the formation of space. Due to the increasingly diversified and complex social structure, that is, with the effect of urbanisation, different movements have emerged, and palaces, i.e. administrative centres, have started to be designed as spaces to manage these (Frankfort, 1970: p. 145).

Since the Middle Ages, Europe has been one of the most urbanised continents on the planet. In addition, Europe cities have stamped their imprint on the continent's economy, social structure, political structure and cultural life. Like today's megacities in Latin America or Asia, European cities developed in a compact and interconnected manner. However, when these cities are evaluated as a whole, the increasing waves of immigration and high death rates should not be ignored. In addition to having administrative powers and political autonomy, these cities also functioned as commercial and business centres. Furthermore, cities played a central role by distinguishing themselves from other regions regarding religion, education, leisure activities and distinctive urban scenery. These cities were generally classified as chaotic and threatening as they were noisy, smelly, crowded and anonymous (Clark, 2009: p. 1).

Due to the economic decline of the post-Roman era, early medieval towns saw an exodus of particularly elite classes to the countryside. When the ruling and landed classes visited the towns, it was only for religious causes and festivities. However, migration to the city began from the tenth and eleventh centuries. Especially between the 10th and 12th centuries, Italian cities were exposed to intense migration. Elite classes among the immigrants took their place in the city's administration, economy, and social life. The role of the elites who migrated back to the city increased in the shops, stores, market areas, executive boards, financial institutions and religious boards that were opened. Returning elites in the city have also taken steps to own the rent areas of the city and transform them into housing areas where the increasing population can stay. The medieval city gradually began to gain its urban space around the elite (Clark, 2009: p. 44). Between 60 and 70 per cent of the population living in cities in the 13th century consisted of day labourers from rural areas, poor peasants, the unemployed poor as well as journeymen in poor trades. A large part of the city has been marginalised and alienated from official political and economic life. Temporary problems regarding livelihoods caused by the annual harvest shortages in the city, as well as increasing food prices for the long term and the competition between workers from rural areas, caused urban crises (Clark, 2009: p. 65).

Civil fortifications were generally built in the third and fourth centuries. As public buildings and temples remained behind the walls, they were protected from raids by groups attacking the city. In this process, the city's public monuments were demolished to make more fortifications. Urban space had to relinquish its coherence, and the number of citizens living inside the fortified area decreased. Due to the lack of space, the majority of the city has built their homes beyond the walls or further away. Walls and gates are often owned by private organisations. The city's water and drainage systems proved insufficient and collapsed. In some cities, palaces and temples began to be used as squatting houses during this period. However, as the administrative and civil functions of the cities decreased, their religious activities became livelier than ever. For example, churches gained importance in Europe starting from the fourth and fifth centuries, and the silhouettes of cities were equipped with the spaces provided by the churches (Clark, 2009: p. 76). The urban revival that began after the 11th century coincided with the gradual growth of European cities; in this period, cities extended their networks to distant regions and expanded their economic and political importance, allowing them to host rural peasants, workers, knights, landowners and elites. In this period, the polycentric plan became dominant in cities, and even suburb developments were observed (Clark, 2009: p. 78).

Gradually, European cities began their spatial articulation with public buildings and residential areas. A new form of housing emerged in Italian cities, especially Florence, Pisa and Bologna. Low-income families who started to live in the towers, which were up to 75 meters high, were affecting the spatial transformation of the city. These towers were built by the elite as the living quarters of the poor. During this period, it has been determined that there were nearly 150 towers in Florence and almost 200 in Bologna. Southern France, Spain and Portugal followed this architectural and spatial development. The fact that the borders of the new city centres are not wide, and the increasing population and migration have caused the cities to show such a spatial development. While the space was designed for the poor in this way, it is known that the houses designed for the rich have wooden structures and a very aesthetic appearance (Clark, 2009: p. 81). While urbanisation was progressing at a high level, it was essential to have some changes in terms of the management of the city. It was a milestone in the life of cities as certain boards, which we can consider the first municipalities, became operational. In this period, the councils formed to ensure the effective and efficient continuation of the services provided to the citizens were generally in the hands of the elites. In fact, complaints and thus revolts, namely urban mobilisations, were seen among the poor segments who could not receive effective service for this reason. However, religious representatives who were influential in the cities during this period effectively reduced the tension of these movements. Other people who were seen as influential in the cities were kings and princes (Clark, 2009: p. 93). The civil oligarchy established in the city was the locomotive element in the management and spatial development of the city. The municipal development of the communities restricted by the boundaries of the space seems far from that of today. During this period, low-income families, minority groups and women with limited means of paying taxes did not have a say in the fate of the places where their lives would be administered (Clark, 2009: p. 95).

The Netherlands Revolt of the 16th century had severe urban consequences, including disrupting trade, military charges, turmoil and destruction. As a result of the revolt, there was an intense wave of immigration towards the north of the country from the southern region of the country and the city of Antwerp, which was affected by the financial results. Capitalists, merchants, and skilled artisans poured into the nation's capital. Amsterdam's population exceeded 100,000 in 1622. The merchants increasingly dominated the trade between the Baltic Sea, Asia and the Americas. The raw materials and intermediate products obtained were converted into final products in Dutch cities and exported. The Dutch urbanisation rate in 1670 reached 42 per cent, which is the highest figure in Europe. Due to this rate of urbanisation, Dutch cities were teeming with economic and political developments as well as hosting many urban movements. In particular, the interaction of artistic and social developments is still in effect (Clark, 2009: p. 114). The period between the Renaissance and the French Revolution was the time of the critical transition of European cities. By the late 18th century, a loose urban network was becoming consolidated. Influential capital cities, Atlantic ports, industrial cities, and recreational spaces became parts of the spatial network that developed within cities. Increasing trade with Asia and America since the 1700s triggered the transformation of European cities. Cities were increasingly becoming spaces of innovation and secular relations. And the actors trying to influence the city were increasingly the bourgeois and poor rather than religious leaders and royalty. Cities were reviving not only economically but also politically and socially (Clark, 2009: p. 109). When we look at the urbanisation that developed in this period, it had a faster and more intensive place than the Middle Ages. Second, there was a growing trade-off between the chronology and pattern of urban development across the continent. Finally, the urban achievements of the 18th century were very fragile, and political and economic struggles due to urban movements such as the French Revolution were affecting the spatial transformation of cities at a breakneck pace.

State power and patronage played an influential role in the distribution of capital in the city. The city began to change with the effect of not only the businesses operating in the city but also the rental income from the rural areas. While the elites and nobles took steps for urban rent, they did not renounce their existence in the rural areas as well. People with high economic and social status were increasingly meeting in taverns and coffee houses to discuss the agenda, talk politics and sign commercial agreements. Officials and nobles struggled for influence in the housing market, industry, retail and service sector. Another area was opened for the city during this period: recreational spaces. With the Age of Enlightenment, popular cultural life such as music, theatre and meeting was transforming into a spatial identity under the title of metropolitan life. Although the high level of consumption gave information about the city's economic activities, the increasing number of beggars and the poor in the same period also made it possible to see the effects of social and spatial differentiation on the cities, like the sword of Damocles. Increasing polarisation introduced the city's most sumptuous wealth and the most deplorable misery (Clark, 2009: p. 131). This was prevalent in many continents of the world, but it was most common in Europe. For example, if we look at the Americas, the urbanisation rate was only 6.1 in 1800 after the American Revolution. However, Europe was living in its golden age. Neoclassical style public buildings, theatres, assemblies, concert halls, promenade areas, coffee houses, clubs and communities triggered the spatial transformation of cities. However, in an environment where urban spaces are so diversified, the ordinariness and similarity of the poor areas in the city should not be overlooked. The more wealth and ostentation revived, the more deplorable the poverty became. Especially the short-term and long-term depressions experienced by the cities mainly affected the poor (Clark, 2009: p. 136). The crisis that emerged in a city due to the network between cities gradually affected other cities so that when interregional problems arose, cities turned into uninhabitable places.

After the 1700s, we see the existence of places that hosted public alcohol and coffee consumption. Coffeehouses spread to London from the Ottoman Empire in 1650. And they soon became fashionable. Paris was introduced to coffeehouses in 1670, Venice in 1683 and Vienna in 1685. Paris had 300 coffeehouses in 1714, and just before the revolution, the number had reached 1800. While there were 500 coffeehouses in London in 1700, the number began to decline in the next century. Because there was an increase in public alcohol consumption and the number of places serving it in England. The situation in Russia was not different from England. However, Russia's places serving alcohol consumption were under state control and operated as public enterprises. In the 19th century, two new actors joined the service sector and thus spatial development. Hotels and restaurants. Hotels were paradise gardens created in crowded cities, especially for high-income citizens, merchants, and nobles. The first restaurant opened in Paris in the 1760s. We know that there were 600 restaurants in 1804 (Clark, 2009: p. 156). Alongside this spatial development, which was particularly intended for the elite, the changes that would apply to the poor were limited. In fact, the number of houses having spatial conditions as seen in previous centuries was increasing. Despite this increase in housing, the increasing population and migration also triggered the mobility in the city. For example, in Spain, one out of every ten people changed their place of stay in the cities every year. In London, the number of people living in the same house for ten years was only 25 per cent (Clark, 2009: p. 164). The development seen in art and theatre was also important for the cities. Like every activity for the rich, there was a positive trend in these areas. Fine arts became visible in spaces, artist societies were established, workshops were opened, public exhibition spaces were designed, art exports began, and an increasing number of printing houses were established.

The commercialisation of the art market was at its peak during this period. Theatre halls were started to be built for theatrical plays that were previously performed in hostels or hotels, municipal buildings and open spaces. All fields of fine arts were used for the construction and design of these spaces. And these places were filled with many sub-spaces that served them and vice versa. The fastest and most influential art movement was seen in London after the 18th century. With 3,000 people, the most crowded theatre of that period belonged to the theatres built on Coventry Garden and Drury Lane. Opera, ballet and the most contemporary plays were played in these places for the rich. Theatres became places where the latest fashions, language, morals, and styles were displayed. An increasing number of coffee houses, bars, restaurants, shops and markets were located around the theatres (Clark, 2009: p. 192). Outdoor activities were also increasing in this century. Since the 17th century, many European cities have had tree-lined walkways and promenades that they will eventually reach. Areas that were not used before except for some secret relations other than hunting were now undergoing spatial transformation. In these places, the notables and rich people of the city were meeting, gathering and chatting with each other. It was a completely new definition of space. Such places were observed in the 18th century, especially in France and England. Especially the cities of regions such as Italy, which hosted rapid and intense urbanisation in previous centuries, were criticised for being deprived of such spaces.

Population growth and migration were unavoidable for the cities of the 17th century. Urban density caused the urban open spaces in the city's centre to be occupied by the crowds, and the city's lungs were closed. The city developed a new solution to this. Gardens and parks. Often and until recently, these were places that the citizens of the city could enter with money. In these places, visitors could take a walk as well as spend time in company with a green vista. Redesigned in the mid-1700s, London's Spring Garden sometimes hosted activities for up to 10,000 people. The steps taken by the royal family have an important place in the spread of such parks. The royals, who needed places where plants from different geographies were exhibited, started to invest in such parks. In addition, the number of such places has increased gradually due to the increase in the city's population, the crowding of the public space and, of course, the movement of industry into the city. Hyde Park in London and Djurgarden in Stockholm are examples of such parks (Clark, 2009: p. 193).

While talking about the urban landscape, it is necessary to mention the transformation of the streets surrounding the central areas. The popular social spaces created for enlightened cultural activities enabled the streets to be illuminated and the necessary infrastructure services for recreation built. Starting from 1720, the streets of London began to be illuminated, the roads were widened, and pavements and stone pavements covered the streets. Drainage systems were installed, and pedestrian walkways were built. The city walls and gateways, which had formed the silhouette of cities since the Middle Ages, had begun to be demolished. Fortification walls and passages were demolished to create the spaces necessary for the city's increased cultural activities. For example, in Paris, the old fortification walls were converted into boulevards. These changes also triggered new designs of urban spaces in central areas. Urban design, which emerged in the Italian Renaissance cities, began to spread to Western Europe with the Baroque and neo-Palladian architecture of the 18th century. New public buildings were built using brick and stone. The venues of the new construction were theatres, opera houses, hospitals, mansions and churches. New construction techniques were also reflected in residential architecture. Unlike previous centuries, the houses had private gardens and parks (Clark, 2009: p. 195).

Cities gained a new urban space from the beginning of the 19th century. Public transportation has given cities a new silhouette. Until that date, transportation in the cities was generally carried out on foot or by horse-drawn carriages of the rich. In 1820, horse-drawn omnibuses arrived. In 1860, horse-drawn trams with horses again became visible in cities. Cities began to reserve more and more areas for public transport. Stores, shops and markets clustered around the stops promised a new spatial development. Towards the end of the 19th century, municipal affiliates began implementing public transportation systems in cities. Towards the end of the century, the number of people using the bus, tram and train lines reached one million in some cities. The new century also evoked the birth of another place. The subway systems. For the first time, the underground was gaining importance in cities. Four hundred million passengers used the Paris metro network in 1914. Due to this new space and the spatial network woven around it, a new line of business was emerging. The London shuttle service, for example, had 70,300 staff in 1933. By 1947, the number had reached almost 100,000. Public transport continued to develop after the Second World War. In fact, the number of passengers travelling in Paris in 1971 exceeded 1 million in one day. Cities gained another vehicle between the two world wars, thus a new location. Private cars. The use of automobiles paralysed the traffic in the city, and attempts were made to create new spatial areas. Between 1918 and 1930, the number of cars in Stockholm quadrupled. While Hamburg had 80,000 vehicles in 1938, 430,000 vehicles travelled in the city in 1968. The development of private and individual means of transportation has had significant economic and environmental impacts on the city. While the gases emitted by the fuels used for automobiles made the city's air unbreathable, the increase in the number of vehicles caused a traffic jam that made everybody unable to move. The increasing number of cars also revealed another spatial problem: parking area. The number of garages for cars quadrupled in Berlin between 1951 and 1979. Another problem was the insufficient parking areas in the city centre, which led to the emergence of multi-storey parking areas (Clark, 2009: p. 272).

Going back to the 19th century, political changes were causing significant spatial changes in the city. For example, cities were making room for new spatial areas due to the urban movements in Paris in 1830, 1848 and 1871. The number of official offices and employees of the city had increased due to the increasing pressure of the people on the city administration. And new spaces were being created in the city for such buildings and those working in these buildings. New central districts were beginning to emerge within the city, and the monumental designs that would spread over these areas led to the replanning of the space. For this new monumental and modern planning, many old neighbourhoods and buildings with historical identity had begun to be demolished. For example, since its independence in 1830, Belgium started to create modern spaces by demolishing many neighbourhoods for the administrative and social spaces it needed. But the most transparent and most famous example of this came from Paris. Haussmann, appointed during the era of Napoleon III, started to create new city centres that divided the city centre into pieces. In Paris, where wide boulevards were built, neighbourhoods bearing the traces of the past were being demolished one by one. New and modern urban spaces and buildings were being built, and the region's low-income families were exiled to other parts of the city. Of course, the only reason for this intervention was not the desire to have a modern city.

The ensuing urban movements glowed, enlivened and breathed in neighbourhoods with narrow streets and organically intertwined buildings. State forces were struggling to intervene. And the inhabitants of the region occupied their place as potential participants when the urban movements were trying to shine, as well as when they were not. And the urban space gave up adopting this style of politics and wanted to transform these places of danger into places where the citizens of the city would live, which would not cause them any difficulties. And for any military intervention, the streets and roads were no longer as narrow as they used to be. The boulevards began to dominate the centre of the city. In the event of an unpredictable situation, effective intervention should have been done as quickly as possible (Clark, 2009: p. 324). The clearance activities that started in the city in the 19th century were called 'sventramenti'. The use of this word went back to the actions carried out by Haussmann in the city for his plans. 'Sventramenti' originally meant a potent drug and massive surgery as a medical term. It also meant destroying severely inflamed urban organisms and transforming them into healthier spaces, in line with the planning (Kostof, 1994: p. 10). Not only those who wanted to get rid of the old buildings in the city's centre benefited from the demolition. The citizens, who were bored of the crowd of the city and wanted to get rid of the polluted air that comes with the traffic jam, wished to move towards the outer sections of the city. A new urban design and urban space were born: the Garden City. This new spatial development, theorised especially by Ebenezer Howard, became a recipe for salvation for many European cities for a while. These new settlements, where new spaces and buildings would be established, promised peace, away from the chaos and hustle & bustle of the city. And it also meant getting away from the growing dangers and crises that urban movements would create. Of course, new public transportation networks and systems followed this development. Time meant the abandonment of cities once again. However, it was not. Of course, many people followed this development and organised a new network of spaces to continue their lives in new rent areas, but they could not break away from the city and always maintained their relations. Cities are now indispensable. No matter what, the rights and comfort would remain the fate of the cities.

During the Renaissance, cities changed based on mutual agreements and bargains between landowners and contractors. The landowner or proprietor requested changes in the place he owned by consulting the city councils and bargaining with them. Where the streets would pass and what would be located next to the land were determined by mutual understanding in this period. The designs of the planned spaces were usually plotted on the city plan in the form of a square or rectangle. As it became impossible to find space in the city with the rate of increase in the population, an old tradition was applied, and multi-storey buildings started to be constructed, which affected the silhouette of the cities. With the Baroque period, the concepts of dynamism, impetuous reach, sensate passage and grand vista came into urban planning, and thus to spatial transformation. Renaissance streets were straight, connecting channels of communication. Streets regulated traffic and encouraged the exploration of sub-spaces created. However, during the baroque period, roads started to be arranged as much larger corridors or landscapes. Secondary roads were designed to lead the main roads, determined according to the positions that overlooked the city's silhouette, towards the city's critical stopping points. In this way, some points and areas in the city became essential places for each citizen. In particular, they were turning into monumental places over time. Haussmann would also use this understanding centuries later (Kostof, 1994: p. 16).

After the 1750s, a cultural revolution took place across Europe that would affect every city. An urban space arrangement that went beyond the precise and permanent planning of Renaissance architecture began to take place. This understanding, which intended to preserve an identity that history bestowed

on cities, was actually destroying the strict lines of planning as well. The importance of the urban spaces built until that time has also been effective in the
importance of this understanding, which would respect the past of historical
areas and preserve the structure of the neighbourhoods. The city was saturated
with new spaces, and there was no question of feeling hungry. Of course, this
was not true for every city, but such an understanding had become dominant,
especially in the west of Europe (Kostof, 1994: p. 17). However, the political and
military revolutions at the end of the century caused the bourgeoisie and capital to gain importance for the reproduction of cities. After the revolutions, the
bourgeoisie, which expanded its position in social and political life, wanted to
change the city in line with its own needs. They wanted to replace the palaces,
official buildings, and churches of the Baroque period with their own workplaces, residences, entertainment venues and monumental structures. They
also wanted the sewerage and drinking water infrastructure to expand into
the city. Just in this period, Haussmann, who was working for the emperor,
became the new representative of the changing political structure, namely
the bourgeois, and began to overhaul the city centre and its nearby geography.
He started demolition activities to limit a more profound urban movement
and turn the city into the living space of the bourgeoisie, which was the ruler
of that era. Old spaces, neighbourhoods with identity, and living spaces that
were important for the poor gradually decreased, and business centres, market
areas, and recreation and entertainment venues for the bourgeoisie were being
built in their place (Kostof, 1994: p. 18).

Haussmann's work was followed and applied throughout the following
years. Neo-Haussmannism, which emerged primarily in the middle of the 20th
century, aimed to destroy the ageing neighbourhoods as well as the poor and
deprived areas of cities. They wanted to fulfil the requirements of the global
system and create a spatial expansion for the owners of the rising global capital by demolishing not only the ancient neighbourhoods or spaces of the
city, but also many settlement centres built in the 19th century (Merrifield,
2014: p. 10). What neo-Haussmannism wants to do today is not to change the
fabric structure of the city by creating wide boulevards in the centre of the
city. On the contrary, they aim to build new settlements of the bourgeoisie
who settled outside the city in the past, which are no longer just national but
international. New spaces do not require vast openings. They aim to demolish
impoverished neighbourhoods, which gained an identity in the city's centre
and build sheltered, secure and isolated residential areas, namely residences,
in their places. Of course, this includes not only residences but also business
centres. They change the silhouettes of cities to work and live in today's version
of the towers of the past, which were intended for the poor, with a height up to

75 meters. High-rise buildings, which completely change the city's landscape and even change the historical places, reveal the new goals of the Neo-Haussmann approach. Of course, the sub-spaces built around high-rise buildings are a kind of space syntax, restricting the users of this area without fences or electrical wires. While people who do not have a certain economic power have the right to come to these places, they cannot do so. Worse still, the construction of such places obliges many people to be exiled to another corner of the city, completely destroying their memories. This understanding is another step of planetary urbanisation under Bonapartism (Merrifield, 2014: p. 29).

Today, therefore, no space is far from being called physical or central. People can now easily breathe in the city spaces and communicate offline, that is, in digital spaces. However, this actual situation does not explain the reality. Although the distinction between private and public remains in a grey spot, spaces retain their definitions while also losing their definition due to imaginary boundaries. Areas of sovereignty are now more transitive than before but still not public in use. And although it is still not in the centre of the city, there are 'dead zones' on its peripheries. Due to the dynamic communication prevailing among people, social media (i.e., digital spaces) gain more importance than physical spaces. However, people still live and work in physical spaces. And for this reason, they share in these places. However, not every citizen can be a user of every digital space, nor can they experience every physical space, although there is no legal obstacle. This development is progressing so rapidly that it is difficult for the citizens to use it due to the imaginary boundaries set without really changing the physical properties of the spaces. This development envisages that the users of public spaces will gradually change after the occupation of urban centres. Citizens, who have already been expelled from the urban centre and have to live on the city's outskirts, are compelled to stay away from infrastructural developments. The water and natural gas network are more backward in the peripheries compared to the centre. Means of transport are more limited and tiring. Urban service spaces are increasing towards the centre, whereas they are almost non-existent on the peripheries. Even the internet infrastructure worsens towards the periphery. Housing structure and living spaces appear to be unhealthier. Recreational and entertainment areas to serve the citizens are also very limited in the city's peripheries. The only thing left in the hands of the citizens in this competition and struggle is the public spaces visible in the urban centres. And by occupying these areas to win their struggle and at least keep what they have, they spatialise their actions, namely their urban movements. The urban movement, which started with Occupy Wall Street and Zuccotti Park, a semi-private area in America, and is reflected in the city's squares, is the product of this spatial occupation, objection and ownership (Merrifield, 2014: p. 83).

The fact that the city is divided into different regions causes the emergence of various 'villages' within the city. These 'villages' are not designed as rivals to the city's existence but rather for the citizens' idealisation of the urban social space. We see that 'villages' develop automatically and synthetically in line with cultural ties, production of dreams, politics and goals. For this reason, they come across as the codes of social and spatial separation as new 'quarters' and 'villages' within the urban space system as the space market of a new strategy that we can imagine as a network of urban villages, especially in big cities (Tonkiss, 2011: p. 18). Social mixes require and demand a mix of spatial uses. For this reason, in today's urbanism, the separation of residential areas and the living areas of the city, unfortunately, cut off the citizens' communication. Different types of people and places are indispensable elements of cities. For this reason, it is vital for the citizens and their spaces to be together in a mixed order. The fact that the city continues to live in the company of the separated 'villages' kills this urban form. Moreover, the removal of the houses included in this plan from the streets and the intensification of the living spaces inside the rooms is the product of urbanisation without a city (Jacobs, 1964: p. 256).

Under this siege, the spatial organisation of sameness fortifies alienation and insecurity in the sense of reproducing the communities within the city. The fact that daily life revolves around the streets increases the trust and tolerance of the citizens towards each other. Citizens get to know and meet other citizens through the places they visit and their neighbours. However, due to the increasing globalisation, cities are losing their sub-spaces through sameness. While each space and its users continue their lives through the same values and designs, people and places with different styles and understanding of life become marginalised (Jacobs, 1964: p. 66). This new urbanisation separates urban space and social groups. The link between spatial locations and social identities is an important development in urban policy. Losing the connection between these two concepts makes the lives of the citizens ordinary and homogeneous. In areas where this link is broken, marginalisation and alienation occur. For this reason, urban ghettos and worn-out neighbourhoods emerge in the inner cities. And even not limited to this, the city's peripheries gradually begin to break away from the city's centres. Urban poverty and inequality arise due to the ineffectiveness of the prominent institutions and organisations, as well as the environment of distrust exceeding the physical borders, and the gears of social exclusion begin to turn (Tonkiss, 2011: p. 30).

Power can be a complicated phenomenon to observe, but it can easily manifest itself in space. One of the most visible ways of exercising power is to control or occupy space. It makes architectural power legible in material forms. From this point of view, cities are the major areas of official power. Political, legal, constitutional, economic, police and military authority materialise and embody on space. They ensure the concentration of power by giving physical form to formal architectural spaces. While the elites in power turn the city into a living space for themselves with the weight of their established institutions, they turn it into a hell for the poor. The geography of political and economic privilege maps the organisation of existing power in urban space. As Zukin (1993) mentioned, urban architecture can be seen as a landscape of power. Constructed areas that are dominant and submissive can become the production area of urban industry with legal associations from the underground up to the sky, as well as revealing 'dead zones' in which deprived areas are located. For this reason, the places targeted by urban movements in the past were palaces, government buildings, central banks, ministries, or intelligence centres. The centres of power, which later turned into a global union, changed. So the protests concentrated more on the physical and digital spaces of organisations such as the IMF, the G8 or the World Trade Organisation. The geography of protests and demonstrations became the spatial expression of the elongated dome of politics. And the urban movement activists targeted the city centres and places that are important for the city, which remained in their hands and where they could make their voices heard. The use and sometimes even occupation of these spaces was a symbol for the city they would gain, and it also showed that the same spaces still belong to them (Tonkiss, 2011: p. 60).

Urban movements directly connect with the public area, i.e. the public space. Although the line between private and public space is getting fuzzy today, it is necessary to define public space here. We can classify public space under three headings: squares in terms of representing the common sense of belonging; restaurants and coffee shops as they represent social change and shopping; and Streets representing informal encounters. Therefore, the most basic public spaces are squares, restaurants, cafes and streets. Even though these spaces are provided and secured by the state, they are free spaces for the citizens, and no distinction or privilege is given in terms of entry and use (Tonkiss, 2011: p. 66). The most ideal basis of public space is its accessibility. In terms of these spaces, control will not always be at the hand of the citizens, and there will be no such thing as exclusion. When we look at today's cities, we see an unstable and variable border between private and public spaces. When we look around today's cities, we see that places are becoming more and more privatised. This is not a re-acquisition or development gained by the private enterprise by taking a step. Still, it results from the use or operation of public spaces being offered to private enterprises for the sake of rent.

While the public transportation is in the hands of private enterprise, private enterprise can intervene in the planning of the roads and spaces in between where public transportation will pass, and even when the need or obligation to consume within the time spent in public space is sprouting as profit in the hands of private enterprise, the reason for the struggle for public space can be understood. With this perspective, the economic and cultural privatisation of cities not only changes the ownership of urban space, but also transforms its dimensions in urban experiences (Tonkiss, 2011: p. 72).

GIS (Geographic Information Science) is vital in terms of spatial representation, both as a digital tool responsible for the production of projects, an interdisciplinary object, and a digital method that allows us to establish visual connections between the dimensions of urban phenomena. The inclusion of destinations and locations on the screens and the introduction of promotional activities to add value to the recognisability of these places in terms of branding is the clearest example of how the space has become digital. People who exist with space as digitalised cities are now more familiar with the geography of the city in which they live through digital layers than on the real plane. Finding the places to go and creating the route to be used becomes more manageable thanks to digital tools, as people rely on technology rather than intuitive features. Geography is gradually shifting from the real visual to the artificial digital environment. This proves how dependent we are on digital media for our cities at the beginning of the 21st century (Fraser, 2015: p. 56). This century is called the age of information. In this age, it is seen that the political, economic and social developments of information and communication technologies have become very basic. The Internet is changing power. Access and control of symbols, norms and interpretations play a critical role in today's societies. For example, the most obvious example of this is the loss of social control for a while by the national governments that stand against WikiLeaks after thousands of pages of confidential documents have been published. Despite all kinds of interventions, the spread of social networking and microblogging practices may result in the expansion of political, social and economic freedoms (Milan, 2013: p. 3). It was a special case of the 1990s when non-governmental organisations, individual media activists and professionals first appeared in the media and communication channels as a coalition. This coalition founded organisations such as the MacBride Roundtables and made announcements and associations such as the People's Communication Charter and Platform for Communication Rights. In the 21st century, non-governmental entrepreneurs have gained momentum and paved the way for multi-stakeholder governance diffusion. The appearance of communication activism has emerged and begun to be confronted with the pieces of training and notifications of WSIS (UN World Summit on the Information Society) (Milan, 2013: p. 7).

Individually, new technologies have caused radical changes in individuals' social ties. In the past, friendships allowed sharing information in moments, limited to minutes, shared in cafes, restaurants, and activities such as sports. People meeting at a friend's house or students meeting at school desks mediated the flow of information. In fact, secret note pages sent from desks to desks were the most mysterious method of communication. Then, the means of communication with receivers and transmitters were discovered. A new tool of knowledge was introduced into our lives. But the 21st century has completely changed our means of communication and the flow of information. While communication has changed, our line of intimacy with the people we communicate with has also changed. Of course, our communication density has changed too. For example, according to a study on young people living in the United States, in 2009, an average of 3000 messages were sent per month for the 'Twitter' application alone (Carty, 2015: p. 1). In the information age, which results in the opening of digital space to all kinds of users, social media applications are an important factor in urban movements' emergence, spread, and effect. According to this new type of action, called cyberactivism, participants make digital spaces their home, sparking face-to-face relationships. Face-to-face civic belonging is expanding and becoming widespread with 'clicktivism'. Notices regularly reach more and more citizens than in the past, and actions become more attractive.

The synergy created by people who cannot physically participate in the digital space deeply affects the fate of the actions. New communication technologies cause us to call people who use digital space as new generation journalists. While this new trend, known as the civil media, causes the facts to be published directly without comment, it heralds a new media age in which sometimes distortions or momentary deceptions are easily made for propaganda purposes (Carty, 2015: p. 32). Those who use new activities such as civil media most actively are members of non-governmental organisations. These people can both reflect the developments most actively and easily announce the rights they demand. For example, the struggle of the participants who organised to lift the ban on women driving in Saudi Arabia is an example. Mass demonstrations are prohibited in Saudi Arabia and are a serious crime. For this reason, the citizens of the city cannot make their wishes heard as they wish. However, since a female citizen could not go out to the streets to remove this sexist ban, she prefers to show herself in the digital space and defend her case. The struggle she started on his Facebook page found a lot of support. It even received support from international platforms. For example, the petition with 10,000 signatures that reached Hillary Clinton, who declared a decision to lift the ban and took the initiative, shows how women's rights defenders effectively use social media, i.e. digital space (Carty, 2015: p. 47).

However, like every other place, the users of the digital space continue their criminal acts in the new place. Initiatives called 'Hacktivism' access the data of individuals and organisations and cause the information obtained to be used for malicious purposes. By using computer viruses, bugs and Trojan horses, the digital space of the citizens and important organisations is opened for unauthorised use, and information is shared. Sending thousands of spam emails (email bombing) causes servers to become unstable. On the other hand, attacks called cyberterrorism are digital attacks actively launched by terrorist organisations against people or institutions that they see as their opponents or targets. These activities also result in the destruction of the digital space for the society and the touchstone institutions that concern the society (Carty, 2015: p. 36).

CHAPTER 5

The Case Study

Beyoğlu, Istanbul

The Pera district is where Istanbulites experienced many things for the first time. The development process for Beyoğlu is in line with the socio-economic structure of Turkey. Istiklal Street, the so-called "heart of Beyoğlu", was affected by political instabilities and economic crises. Every twenty years, the street went through a social and an economic crisis before being revitalised. Indeed, Beyoğlu has always been Turkey's gateway to the West, but its most significant development was during the Crimean War in 1854. The protracted stay of French, British and Italian soldiers in Istanbul due to war marked the beginning of Beyoğlu's modern appearance. After the Crimean War, the Ottoman Empire borrowed from Europe by selling bonds and constructed almost three hundred palaces, mansions, and pavilions primarily in the Bosphorus as well as in Göztepe, Erenköy, Büyükada, Çamlıca, and Bağlarbaşı with the funds acquired from these bonds. The accessories of these structures were entirely of foreign origin. In addition, infrastructure projects such as Karaköy Tunnel, Karaköy-Şişli tramway, Galata Pier, gas lighting for the city as well as Baghdad railways were carried out with the build-operate-transfer model. Many businesspeople, industrialists, stockbrokers, bankers, technical personnel, and engineers from Europe settled in Istanbul to make a living. Levantines, who aimed to supply products unavailable in the Ottoman Empire for use and sale, settled in Galata and Beyoğlu. The number of Levantines who settled in Beyoğlu at that time was known to be 12 thousand. The lives of Levantines changed Istiklal street and its surroundings. Restaurants, pubs, operas, theatres, and shops were opened on and around the street. The first municipality in the Ottoman Empire was established in Beyoğlu in 1858. With its clean and tidy streets, sidewalks, and municipal gardens, Beyoğlu became the most beautiful district of Istanbul. The citizens of Beyoğlu began to live in Western-style masonry buildings, in apartments with Western-style decorations, dining tables, and armchairs. The households' clothing, table manners, and education changed, and pianos appeared in many homes. However, events such as the declaration of the 1st World War, the Gallipoli Front, the loss of the war, the occupation of Istanbul, the migration of the White Russians, the liberation of Istanbul, the proclamation of the Republic, the Wealth Tax, the Events of 6–7

September and the Turkification of Istanbul triggered the urban movements of Beyoğlu dramatically (Akıncı, 2018: p. 13).

It is narrated that the name "Beyoğlu" comes from Luigi Giritti's mansion. It is claimed that the mansion is somewhere around Taksim Square and Tophane. The origins of the Venetian family of Andrea Gritti are based on the island of Crete. Andrea Gritti was the Istanbul representative of the Venetian State and a businessman. A person of high commercial income, Andrea has made remarkable contributions to improving relations between the two states. Andrea was later made the Governor of the Venetian State. However, while his four children were accepted to Venice, his illegitimate children were not. In turn, Luigi Gritti returned to his father's residence in Istanbul and continued to engage in trade. Being successful in trade, this boy later became a Muslim. Due to the respect he gained in the district, the area around his mansion was named Beyoğlu over time. The name "Beyoğlu" ("Son of the Governor") comes from the son of the Governor, who was denied entry into Venice. The central axis of the ongoing development of Beyoğlu was Cadde-i Kebir. Today, this road, known as Istiklal Street, was transformed into its current form with the development of the pathway connecting Taksim, which is at the top of the region, to Tünel. The most lively location in the district is Pera. Pera means "opposite shore" or "the other side" in Greek. Pera, which was built around Tünel, the end of Istiklal Street, was particularly notorious due to the sufferings of Turks in the hands of minorities and occupation forces during the Armistice period. Due to these sufferings, the name of Cadde-i Kebir, known as 'Grande Rue de Pera' for 55 years, was changed to Istiklal Street following the liberation of Istanbul from the occupation forces after the War of Independence (Akıncı, 2018: p. 15).

The fate of Beyoğlu changed after the French ambassador settled in Beyoğlu following the conclusion of the Ottoman-French Trade Agreement in 1535. Until those years, there was no structure in Beyoğlu except for the Genoese Area surrounded by the walls in Galata. Beyoğlu was a place with vineyards and gardens and a cemetery located out of town. Şişhane Hill and Tepebaşı were predominantly Muslim cemeteries. They were not liked very much, as the area near the water distribution tank in Taksim was prone to northern winds. In time, Muslim cemeteries began to form in Ayaspaşa. The French embassy was not the only one settled in Beyoğlu. Following the French, all embassies settled in Beyoğlu. Neighbourhoods built around the pathway that developed from Taksim to Tünel were the first residential areas of Beyoğlu. However, Turkish and Muslim populations were in the minority in the area. The newly established settlements were unplanned and unscheduled. The streets were very narrow and derelict. The houses were wooden and had three or four floors. The masonry buildings were thick-walled, damp, and gloomy. Food was eaten at floor tables, and people lived on sofas. Houses were heated with floor furnaces.

By the 1830s, there were three to four thousand people in Beyoğlu, where minorities and Franks lived in derelict neighbourhoods. In the 1830s, Beyoğlu was a district with coffee houses, taverns, inns, and neighbourhood shops on its streets. There were also three churches and two monasteries in the area. Beyoğlu was quiet most of the day. Sounds of prayer calls (Adhan) were among the only things that broke this silence. Church bells did not ring. They were only heard if a critical visit was to take place. The most significant development in Istanbul took place in Beyoğlu after the proclamation of the Tanzimat Edict in 1839. National revolts and urban movements before the Tanzimat caused the state to decide to renovate itself. Now, the rights that spread in Europe after the French Revolution also applied within the Ottoman Empire. After the innovations and vitality brought by the Tanzimat in trade and social life, the arcade culture began in Beyoğlu in 1840. This was a new shopping culture. The stores that could not find themselves a place on the street were able to do so in the arcade. Over time, 29 arcades were built in Beyoğlu. As of 1850, 50,000 Levantines lived in Beyoğlu. The people of Istanbul were influenced by this population's lifestyles, homes, and workplaces. Everyone, especially the Palace, was trying to implement the Levantine lifestyle.

The word Levantine is a French term used to refer to the Eastern Mediterranean. Levantine is a term used by Europeans to condescend to people of European descent living in the East. In particular, it was used to describe the Christians living in port cities and dealing with trade in the Ottoman Empire. European-style city management was required for the activities of the Levantines in the city. Thus, the Ottoman Empire initiated municipal activities by taking Paris, the capital of France, with which it had close relations, as an example. It took the 6th District system of Paris as an example, and for this reason, Beyoğlu Municipality was named the 6th Department of the Municipality. Due to the influence of the Levantines on the district's life, the Cadde-i Kebir was renamed by Server Bey, the Mayor of Beyoğlu, as Grande Rue de Pera in 1867. During this period, it was clearly seen that Beyoğlu was the heart of Western-style development. Street lighting was first used in Beyoğlu. The first apartment building was constructed in Beyoğlu. Beyoğlu was the central core of modernisation in the Ottoman Empire (Şenyurt, 2018: p. 235). In the course of this development, groups against modernisation started taking action as well. Beyoğlu was home to those who stood against this urban movement, defending a Western lifestyle. Therefore, Beyoğlu was a district that gave rise to urban movements and became the point of origin for this movement. The coffeehouses and taverns in Beyoğlu became places where the following steps to be taken concerning the internal affairs of the palace were discussed and were also transformed into places where solutions were sought against social problems. In particular, the coffeehouses were the centres of urban movements (Berkes, 2018: p. 44).

During the Great Fire of Pera in 1870, approximately 3,000 buildings burned down. According to the investigations of the Beyoğlu Municipality Office, it was stated that 65 streets, 163 neighbourhoods and 3449 buildings were burned. According to the municipality's plans, all the buildings built after the fire were constructed. In the next 40 years, the appearance of Beyoğlu changed. The tram line connecting the Karaköy-Beyoğlu Tunnel and Istiklal Avenue to Meşrutiyet Avenue was added to the arcades built by the architects' group, whose majority was constituted by Europeans. While there was only one hotel in Beyoğlu in 1840, new accommodation centres were built, including very luxurious hotels. Exquisite shops, restaurants, pubs, patisseries, and coffee houses were opened. Nine theatres and fifteen cinemas were opened on the street (Akıncı, 2018: p. 22).

Although Beyoğlu lost its liveliness for a period due to the grim events at the beginning and the middle of the 20th century, it never lost its significance. In particular, the student movements that occurred in the '60s changed the face of Beyoğlu and, most specifically, Istiklal Street. The workers' movements that occurred in addition to the student movements increased the vitality of Taksim Square. Beyoğlu had now become the central point of urban movements due to the spaces and squares it offered. Art, culture, identity, and urban political movements became a current issue throughout the country, especially in Beyoğlu. However, this process was interrupted due to the revolution of 1980. Beyoğlu was now only a leisure and shopping location. Only the artistic activities continued. On one condition: Under state control. However, in the 1990s, Beyoğlu once again became known for urban movements. With the increasing number of young population and the rate of urbanisation, in particular, the actions of the citizens once again came back to the urban scene. Due to the increase in global relations and communication technologies in the 2000s, urban movements were revived even more. However, due to the central governments' approach to these movements, what was inevitable did happen, and the social explosion began with Gezi Park in May 2013.

With the increase in the urban crises created by the main problems in the city, the urban movements in Beyoğlu gained momentum after the 1960s. Actions against housing, education, health, transportation, urban planning and design, preservation of historical and cultural areas, social life and political problems were organised within the urban movements of this period, which we can consider as a period in which urban protests merged with political demands. Considering the housing problems, we see a demand for new, suitable, and affordable housing. Many of the protests are made against the poor living conditions of the housing. It is demanded that derelict and worn-out buildings, which have completed their useful life, are inharmonious with their surroundings and are not earthquake resistant, be replaced with more suitable structures. Another demand is to take the necessary steps to improve payment conditions. Neighbourhoods demolished within the scope of urban transformation projects, and the situation of families exiled within the city are also the focus points of the actions. In terms of education, there are demands regarding public schools' infrastructure and education conditions. The urban movements focus on the demands of young people who wish to study in schools closest to their residential address at an equal level of education and the wishes of their families. Within the scope of health services, the infrastructure of health facilities and the number of doctors is the main topics of the complaints. The inadequacy of doctor appointments regarding their times and the prices of drugs cause an increase in complaints. The demands of those without a sufficient budget to have health insurance are also the subject of protests.

Transportation is a topic that is particularly important for Istanbul. The inadequacy of the metro network, the tram and bus lines, and the intense use of the *metrobus* with its limited lines trigger the transportation demands of the citizens. The fact that public transportation is expensive and not affordable in a city with a traffic mess is another cause of complaint. It is also the subject of protests that the lines for sea transportation are insufficient. Another complaint is the number of stops and lines, lagging behind the requested amount. The demand for more open spaces is among the top demands of Istanbulites. The inadequacy of green areas, recreation areas, protected areas, and urban and neighbourhood parks are among the issues citizens complain about. The lack of roads planted with rows of trees, i.e., a city that is insufficient in terms of green space, is frequently mentioned in the protests. The preservation of historical and cultural sites is vital for the people of Istanbul and especially for the citizens living in Beyoğlu. Istanbul's historical and architectural inventory, which has hosted many civilisations, is extensive and numerous. Of course, preserving this inventory and making it available to citizens is essential. The fact that these structures and areas cannot be preserved, or preserved through privatisation, increases the complaints. There are also actions taken to maintain social and neighbourhood life. The main reason for the complaints is the problems regarding the organisation and space for street festivals, historical and religious holidays, sports activities, and weekend activities for children and youth. Even the inability to find areas for urban movements is a matter of complaint. Another social need and demand is related to the fact that neighbourhood life is slowly ending. Of course, there are also urban move-ments whose demands are oriented toward political goals. The essence of political goals does not actually change, even in case of a change in political power. A free society and individuals and a more democratic political order and power are the foremost political goal which forms its core.

The restructuring of economic organisation and urban re-development are the reasons behind the increase in the mobilisation in cities. The global tran-sition from industrial to post-industrial cities after the 1980s has made urban space the new strategic institutional arena. The central and strategic role of cities as part of the global economy turns urban space into an area of strug-gle. A series of urban renewal and transformation projects were included in the agenda of the new urban policy, particularly in urban centres, after the 1990s. This new urbanisation transforms the city's urban environment and socio-economic structure to make it more convenient and attractive to private enterprises and global powers. This process causes an increase in gentrifica-tion projects and the urban exile of low-income citizens. The city centre and its immediate surroundings are increasingly occupied by wealthy, privileged and global powers (Andretta et al., 2015: p. 203). Istanbul is one of the main cities where this process is implemented. In particular, the Beyoğlu district is becoming the target of this new urban policy. This district, a historical and cultural centre of the city, is increasingly being transformed into venues suita-ble for privileged citizens and tourists. The living spaces of low-income people in the district are gradually becoming the playground of national and global high-income people. In this competitive and unequal race, conflict is increas-ing among the citizens. Such a rapid and unequal change in urban spaces clearly explains the difference between use and exchange values (Brenner et al., 2012: p. 204).

Considering the old, nostalgic appearance of Beyoğlu, which dates back to the mid-1900s, Beyoğlu Municipality began its renovation and restoration activities at the beginning of the 2000s. The task, called the Beautiful Beyoğlu Project, was a collective renovation operation where the municipality sought to give the Beyoğlu district, its big shops in the streets, an antique yet mod-ern look and bring back the former inspirational and prestigious days of this district. In particular, the 1980s and 1990s are the years when Istiklal Street lost most of its dignity and splendour compared to the past. Although not openly discussed, this district, like New York's Times Square, had been plagued by homeless people, gangsters and drug addicts, particularly in the evenings. Well-known brands and other essential brand names started to leave Istiklal Street due to the loss of brand values and significant decreases in sales. Thus, the Beautiful Beyoğlu Project aimed to reintroduce and restore the historical identity of this region. In keeping with this operation, the hot food wagons were redesigned in an old-fashioned style and painted mainly in red colour. Several old and derelict buildings have had their facades renovated.

The legendary and nostalgic trams passing through Istiklal Street were redesigned in red to match the old-fashioned style and made operational again. In addition, plants in wooden pots were introduced to support and affirm the old, nostalgic identity of the streets. The only diversion in this project was the appearance of the leading taxi stands and commercial cinema venues, designed in a modern way. The project also impacted visual appearances; in terms of signage, the front panels and facades of all shops and stores on Istiklal Street were required to conform to a single visual style, in line with the project's principles. As a result of these instructions, most stores have abandoned their original front panels and adopted the required visual codes. This meant that contrasting elements of visual perception were removed from shop signs. As with almost every new application, the Beautiful Beyoğlu Project received both positive and negative reactions: Some believed that such a project had a sense of disorder, that it acted in a way that was not harmonious with the chaotic and confusing visual system on Istiklal Street, thus making it lose its identity. On the other hand, the project drew more criticism than admiration from architects and urban planners, who harshly criticised these profound visual arrangements in a historically and culturally significant area.

The Beautiful Beyoğlu Project may not represent an entire Disneyification case, as it lacks the concept of simulation. However, based on this definition, it can be indisputably argued that most shops in this area have been stripped of their original visual character and repackaged in a sterilised form. Unfortunately, this urban transformation project has depersonalised Istiklal Street to avoid visual chaos. Furthermore, the chaos continued more seriously, causing it to lose its current identity as well. Display techniques became deformed and lost their foundation in space more than in any of the world's leading global cities (Ertep, 2009: p. 269).

It is observed that cities are local areas that carry diversity, multiplicity and even contradictions within themselves; they are not homogeneous units of a single sound, tone or flavour. This makes our cities unique, energetic, vibrant, and culturally rich. Beyoğlu has always been known as a brand of Istanbul, which provides opportunities for pluralism in expression and representation; every Turkish citizen associates the word Beyoğlu with the richness, diversity and even contrast in culture and civilisation. The unique character of this critical point has been reduced, and even de-energised as a result of the projects carried out. Standardising the front displays of the stores, as was first attempted on Istiklal Street, can be perceived as a beautifying task to recreate the old, nostalgic spirit of a particular area. However, such a standardisation serves as a tool for visual homogenisation up to the point where visual language and cultural codes are unified. From urban planning or environmental architecture point of view, making certain adjustments to the visual message system of a significant street, district or area may look like a reasonable argument. However, unifying all store visuals and signs on the street not only destroys the local characteristics of the business but also harms the urban fabric and, therefore, the city (Erdi-Lelandais, 2014: p. 46). In social communication, form is affected by content, whereas content is affected by format. Logos and company marks are designed for specific and defined purposes; therefore, colour, format and visual standards are unique and cannot be changed. There are many various shop signs on Istiklal Street. These include both multinational brands and local companies. However, the truth is that the magic was long gone, and this project, which is instead a rescue operation, does not serve as a solution to the problem. Any city district like Beyoğlu, which grows culturally and therefore naturally, suffers from artificial interventions such that a fast-food logo will be defaced on the grounds of adaptation to the environment. However, the future authenticity of urban space is determined only by its dynamism (Gökmen and Özsoy, 2014: p. 146).

Since 2001, there has been a radical shift from populist to neo-liberal fashion in Turkey's urban land and housing markets governance. Major urban transformation projects are the main mechanisms of establishing a neo-liberal system in urban areas that are entirely commodified. It shows that urban transformation projects predominantly aim at physical and demographic upgrading of the properties rather than improving the living conditions of existing residents, thereby initiating a process of property transfer and relocation. It also shows that an area's ownership/duty structure plays the most crucial role in determining the form and efficiency of grassroots movements against urban transformation projects. The complex relationship between neo-liberalisation and urban transformations has received considerable attention since the 1980s. These developments, which are focused mainly on the global cities of advanced capitalist states, show how the exigencies of capital have caused new forms of urban segregation and inequality to arise in the post-industrial economy. As the urban area becomes one of the most profitable sources of investment and as cities adopt aggressive place marketing strategies to draw capital, it becomes complicated for the urban poor to survive in their living spaces due to the rising cost of living. Numerous case studies have shown that these processes have led to widespread displacement and transformation of these areas into commercial and/or high-end residential districts.

A new form of management is observed in which local governments assume an entrepreneurial role either directly or through partnerships with private actors. Large-scale reconstruction projects play an important role in this system change, as they are often invested through direct government action in high-profit areas (such as former industrial zones, waterfronts, and inner-city slums) that have not been fully exploited economically. Existing research on such projects shows that these have unequal socio-economic consequences for different groups. While these investments provide rapid returns for investors and local governments, they bring strong displacement dynamics and dispossession to disadvantaged communities (Kuyucu and Ünsal, 2010).

The first set of reforms concerns the current slum policy. With the adoption of the new Penal Code (Law No. 5237) in 2004, the act of building a shanty house was sentenced to five years in prison for the first time, clearly demonstrating the government's zero-tolerance approach. The demolitions of slums, which rarely occur in Istanbul, then accelerated; between 2004 and 2008, 11,543 units were destroyed in Istanbul, a record high for any period. In 2005, the new Municipality Law (Law No. 5393) was adopted, authorising district municipalities to implement old, abandoned transformation projects. Within the scope of these projects to be carried out in partnership with the Housing Development Administration, existing building stocks would be renovated through a demolition/reconstruction method and transfer the beneficiaries (excluding tenants) to public housing projects. Due to their precarious physical, legal and economic conditions, slums have become ideal targets for transformation. The third area of reform is related to the regulation of historical and natural protection zones not sufficiently integrated into capitalist markets due to special protection laws (such as Law No. 2863). With the adoption of Law No. 5366 in 2005, regional municipalities were given the authority to implement regeneration projects in abandoned and derelict areas in conservation zones.

As in other cities, the historical inner-city districts of Istanbul have also undergone rapid declines and are inhabited mainly by a vulnerable population that cannot meet their needs for shelter elsewhere. The new law makes it possible to restore existing buildings in these areas or demolish and reconstruct these areas according to their general historical characteristics and development potential (Geniş, 2007). Tarlabaşı, on the other hand, is like the missing piece of the puzzle in Taksim, the social and cultural centre of Istanbul. Although special zoning regulations have protected the neighbourhood since 1993 due to its proximity to the Taksim district and the housing stock of the 19th century, it is undergoing a rapid socio-economic and physical decline. The ghettoisation and radical abandonment of Tarlabaşı began in 1986 when Dalan allowed the demolition of more than 300 Levantine buildings for the construction of today's Tarlabaşı Boulevard. Disconnected from the social and economic flow of Taksim, Tarlabaşı entered a stage of deterioration as the socio-economic collapse also triggered physical abandonment. However, since 2012, transformation projects for the city's elite, instead of the citizens who have reclaimed the district, have begun to be realised. This has been seen before in Beyoğlu, specifically in the surrounding areas such as Cihangir, Galata and Talimhane. As these areas became gentrified and attracted significant investments, the decline of the Tarlabaşı neighbourhood became even more striking. In the midst of these, Tarlabaşı remained as an inner-city slum. And it was owned by disadvantaged transient populations. However, as of 2012, Tarlabaşı, Dolapdere and Ok Square were forced to be transformed with an aim to be sold to new owners (Ergün, 2004).

The Law on Transformation of Areas Under Disaster Risk (Law No. 6306) was published in 2012 to increase the safety of old buildings and urban areas at risk of disasters. Different names have been given to this law, such as urban renewal or urban transformation laws by the public. Although all these names imply an improvised rehabilitation and re-development of urban land by large-scale activities, the law does not restrict these changes in terms of their scale. They are open to transformations both at the building and the neighbourhood levels. The legislation sets out the details and procedures for the renovation and transformation of areas and buildings at risk. If a district or building is declared risky, the law forces occupants to rebuild or renovate their buildings. Many incentives, such as credit facilities as well as exemptions of tax and fees, are offered to owners and contractors. The demolition of unsafe buildings and the construction of new, safe buildings are encouraged by this law. Although this law was intended for areas and buildings at risk of disaster, many individuals and construction companies have applied it to any building they think they can rebuild for profit to achieve a higher proportion of floor area. For the most part, these urban transformation initiatives were applied to individual plots rather than building an entire neighbourhood that is newly planned. Since 2012, different projects have been developed for the slums of Istanbul. Therefore, action aimed at creating quality constructed environments has become a new tool of economic development for the informal housing stock and their slum neighbours. If a particular parcel cannot be made profitable, several parcels or more are purchased to expand the coverage of the new project. Public spaces have been made smaller than existing spaces, and the density of buildings and residents has increased with the introduction of newly constructed vertical living projects. Undoubtedly, profit is the most potent source of motivation for these urban renewal projects in the reproduction process of physical space. Thus, legitimised houses were demolished to build new, high-density dwellings. However, as a result, certain legal slums are still not purchased and redeveloped because they will not be profitable. In addition to the legal slums, there are still illegal slums built after the 1980s. The intersection and conflict of slums in a specific area and new apartments close to that area have affected the urban fabric and social, cultural and economic relations (Asan and Özsoy, 2018: p. 67).

Thus, the gentrification of slums and public spaces in historical centres became the main reason for the organisation of urban opposition. Moreover, interactions have started in this area as the professional chambers provided technical support to the residents of the slums in their legal struggles. As these ties developed over time, organisations focused on the right of accommodation of slum residents began to participate in demonstrations organised to defend public spaces. However, a third dynamic remained invisible until the Gezi events and was generally overlooked even by the research on urban struggles. In the institutional framework that emerged with the Law I mentioned, there were projects of various scales from the municipalities which disregarded the existing urban development plans and the participation of citizens. Plans that ignored transportation master plans and impaired life in residential areas seemed too trivial to be on the agenda of urban struggles. Discontents of varying degrees were not taken seriously, but complaints were increasing. Moreover, the civilian area they would reach out to announce these complaints gradually narrowed (Batuman, 2018: p. 158). It is possible to include infrastructure services in complaints. Even in 2020, people are almost devoid of drinking water. According to research, Istanbulites still use packaged water as drinking water. Unfortunately, the tap water supplied to their homes is not considered drinking water. Even this is a significant issue of inequality in the city. The annual total consumption of packaged water in Turkey was more than 10.7 billion litres in 2014. And per capita usage is increasing. We can say that, on average, one-fourth of this amount is used in Istanbul. It corresponds to 2.675 billion litres. This reveals that the average daily consumption of packaged water for Istanbul is 7.3 million litres. Alternatively, it can be said that the daily consumption of packaged water in Turkey is around 30 million litres. On the other hand, the daily use of mains water could only reach 3 million litres in 2016 in Istanbul (DHA, 2020; SUDER, 2020). Even obtaining drinking water is difficult for the citizens, and this is the case even though the infrastructure services provided are not that old. This creates inequality between those who can consume packaged water or can afford it barely and those who cannot. This is an example of why urban dynamics take a leading role in complaints.

Occupation of unused buildings in the city is one of the methods used by urban movements. This is a somewhat local practice called squatting. However, if this squatting lasts too long, it will attract both moral and legal reactions. The building owners become uneasy about the squatting of the building, although it is not in use. This is also not received well by society. However, the cases of political squatting are the most explicit expressions of the reaction against the urban politics and urbanisation process prevailing in the city. The attitude adopted through squatting houses against the globalised capital and the city centre occupied by its representatives is very beneficial in terms of socialising and taking action of the citizens who react to this process in the city. It is an illegal but justified response to the legal but unequal occupation of urban spaces (SQOK et al., 2014: p. 207). In general, squats are apartments that are unused, empty and derelict. They are being squatted to serve their users as a sanctuary that opens the path for social activities and cultural developments. Actually, squats are not a new phenomenon. Although the houses squatted by those who direct the urban movements stand out, the history of the squats goes way back. Unused and derelict buildings and apartments, particularly those in the city centre, are mostly owned by low-income families and immigrants. The actions of these citizens, who took advantage of the order that did not provide them with the means to live, set a precedent for the participants of the urban movement. Squats are typical in Berlin, Hamburg, Amsterdam, Copenhagen, Paris, London, and Zurich, central and northern European countries. However, squatting has become common in southern European countries after the most recent last economic crisis. Madrid, Barcelona, Milan and Rome can be considered particular examples (Mudu, 2014: p. 158). For example, following the reaction against the housing market in Barcelona in 2009, the number of squats increased. The Platform of Citizens Affected by Mortgagee (PAH) is the pioneer of this movement. Similar movements and organisations are also seen in other European cities (Andretta et al., 2015: p. 210).

Beyoğlu, on the other hand, has more than half a century of experience in squats. Many of the minorities living within the borders of Beyoğlu left their homes due to the population exchange Greece insistently requested. The government's subsequent economic sanctions against minorities also caused a group of Greeks to leave their homes. When Turkey's relations with Greece were tense, a group of people engaged in acts of violence against minorities. In fact, this influx, which started as an urban movement, lost control due to the persecution of the Turks in Greece and Cyprus and turned into acts of violence (Örs, 2017: p. 137). The minorities, disturbed by this reaction, finally left their homes. After 1950, Istanbul accelerated its urbanisation and received an intense flow of immigrants. Due to the expensive and inadequate housing, the immigrants who have newly arrived in the city also found solutions by squatting these vacant houses. However, since the beginning of the 2000s, many neighbourhood residents have been displaced for legal occupation, i.e. for developments aimed at global markets, due to the area's economic value. However, in response to the legal occupation of these spaces, these buildings are being transformed by urban movements into squats from time to time. In this regard, urban movements are transformative actors of urban space and participate in the production of urban resources, as if showing that the citizens are the owners of the city. It is clear that the political structure narrows the field of urban movements; however, as it cannot provide solutions to urban problems, it also provides a manoeuvring space for urban movements. Urban spaces are areas of social, cultural, political and economic production, and in terms of the transformation of space, urban movements are essential for the participation of every citizen in this production and subsequent consumption.

The understanding and practices of democracy have been brought to the agenda by global justice movements, emphasising the importance of participation and discussion. It must be possible for every citizen to engage in participation and discussion. When they are unable to engage in discussions, and there is a lack of participation, urban movements explode, as is the case in Tahrir Square, Puerta del Sol Square, Syntagma Square and Zuccotti Park after 2011. These explosions take place during periods when the guidance of democracy is not resorted to. An example of this for Beyoğlu is the urban movement in Gezi Park. Those who desire a more egalitarian political life demand real or direct democracy (della Porta, 2015: p. 774). The spaces of squatting are the spatialisation of the spirit of solidarity as well as the reaction against the insensitivity and the policies adopted. Moreover, these areas are increasingly becoming 'vibrant sites', both for the urban movement and raising complaints. However, due to the police intervention and the fact that the settlements created are often in the form of a temporary camp environment, these areas do not last long. Nevertheless, it will not be possible for urban movements actually to occupy these spaces for a long time. Nonetheless, the movement and the set of ideas created show that the struggle for these spaces will continue and will repeat if the demands are not met (della Porta, 2015: p. 775).

Although technological innovations trigger the occupation of such areas, such innovations also prevent the extension of their duration. Even for a short time, the actual occupation of the space is encouraged and directed by social media. However, after the interventions, and as the conditions become difficult, the participants actively take action in the digital space, which is an extension of the actual space, and continue the urban movement in the digital space (della Porta, 2015: p. 777). An increase in violence occurs when the duration of urban movements exceeds the optimal level. Terrorist organisations trying to take advantage of the outrage caused by the just demands of urban movements easily infiltrate the participants. However, since the spaces occupied are the city's favourite and intensely used spaces, they are already chosen as targets by terrorist organisations. In the case of Beyoğlu, urban terrorism often intervenes in the life of the citizens. These actions limiting the space of urban movements typically occur in places that often host urban movements. For example, the nationalist terrorist organisation PKK, radical Islamic fractions and non-Kurdish nationalist left organisations have caused more than 200 citizens to lose their lives and more than 1000 citizens to be injured in the last 50 years (della Porta, 1995; Savitch, 2008: p. 29).

With its rich cultural heritage, creative industries, and historical and cultural diversity, Beyoğlu, the cultural centre of Istanbul, has hosted people from different cultures who have lived together in harmony for centuries. Each day, more than 1 million people pass through Istiklal Street. The district has a population of approximately 250,000. The physical expansion of the urban area now extends up to the northern side, the Black Sea (Erkut, 2014: p. 82). Urban density is a fundamental problem for Beyoğlu as well as for Istanbul. Particularly, during certain hours of the day, Beyoğlu hosts not only the citizens residing within the borders of the district but also the crowds from various parts of Istanbul, Turkey and the world. Density results from the effect of topographical limitations as well as public transportation and other infrastructures and the traditions of urban planning and development inherited by each city. Compared to other European cities, density levels are higher in Istanbul and Beyoğlu. The densest location of the city, with 68,602 people per km², is well above the peak density of Manhattan, and the average density within a 10 km radius is at least 30 per cent higher than other American and European cities (Erkut, 2014: p. 83).

The first demographic boom occurred in Istanbul between 1950 and 1960 as well as factors such as industrialisation, the mechanisation of agriculture and the improvement of the road network affected the growth to a large extent. However, these changes would not have been possible without the pull factor and the government's efforts to attract rural migration to the city in return for employment opportunities, access to education and health care. A new industrial phase in the 1980s represented the growth of that period, resulting from changes in economic and political reforms. This growth was the second demographic boom of the city, which was realised by the new global order of the period and the rise of state financial enterprises. These factors increased the economic presence of Istanbul in Turkey; however, it had weak links with the outside world. This type of demographic explosion in Istanbul did not occur only due to the changes mentioned earlier and migration from rural to urban compared to previous years. In addition to this development, it is also important that citizens of a higher social class from the Marmara area immigrated to Istanbul. These years represented a critical phase in Istanbul, in which not only the factors mentioned above but also social, economic and political factors would lead to a shift in the vision represented by cohesion and infrastructure. The peak of Istanbul's urban density occurred in 1985. Until this time, the city's population density consisted of many immigrants, street vendors, and slum dwellers, who would be driven out of the city under the changes of the coming years. Population density increased at the beginning of the 21st century, especially in certain districts and regions. It is clear that this urban density has not yet decreased despite the expanding borders of metropolitan municipalities (Erkut, 2014: p. 79).

Beyoğlu is one of the leading districts of Istanbul both in terms of structural density as well as urban density. Therefore, its spatial development and diversity are essential. Public spaces of Beyoğlu can be analysed under four categories, namely religious spaces, civil spaces, touristic spaces and semi-public spaces. The identity is formed with the coexistence of the elements in the space and the people who use these elements. In Beyoğlu, this integration can occur in mosques, markets, cafes, or on the street. Mosques are the most common religious public spaces in Beyoğlu. Due to its character as a sacred place, religious space can never be compared with other categories. Religion is a part of Beyoğlu's historical development and culture. Although most of the population accepts Islam as their religion, the residents of Beyoğlu can mainly be classified as two groups: Muslims (98%) and citizens of different faiths. Christian denominations constitute the majority of the citizens of different religions. Strong religious beliefs were considerably crucial for the development of Istanbul and influenced the whole culture in many ways. Courtyards and pointed domes are typical elements that create cultural landscapes. Mosques are holy places that incorporate these and other religious elements. According to the report prepared by the Istanbul Metropolitan Municipality in 2008, there are 3,028 mosques, 40 churches and 16 synagogues in the city. Moreover, Beyoğlu is the most critical district where this diversity can be observed. Catholic churches and synagogues influence the cultural landscape by highlighting the presence of other forms of religion and culture in the middle of an Islamic city (Erkut, 2014: p. 94).

A civil public space such as Istiklal Street or Taksim Square is integrated into the daily routine of the inhabitants. It can be a street, a pavement, a park, or any other open space that usually belongs to the government. The private sector manages typically touristic and semi-public areas. In a touristic area such as Pera Museum, the economic activities around the space appeal to temporary visitors. On the other hand, a private or semi-public area, such as Çiçek

Pasajı or any other shopping place, is offered to the public in exchange for economic interaction. Public spaces can also be a mix of public, private, touristic and civil spaces. One of the most significant of these is Taksim Square, considered the city's busiest and most active area. As the heart of modern Istanbul, it symbolises its urban inclusion. On the other hand, Istiklal Street is a pedestrian street with a length of 1.5 kilometres, which has become one of the most famous touristic centres of Istanbul. The street lies along the old tram tracks between Tünel and Taksim Square and is connected to various places with particular purposes (Erkut, 2014: p. 95). So, considering Beyoğlu, among the places that host urban movements, which ones are chosen as areas of struggle? How do these spaces transform and change? Let us examine how urban movements in Beyoğlu spread spatially.

Istiklal Street is a long promenade, with a length of 1.5 kilometres and a width that occasionally narrows down to 15 meters. Every day, millions of people visit Istiklal Street. It is home to Istanbul's most exquisite buildings, art, and culture venues. Many squares are located along Istiklal Street, and the buildings built around these are home to activities that keep the art and cultural life alive. The freedom and exchange of thought needed by the urban movements is made possible through numerous coffee houses, restaurants, bars, taverns and theatres along the street. Many political, social, cultural and even technological issues, needs and solutions come to life by breathing the air of the spaces spread around this street. Many types of urban movements, ranging from headscarf protests to those related to the difficulties of transgender life, colourise Istiklal Street. Istiklal Street hosted the Gezi Park protests and the demonstrations of anti-capitalists objecting to the practices of the United States of America, who supported Israel's unfair behaviour and occupation. In protests against gender discrimination, they made their voices heard on Istiklal Street. Although the demonstrations and meetings of LGBTQ individuals are primarily concentrated in the Cihangir district, demonstrations ranging from the Pride parade to many others took place on Istiklal Street. Environmental demonstrations and protests for violence against women are also examples of urban movements observed on Istiklal Street. From the protests of families who have been victims of terrorist acts to complaints about housing problems, Istiklal Street is used as a venue for a wide range of urban movements. Most of the NGOs operating in Turkey were either established in this area or opened branches on this street. For this reason, the presence of places where non-governmental organisations actively operate invigorates the street.

Tünel is another vital space of urban movement. After London, Istanbul has the second oldest subway globally, and this breakthrough took place in Beyoğlu. The area in front of this metro station, called Tünel, forms the Tünel

Square. This square of Istanbul's first metro is also where urban movements in Beyoğlu meet and take their first steps. Urban movements usually gather here or in Galatasaray Square, located nearby. Just as observed throughout Istiklal Street, a wide range of urban movements occur in this square as well. For example, women's movements use this square actively. In order to defend the rights of women, who have been subjected to violence and killed, and to raise their voices against these acts, women's movements use this square and expand their movements throughout Beyoğlu. Tünel, which is the point where NGOs start their demonstrations, host protests every year for World Peace Day on 21 September, for example. However, just like the others, these demonstrations are subjected to violent interference. Official permission is not given for demonstrations of associations and users from the public spaces around the square, although such demonstrations are peaceful.

Galatasaray Square is the second most well-known square in Beyoğlu, after Taksim Square. In the Galata Palace Imperial School institution, high-level officials for Enderun (a special school in the Ottoman palace) received training. People who would serve and advise the Sultan in the palace were trained in this institution. From the end of the 15th century (1481) to the beginning of the 18th century (1715), it was one of the most important institutions of the Ottoman Empire. After 1820, it was used as a Medical School and Military Barracks. It became a symbol of the Westernisation period and Tanzimat practices. Because this time, the institution became the centre of the western-style education necessary for the education of the personnel who would realise the innovations to be implemented in the legal, political and social fields in the Ottoman Empire. Students from many nationalities, who were citizens of the Ottoman Empire, were educated in the institution. The institution started to operate as Galatasaray High School in 1924. The square located in front of this institution, which has witnessed and even directed the development of Turkey, is called Galatasaray Square. Galatasaray Square is the point where many urban movements start their actions. NGOs gather here and make press statements. They start their marches from here. One of the most persistent demonstrations of the Turkish political scene started in this square. The protest, named Saturday Mothers, is organised as a sit-in in Galatasaray Square and aims to find relatives who disappeared in custody and those who were victims of unsolved political murders. Due to the interventions, these past and present protests, which were not affiliated with any organisation or agenda, had to end after the 700th week. Galatasaray High School is also the home of Turkey's most prominent football club. Galatasaray Sports Club was founded by high school students and became the biggest club in Turkey. The successes and failures of the club are celebrated or protested by the fans who gather in this square. The square hosts not only urban movements for political and social issues but also issues related to sports. The square is surrounded by places where the citizens coming to Istiklal Street can rest, talk and share. The participants of urban movements spend their lives in these spaces and stream towards the Taksim Square. Hosting ideas of freedom and enlightenment and ideas opposing power, these spaces are also home to a life free from taboos.

Emek Cinema is another crucial venue that used to be the centre of cultural and artistic urban movements. The first building in Yesilçam Street No. 5 was constructed in 1910 under the name Nouveau Cirque. This building also incorporated the Skating Palace and ballroom venues. These were subsequently demolished and replaced by the New Theater in 1918. In 1924, the place began to show movies under the name Melek Cinema. After the cinema operated for 33 years, the Retirement Fund bought this arcade and Emek Cinema started operating in 1957 (Akıncı, 2018: p. 224). Over the years, Emek cinema became unable to cope with modern movie theatres that were more organised. The number of users decreased. However, Emek Cinema did not lose importance thanks to the building's architectural structure, history, and identity. Due to the increasing economic activity in the 2000s and the area visited by many tourists, Emek Cinema also had its share of urban transformation activities. Emek Cinema was to be demolished. Despite the urban movement on 14 April 2013, with the intense participation of activists and artists, the cinema was demolished and turned into a shopping mall. Emek Cinema, which is not a square and has become one of the most significant points of urban movement on Istiklal Street, is also an example of urban movements centred on art, culture and architecture.

Gezi Park, on the other hand, is a space of urban movement that has emerged and globalised in recent years. Until the 18th century, Taksim Square was just a vast space that did not even have a path. In 1731, a cistern (Maksem) was constructed to meet the water needs of the growing population in Beyoğlu. The name Taksim refers to these constructed structures. Later, during the reign of Selim III, Artillery Barracks were built for the artillery class of the Kapıkulu soldiers. The barracks were located in the area where Gezi Park is present today. There was a three-storey building and stables in the part where Atatürk Cultural Centre is located today. The open area opposite the barracks was the training ground for his soldiers, where the name Talimhane (training ground) comes from. The artillery barracks were evacuated in the 1920s and 30s. The barracks were used as a football field for a while. With the Taksim Republic Monument being placed in the square in 1928, it began to host official ceremonies. During the mayorship of Lütfi Kırdar, the barracks were demolished, and Gezi Park was created. Becoming an area of attraction with Gezi Park, the square gradually became the symbol of Istanbul. Lots of interventions were made in the area around Taksim Square. The destruction of Tarlabaşı followed the destruction during the term of Adnan Menderes during the term of Bedrettin Dalan. However, Taksim Square continued to be the most active area of Istanbul. Since the 1960s, it has become a centre for mass demonstrations. Particularly in the 1970s, worker and student demonstrations took place in Gezi Park and in Taksim Square, which is considered the symbol of the Republic (Gül, 2017: pp. 167–8).

The zoning of Gezi Park for development was not discussed in the Metropolitan Municipality Council. This was a direct plan of Prime Minister Recep Tayyip Erdogan. By order of the Prime Minister, the project was presented to the Ministry of Culture. However, the Regional Board No. 2 for the Conservation of Cultural Heritage of Istanbul, affiliated with the ministry, unanimously rejected the reconstruction of the Artillery Barracks, as Gezi Park was a place that witnessed history. The Prime Minister ignored the board's decision, saying "those who refuse will themselves be refused". This time, the project was referred to the High Council for the Conservation of Cultural and Natural Heritage in Ankara, and permission was granted. Being afraid of public backlash, local administrators (particularly Kadir Topbaş, the Mayor of Istanbul) stated that the barracks would become a culture and art centre. However, the Prime Minister stated that the building would serve as a shopping mall or a residence. At the end of May, as the dozers entered the park and began to remove the trees, it was understood that the Prime Minister was determined in his project. However, a group of young people aimed to protect Istanbul's green spaces, and cultural and historical values united to defend Gezi Park. As the trees began to be removed in Gezi Park, the Taksim Solidarity Group set up a tent in Gezi Park with the participation of 40–50 people on 27 May and slept inside the park. On 28 May, the city police and the municipal police arrived and tried to disband the group. After this intervention, the number of participants began to increase.

On 29 May, the police intervened again, and the tents in the park were burned. The police intervention that took place on 31 May was very violent. As the number of participants increased, the protest spread all around Turkey. On the same day, the 6th Administrative Court of Istanbul decided to stay the execution of the Artillery Barracks Project. On 1 June, the activists gathered on the Anatolian side and marched over the Bosphorus Bridge. The police intervened. After the harsh intervention, the number of protesters increased, and Taksim Square became occupied the protesters. The Gezi Park protests, which lasted for 20 days, were among the events that left their imprint on the history of Turkey. Protests in support of the Gezi Park took place in all provinces of

Turkey except Bayburt. Nearly 4 million people attended these demonstrations. However, non-governmental organisations argue that the number of participants was higher. Eight people, including a police officer, lost their lives. Nearly 10 thousand people were injured. Hundreds of people were arrested, and more than 120 were prosecuted (Tayfur, 2014). With the participation of activists in pursuit of violent and ideological actions which, despite being of urban origin, were outside of the sphere of urban politics, these actions brought by urban problems and policies could not remain as peaceful as they were in the first place. However, it was not a movement that was entirely dominated by violence. Reacting against the protests, the government claimed that they were a blow to its legitimate authority.

As a result, the intervention in Gezi Park remained inconclusive. The construction of the barracks stopped, and the park remained untouched. However, interventions such as pedestrianisation projects are still ongoing and what will happen in the coming years is still unknown. Gezi Park is being preserved with its layout before the events, but the pressure on the surrounding areas has increased. The central government's interest in Gezi Park causes local administrators to focus on transformation projects and zoning activities that conflict with the area's urban culture and spatial structure. However, the touristic value of the area and the fact that the capitalist economic system has become the dominant element increases the value of Gezi Park and maybe allows it to be preserved. However, when evaluated spatially, the area's relationship with its surroundings changes.

Taksim Square takes its name from the maksem (cistern – a building used for water distribution) built by Mahmut I in 1731 to distribute the water of Beyoğlu. The maksem has dried up today, but the building constructed is still located at the entrance of Istiklal Street. The Republic Monument, made by Italian sculptor Pietro Canonica in 1928, has become the symbol of Taksim Square. Assuming the public function of Sultanahmet and Beyazıt Squares, the Taksim Square was seen as a symbol of the new regime. Taksim Square has always been subject to interventions due to changing governments. In particular, the interventions made by Adnan Menderes and Bedrettin Dalan by changing the zoning plans completely changed the spatial development of the region. A concrete jungle and multi-lane roads now surrounded the square. Increasing urban movements were coming to life in Taksim Square. Mainly chosen for the celebration of 1 May Labour Day, Taksim Square saw pressure from the governments. There were constant disputes over the use of the space. The 50-year ban ended in 1976. The following year, 1 May, Labour Day, was covered in blood. In 1977, about 500 thousand people gathered in the square. In the stampede caused by the fire opened in the area, 34 people lost their lives, and 130 people were injured. That day went down in history as the Bloody May Day. The square was reopened to the masses on 1 May 2009, after 32 years. However, in the following years, the use of the square was again left to the government's discretion. The square is chosen as a place to celebrate official holidays, on New Year's Eve and particularly for Galatasaray's football victories. The urban movements around Galatasaray Square and Tünel end in Taksim Square. In fact, it is the place where the police joined hands during the Gezi Resistance in 2013 and formed a chain of peace and brotherhood for days. Since the area is used by urban movements and is a point of attraction, the Metropolitan Municipality wanted to carry out the Taksim Pedestrianisation Project. Within the scope of this project, it was aimed to intervene in the area under the pretence of demolishing Gezi Park and rebuilding the Artillery Barracks. Non-Governmental Organisations objected to this project. Making the entrance to the square from a single point indicates a more controllable space design with this project. In this way, the government wants to intervene in urban movements more closely. As a matter of fact, despite the demonstrations that started and ended peacefully on 1 May 2012, the government did not allow demonstrations on 1 May 2013 and violently intervened in the groups gathered under the leadership of the Taksim Platform. The demonstrations, which were banned on the pretext of construction activities, were not held again. In fact, the violence against the protesters on 1 May and the spatial interventions in the square also drew a reaction from the citizens, who are the users of the area. The interventions expanding to Gezi Park triggered the start of the Gezi Events.

Of course, Beyoğlu was not actively present as a space on the night of 15 July but subsequently participated in and hosted another urban movement. It was a kind of celebration in Taksim Square for the wins made due to reactions to the junta who took up arms against the legitimate government.

> As expected, Taksim Square was one of the most important places designated for the democracy watch in Istanbul. Logistically, everything was thought out to the smallest detail; Municipalities set up mobile toilets in areas designated as places for democracy watch, and participants were given food and drink free of charge. There was an atmosphere reminiscent of traditional Ramadan celebrations, especially in terms of the participation of women and children, but the anthems played frequently added a militaristic atmosphere to these watches.
>
> BATUMAN, 2018: p. 197

With the Republic, the Taksim Square developed by taking on the role of other squares of the city. The square is surrounded by places where the seeds of unanimity that host urban movements are planted. In addition to art and cultural centres, coffee houses, restaurants, and bars serve as places where public opinion is formed. Citizens gather around Taksim Square and meet in these places to exchange ideas. Istiklal Street and Taksim Square are the city's backbone in terms of the formation and organisation of urban movements.

Tarlabaşı, on the other hand, is a subject of research as it hosts spaces that foster urban movements. Tarlabaşı district, which was opened to settlement after the 1870 Beyoğlu fire, was an area where minorities had been living for nearly a century. After the 1924 population exchange, which Greece insistently requested, the number of the remaining minorities in the area gradually decreased due to the 1941 Wealth Tax. The events of 1955 would once again reduce the number of minorities in the region. The residences vacated by the minorities would gradually be filled by the Anatolian immigrants who flocked to Istanbul. Tarlabaşı was appropriated by the Roma, Africans and Syrians who settled in Istanbul last. However, this appropriation was not very sincere. So much so that the new owners did not spend any money on the buildings on the verge of collapse. They did not spare any budget for their maintenance, renovation and beautification. For this reason, the buildings have survived to the present day in a dilapidated and derelict state. With the wave of immigration that replaced the original owners, the area had changed. Considering the last demographic change, we will easily understand why this change brought along the squats. In addition, the urban transformation projects of the global and national capital that have set their sights on the area strengthen our understanding. The first squat of Istanbul is the Don Quixote Squat, located in the Yeldeğirmeni District of Kadıköy. Those who took action against the capitalist life after the Gezi Events continued to form a collective life by settling in abandoned houses as a protest against the concept of property and in the name of common life. There are also many unofficial squats in abandoned buildings in Tarlabaşı. In these squats, there are libraries, barter markets, meetings held against the destruction of nature, and forums set up to discuss the problems of the neighbourhood and even the adjacent neighbourhoods. The squats that emerged after or shortly before the urban movements were to stop capitalist exploitation in the city and revive the neighbourhood culture. For this reason, they revive abandoned buildings. They try to find solutions to the spatial problems of the neighbourhoods. For example, they take action to demonstrate the problem of a neighbourhood that needs more green spaces by planting a tree in an area that is used as an informal parking space. The area, which has become more like a park after the tree was planted, has now been turned into a green space after the residents of the neighbourhood applied to the municipality.

After discussing and examining the prominent spaces of urban movement in Beyoğlu, it became necessary to focus on the developments and changes mentioned in the previous sections and this section. How are spaces of urban movement used, and how do they change?

> Unfortunately, the transformation was inevitable for Beyoğlu and its sur-
> roundings. I don't think it's just about politics. First of all, this is an impor-
> tant rent area. It is geared towards a busy tourism and service industry.
> Rather than being a public space, it is literally a district that has been cut
> off from history, where you can exist as much as you can consume.
>
> Personal Communication, 9 July 2020, p. 1

It is stated that Beyoğlu's move away from being a host to urban movements over time may have resulted from the loss of its historical significance. As stated above, the observation that it has transformed from a space that produces to a consumed space is literally a global phenomenon. The participants using the places mentioned throughout Beyoğlu convey their observations that the user of the spaces has changed compared to the past as follows:

> It is a district where even the smallest social demonstration is not allowed,
> and special security measures are taken even in the most apolitical New
> Year's celebrations. Except for symbolic tours, lots of Arab tourists and a
> few nostalgic addresses, Beyoğlu is a place that does not reflect the coun-
> try in general. Spatially, Beyoğlu is an expression, action, and resistance
> area for me. It is a place of meeting for people who have met each other
> with this motive. Of course, what I wrote was valid for a period. For me,
> whether it still has these features is debatable, for most aspects.
>
> Personal Communication, 9 July 2020, p. 1

Another reason for this change in users stems from the fact that places such as cafes, restaurants, coffee houses, association clubs and taverns, which served as the places where urban movements occurred in the past, increasingly approach their customers with a profit-oriented service mentality.

> Beyoğlu has always been important to Galatasaray fans because high
> school is located there, and the club was born in this district. However,
> in terms of giving meaning to the spaces, the stadium's location has been
> more effective than the school where the club was born. Taking Beyoğlu

as the central point of the city, the venues located here aimed at these customers during periods when there is a high number of tourists, but the venues in Levent did not consider the fans as a target customer group, in a way that is completely suitable for us, the fans, in terms of their sound and seating layouts.

Personal Communication, 12 July 2020, p. 2

I think the situation is getting worse now. As the streets have become uglier, being replaced with more and more concrete, the masses we need to reach to create public opinion no longer come to the places I have mentioned. Because the citizens who understand the environmentalist goals now prefer different places as Taksim Square has changed aesthetically after the Gezi resistance. The places themselves have also changed. After the Gezi events, the crowds who used to visit these places have changed. Since the profile of visitors has changed, the business owners who wanted to make money have abandoned all their sensitivities and started businesses with more tourist-oriented venues. The venue called Fıccın in Kallavi was serving through a common kitchen in 5–6 different buildings, and the tables were full. Now people just buy appetisers and go away because the users have changed. Particularly, as Beyoğlu became an area of attraction for tourists, the services and products offered by the venues began to change. As the environment has changed, we started to use these places less and less.

Personal Communication, 12 July 2020, p. 4

It seems that it is not only cafes and restaurants that have changed and transformed. The centres of NGOs are increasingly moving away from Beyoğlu. And there has been a decrease in the number of venues serving arts and cultural activities.

The places I mentioned, which gave the opportunity to gather, share, socialise and allow a person to fulfil themselves and exist in those years, are no longer located in Beyoğlu and its surroundings. These places, particularly the Chamber of Architects, either operate in other districts or are closed. It is observed that the area has now taken a more commercial form, which will bring more income and target people with different expectations and interests. Cinemas, theatres, and exhibition halls are closing, and they are transformed into places such as shopping malls, restaurants, stores etc. Even the scales of exhibitions and similar art activities carried out by a few banks on their own properties are getting smaller, and they are turning into commercial initiatives aimed at selling the banks' own books and publications. Beyoğlu has become a frequent destination for people with different and ever-changing interests and tastes, or a certain group of tourists, and is succumbing to the speculations created by the rapidly-consuming society.

> Personal Communication, 12 July 2020, p. 3

Since Beyoğlu hosts urban movements, it has mainly hosted opposition groups in its venues. However, it is emphasised that this hosting is gradually decreasing.

> Taksim has a historical identity for political opposition, which has been formed over time, and if these places remained without any transformation, the historical memory would also remain alive. At this very point, the government paved the way for the gentrification of the city (Taksim) in order to destroy this historical memory and prevent Taksim from being a part of this identity. At the same time, the intensive relocation of refugees to Taksim and its surroundings after the Syrian war was an important factor.

> Personal Communication, 13 July 2020, p. 5

Another participant's view is as follows:

> In addition, the increase in pressure on activist movements in recent times, the destruction as well as the physical and cultural interventions carried out as if to destroy Beyoğlu's feature of being a place of memory, has brought with it the result that the places of memory here no longer carrying out their former missions. For example, while there used to be certain social events, primarily the May Day rallies of the leftist opposition and the working class, as well as music activities, concerts, exhibitions and fairs held in Taksim Square, these events are now banned, especially those around Taksim and Beyoğlu, and they are replaced by legally permitted book fairs, social events (and even protests), concerts with Mehter anthems and hymns by Islamic groups; likewise, since no opposition activities were allowed in either Gezi Park or Galatasaray-Tünel, opposition groups were compelled to leave these venues, even if they were still wholeheartedly attached to them. In other words, they were, and are still being, deliberately kept away from these venues by the system. Even if people still go to those places where they can socialise, the places of struggle have lost their old mission for now, as they are

banned. Tomorrow, when the conditions are suitable, these places will regain their old values and return to their old days. I am sure of that.

Personal Communication, 17 July 2020, p. 10

Although Beyoğlu serves opposition groups, this does not mean that it serves certain groups politically. On the contrary, the diversity intertwined with its spatial history is reflected in the urban movements and their participants. As participant 10 mentioned, the demand for Beyoğlu and the diversity in urban movements have increased.

During the action we held on 3 June 2011, we realised that Taksim Square enriched our actions in terms of offering diversity. We can count this as the date of a demonstration in which everyone collaborated for a while, regardless of their party. Mis Street, Istiklal and Taksim Square are vital in terms of communication. It was important for us to ask people questions, inform them about our aims and make our voices heard.

Personal Communication, 12 July 2020, p. 4

It was emphasised that this diversity is evident in Beyoğlu. Particularly in the last sentence of the quote below.

These places I mentioned seem to have more social significance than historical significance. They are the most visible places in not only Beyoğlu but also the whole of Istanbul. Moreover, the most important thing is the meaning contributed here by the people gathered here over time and the fact that this meaning is carried as a banner. It is also a historical place where people can gather and express their complaints. It is not a place that is unfamiliar for anyone.

Personal Communication, 13 July 2020, p. 6

One of the answers given by the interviewees to the question of why these places allow such diversity is as follows:

For me, places like these are important as spaces where people from many different cultural backgrounds can come together and spend their time comfortably, where individuals from various socio-economic classes communicate with each other, and where social cohesion is strengthened in this sense.

Personal Communication, 14 July 2020, p. 8

However, to the extent observed, the urban movements (as the subject of this research) transform places with the effect of the city as well as the culture and identities belonging to the city. The reason for the tension is urban and socio-cultural, just like in the Women's movement. Women's rights, which are a necessity and result of urban life, also started in Beyoğlu.

> From the end of the 80s, the feminist movement started to organise in places around Beyoğlu/Taksim, and common spaces began to exist from this date on. Since actions were held in Taksim, the meetings for these actions were also held in spaces located in Taksim, primarily in the venues of organisations or cafes such as Kaktüs cafe, Amargi cafe, the venue of the Socialist Feminist Collective etc., which were used from the 90s until 2015. With the influence of these separate spaces, Taksim/Beyoğlu has a collective political memory. For this reason, the women's organisations that became institutionalised in the 90s established their associations/ foundations in places in the Taksim area. This is why our association has been in Gümüşsuyu since its establishment (1993).
>
> Personal Communication, 16 July 2020, p. 9

It is observed that the cultural change is painful, and the resulting tensions cause disputes and concerns among the types of urban movements.

> Yes, the demonstration of 'Hand in Hand for Freedom' on 11 October advanced from Karaköy and Beşiktaş; although we consider these to be located within the borders of Beyoğlu, I cannot personally describe these movements in Beyoğlu as movements of free thought. When Beyoğlu is mentioned, I think of the movements of communities that are intolerant of opposing ideas, which only impose their own ideas.
>
> Personal Communication, 18 July 2020, p. 12

Urban problems and spatial sharing in Beyoğlu stand out as the cause of tensions. It is understood that there is a struggle within the urban movements since the areas of urban complaints and the struggle to resolve these complaints are almost the same spaces for the people of Istanbul. Therefore, the transformation of places is becoming increasingly important. There are various factors for this change, but Participant 9 made the following observation:

> One of the reasons for the change is the political developments in the country and the inability to take action due to increasing authoritarianism. The second reason is the effort to intervene in the

existing demographic profile with the interventions made in the spaces of Beyoğlu.

Personal Communication, 16 July 2020, p. 9

Urban movements express their problems, concerns, demands, and expectations in Beyoğlu, in increasingly urbanised and diversified groups. Although there are tensions about the sharing of spaces, the expectations of each urban movement participant regarding the spaces in Beyoğlu are similar. Participant 11 expressed this expectation as follows:

> For change to be meaningful, permanent elements must be determined very carefully. Therefore, there is a need for an open-ended environment that embraces all future generations and ensures their participation in the venue. In parallel with this, permanent elements, which will not be forgotten no matter how many generations pass and remind us of who we are, are necessary.
>
> Personal Communication, 18 July 2020, p. 11

Conclusion

Urban Movements and Their Space

Cities are the flavour of humanity. As clearly stated in our study, people cannot maintain their lives without a collective life. What is necessary for the continuation of communal life in a sustainable way is the city. Cities are living spaces where people with different identities and qualities can continue their lives, and new lives are maintained with new identities and qualities. Diversity and originality determine the cities' lifespans. Every citizen wants to build the things necessary for their lives in the city they live in. The city is born, grows and develops around the culture shaped due to these zoning activities. Public works is the expression of this state. But unfortunately, the cities cannot continue their journey by including every citizen in the growth process while growing. The city's threshold value cannot be at the desired levels due to the cultural and economic interests of the groups and communities that make it up. More precisely, this is the result we have seen so far. In this course of the cities, conflicts begin to arise among the groups sharing the urban life. Especially today, the difference in values among groups is more evident. Because most of the world's population now lives together in cities. And as technology has advanced, the cultural, economic, social and technological inequality among urban residents is at a level that cannot be hidden or managed. This difference and inequality create uneasiness in individuals and a reaction for a fairer life. The city now is a more common ground than in the past, so the struggle to dominate the common space is carried out more effectively. The citizens feel more attached to the city that guides their lives, and they expect more returns from the gains the city has achieved. The conflict does not develop solely from political reasons, as it was thought in the past, despite economic or all the other gains achieved. Of course, the citizens of the city could not yet have overcome the economic injustice or fully obtain their political rights. However, examining the development of cities, which we also touched upon in this study, reveals that economic vitality and production begin with urban life. Again, political hegemony and freedom are formed and shaped by urban life. Therefore, the source of these two types of struggles, which have been misunderstood until today, is related to urbanisation, and the city is the place and name of the rights, the conflict, and the struggle to be won, as well as other struggles that have been revived along with these two struggles.

So why did cities disappear in the past whilst in the development process? Or why some of them are prone to extinction today? These approaches, in fact, are an illusion. Of course, cities have disappeared in the past. And this did not happen in a short amount of time. As seen in our study, cities appear as if they suddenly collapse. However, this process finalises at the end of a developmental period. If cities cannot maintain the advantages and gains they previously provided to the citizens, they gradually lose their importance. And if they do not develop policies that will be a remedy for this process, they face extinction. When we look back at history, we see that cities are brought to the brink of extinction due to invasions or losing their economic, cultural and social diversity. In fact, these two reasons are deeply connected. Communities which cannot access the resources to protect the city or which cannot reproduce lose their status in the face of a more robust social and cultural unity, as they continue to live susceptible to external factors. Today, most of these cities have created unique cultures as they did in ancient times. The economic and social ties shaped around this culture never die away. Even if the cities hosting this network are destroyed or vanish, this network, i.e., the civilisation, builds a new city for itself, or it can grow and develop an existing city as it desires. Civilisation means city, city means people. If there is no external factor, which also reveals itself as a result of the second factor as previously mentioned, cities stand with their social, cultural and economic diversity. If this diversity is shared fairly among the citizens of the city, each citizen works for the continuation of this unity. However, from income to other inequalities, which is now called the digital divide, many factors break the citizens away from the urban unity they previously peacefully belonged to. And because of this rupture, people gradually become detached, and cities are running fast towards extinction. Urban movements are the most apparent symptoms that show us such a development process dominates cities. These movements formed against all kinds of injustice and unfairness are the engines that will start the process to bring the developments which will shake the unity of the city to an end around effective policies. If cities do not pay attention to these movements and change their course, they will increasingly polarise and lose their power over time. The subjects and areas that create these struggles exist inside the city and are produced by the citizens. Therefore, these movements are urban, and they are called urban movements.

Humanity has not lived in cities from the first moment they came to life, but they kept the city alive in their minds from that first moment. And the cities they built over time turned into places where they protected their lives, rights, and freedoms. Although injustices occurring in their societies seem to be spreading in rural areas, they are actually related to the living spaces of these people. And even looking back to ancient times, we see that the movements started in the cities, and then the rural areas were preferred as the field for struggle. Even in these moments, the cities have been the fierce defenders and supporters of this struggle. And because of this reason and due to tradition, more and more people started to live in cities. The most recent rural mobilisation to our day is the German Peasants' War, and examining its history reveals that the groups that led the movement are of urban origin. So much so that, we see in the works of those who research the subject that it is a movement that entered a stagnant process with the fall of cities. The famous German proverb is another expression of this development. The city air is liberating.

Our study gives examples from Italian cities, where the most recent urbanisation process started. Later, examples of how French and American cities followed this development line are given. Our study has discussed that the protests that broke out in these geographies spread rapidly to cities in other geographies. Our study also examines why the new movements developed regarding the urbanisation process that we entered in the 20th century have turned cities into flames in specific periods. Why urban movements occur at similar times in almost every geography is explained along with urbanisation spreading worldwide in the 21st century. The term new social movements is out of place, as movements are becoming more and more urban and emerge from concerns about cities. All of these are urban movements, and the urbanite changes as the city changes shape. And they keep on developing by responding to the new needs of the new era with novel methods. Cities are now places of identity, culture and technology. They witness the actions in which they can reflect the wishes and hopes of the citizens on the city agenda as long as they have the economic and political opportunities. Environmental movements, the struggle against gender discrimination and the reactions to income distribution as well should be assessed through the changes in urban life because the source of these injustices and the places where change is desired is the city. The environmental action carried out by a villager group in a remote place is a movement formed in the consciousness of the city dwellers, and it is brought to the agenda more due to the impact of side effects on urban life. Even the media provides its announcement per se, a city production. And the city administrators' decisions will be both the reason for and the factor blocking this development. Gender discrimination is also becoming more noticeable and perceptible in cities. So much so that the living spaces of those who suffer from this discrimination often intersect with the city. And for this reason, the busiest and most popular places of the cities host the urban movement to put an end to this discrimination in every single place. Economic and political inequality is most felt and visible in the city. Because there are poor and affluent neighbourhoods in the city and poor and rich houses within these neighbour-hoods. Although everyone interacts less with each other, they know more about each other. That's why the struggle for the next generation, at least, takes place in the city. Because, especially in developing countries, in other words, in urbanising countries, generations have recently started to be born and growing up in an urban environment. Due to this new development, the interests of urban movements have gained more titles than in the past.

The groups that realised this line about urbanisation and were the architects of the injustice that caused the reaction did not leave the cities for sure; on the contrary, they wanted to shape the cities as they wished. As can be understood from the details in our study, the city has become more of a field of struggle as a place. Due to the increasing number of stakeholders, it has become more desirable and chosen as a field of struggle. With an order in the past and a policy today, central or local governments have had to design the living spaces of those who claim rights to common areas. Groups that wanted equal service and justice not only in common areas but also in their own living spaces had to defend their urban spaces starting from the regions they felt close to. Various topics, such as their users and the way these spaces are used, have been the rea-sons for their actions. Even environmental movements caused by and affect-ing cities are subject to spatial transformation and urban movements of cities. Now the environmental effects have been felt in the cities, and even the areas exposed to the impact have become unequally distributed in the city. While one region suffers less from environmental factors, other regions feel the effect more. For this reason, both the source of and the solution to the complaints about the actions called new social movements are the city. Hence, they are urban movements. And they are one of the most apparent forms of movement in which spatial development is felt most clearly.

Due to the development of technology, another living space of the citizens has now become the digital space. So much so that even as a form of ruling, there are leaders who take this virtual environment for themselves. These spaces have also become areas of organisations, shares and wishes. However, the agora of the past has not yet destroyed the squares of today. In fact, they are shaping this new space to live in these spaces as they have their rights and use these spaces as they wish. Of course, the era we live in is in the offing to new developments, and our cities are open to them. It is difficult to predict what the future will bring, but the acceptance of digital spaces as a reflection of cities has begun.

Istanbul, which has hosted three empires and is one of the oldest living cit-ies, is also exposed to these developments. Considered the heart of Istanbul, Beyoğlu has hosted the struggle for both itself and other cities in its past. Today, it still maintains its importance and influence despite the changing factors over time. While it is possible to observe the adverse developments discussed under urban movements on a global scale in the regions of Beyoğlu we examined, it is also feasible to measure the reactions to these effects again in these regions. Just as we have explained why cities have attracted people over time, we have understood why Beyoğlu has become a centre of attraction for more people as tourists or hosts. Diversity and tradition as well as history, culture and freedom. Even citizens with differing opinions do not hesitate to use these spaces when the day comes. And even this preference clearly demonstrates the extent of urbanisation and the final state of the conflict. So, people come to life in the city, and both the centre and place of their reactions given for the sake of their lives are the city. Therefore, the name of their reaction should be the urban movement.

When you consider their development, no place initially had special meanings for urban movements. Places of urban movements are generally clustered around more deprived areas of the city. However, the places where urban movements take place have gradually decreased in number but become popular due to the legacy of urban movements that took place over time and the ever-increasing importance of city centres. Especially the urban design plans applied, and interventions made to the regions where urban movements occur may have physically disconnected the owners of these movements from the spaces. However, the citizens still prefer these spaces to make their complaints, discuss their concerns, and even have celebrations. These centres are now desirable to more communities due to urban renewal and gentrification projects. And these places often have a historical identity and culture. All of these characteristics attracted the attention of not only national but also international elite communities, increasing the tension even more. Although the participants, associations or groups that have been or are likely to be involved in urban movements have gradually been pushed away from these places due to economic and cultural reasons, these places still exist in their goals and hearts. However, another group that wants these spaces is terrorist organisations, and these organisations cause cities to reshape as a threat to the communities that cause or give birth to urban movements.

The result of urban movements and the number of masses they trigger at times have an impact on the behaviour and policies of city administrations and even central administrations. Peaceful demonstrations are generally tolerated in global cities such as London, which host not only national but also international urban movements almost on a daily basis. For this reason, highly diverse and increasingly more urban movements occur in the city, but with a limited impact. These movements are generally peaceful and intend to create a public opinion. Of course, it has been observed that these actions escalate and cause violent events from time to time. However, such violent action is generally caused by the disproportionate use of force by the security forces, who are also the representatives of the group or administration, or the representative of the current public power against whom the complaint is made. It also happened like this in London in 2011. In that case, we can readily express that the city administration should tolerate citizens' pursuit to find solutions and supporters to get rid of the problems they complain about. If the security of the representatives is guaranteed throughout the movement and it is considered that the requests will be handled rationally and that reasonable requests are fulfilled that will adequately benefit both sides, the probability of the urban movements to burst may be low. Of course, it is not possible to terminate the movements because they go underground and evolve into a more dangerous form. Formally embracing the movements that have emerged as a reaction to the problems, at least under an association and granting it a place in the social life of the city, can direct the will of the citizens, who foresee change against long-term problems, to acts of informing and creating public opinion rather than the actions that will undermine public health. The city administration can question its administration as if it were conducting a survey by leading and following up on these movements. Even if the outlook on the problems is different, the awareness of the problem will create a bond between the citizens of the city and the administration; and accompanied by these features, the urban movements will make the city stand out on a global scale in a range of fields, including tourism, economy, socio-cultural life and even investments to the city.

If this approach to urban movements is supported by a participatory city management strategy, urban movements may cease to take place in history as big explosions. This deprivation, which we witnessed in the Beyoğlu example and also observed in other cities, further increases the problems and reduces urban imagination. However, cities that employ this model and strategy gain importance as a global brand and bring happiness to their citizens. Urban investments and designs can be realised by involving local communities in the process, as in the example of the Superkilen Park and living space designed in Copenhagen. As a result of the Superflex team's design and the city administration's involvement in the process, an ordinary neighbourhood park has gained international prestige and recognition and even revived the local economy. The people living close by the park were Danish nationals from more than 50 countries. People of the region were asked to nominate city objects such as benches, boxes, trees, playgrounds, maintenance hole covers and signs from other countries instead of using city objects and furniture typically designated for parks and public spaces. These objects were chosen from the countries of national origin of the inhabitants or other places discovered while travelling. Objects were produced in 1:1 exact copies or purchased and moved to the site. The area came to life after completing the design of this park and open space. It began to host an increasing number of communities without creating any tension. The city administration focused on new projects as per the needs of the local communities instead of equipping the park's surrounding with gentrification projects by taking advantage of the increasing vitality. The increase of such examples in urban projects and at least awareness of the complaints will reduce the tension between the city administration and elite communities, and communities in deprivation. Undoubtedly, there will always be complaints, but urban movements may remain a peaceful option for reporting the existence of these problems and offering solutions to them.

References

Abendroth, W. (1992) *Avrupa İşçi Hareketleri Tarihi*. İstanbul: Belge Yayınları.

Akalın, A. (2016) *İslam Hukukunda Devlete İsyan Suçu*. Ankara: Fecr Yayınları.

Akıncı, T. (2018) *Beyoğlu: Yapılar, Mekânlar, İnsanlar 1831–1923*. İstanbul: Remzi Kitabevi.

Altınay, A. R. (2010) *Lâle Devri 1718–1730*. İstanbul: Tarih Vakfı Yurt Yayınları.

Altınay, A. R. (2011) *Eski İstanbul (1553–1839)*. İstanbul: Kapı Yayınları.

Alver, K. (2017) *Kent Sosyolojisi*. Konya: Çizgi Kitabevi.

Amin, A., Massey, D. and Thrift, N. (2000) *Cities for the Many not the Few*. Bristol: The Policy Press.

Andretta, M., Piazza, G., and Subirats, A. (2015) Urban Dynamics and Social Movements in della Porta, D. and Diani, M. (2015) *The Oxford Handbook of Social Movements*. Oxford: Oxford University Press (pp. 200–219).

Appadurai, A. (2008) Grassroots Globalizationin, in Ruggiero, V. and Montagna, N. *Social Movements*. Oxon: Routledge (pp. 303–307).

Aristotle (2009) *Politics*. Oxford: Oxford University Press.

Arrighi, G. (2016) *Uzun Yirminci Yüzyıl*. Ankara: İmge Kitabevi.

Asan, H. and Özsoy, A. (2018) The enduring influence of informality, in Istanbul: Legalization of informal settlements and urban transformation. *Berkeley Planning Journal*. 30 (1), 60–81.

Aydın, A. H. (2006) *Kamu Yönetimi ve Polis*. Ankara: Gazi Kitabevi.

Batuman, B. (2018) *New Islamist Architecture and Urbanism*. London Routledge.

Bauman, Z. (2001) *Parçalanmış Hayat*. İstanbul: Ayrıntı Yayınları.

Beinin, J. and Vairel, F. (2011) *Social Movemetns, Mobilization, and Contestion in the Middle East and North Africa*. Stanford (Palo Alto): Stanford University Press.

Bercé, Y. M. (2003) *Modern Avrupa'da Ayaklanmalar ve Devrimler*. Ankara: İmge Kitabevi.

Berkes, N. (2018) *Türkiye'de Çağdaşlaşma*. İstanbul: YKY.

Bilgili, A. E. (2011) *Şehir ve Kültür: İSTANBUL*. İstanbul, Profil Yayıncılık.

Blumer, H. (2008) Social Movements, *in* Ruggiero, V. and Montagna, N. *Social Movements*. Oxon: Routledge (pp. 64–73).

Bookchin, M. (2013) *Toplumu Yeniden Kurmak*. İstanbul: Sel Yayıncılık.

Bookchin, M. (2014) *Kentsiz Kentleşme*. İstanbul: Sel Yayıncılık.

Bookchin, M. (2017a) *Köylü İsyanlarından Fransız Devrimine*. Ankara: Dipnot Yayınları.

Bookchin, M. (2017b) *Fransız Devriminden İkinci Enternasyonele*. Ankara: Dipnot Yayınları.

Boudeville, J. (1968) *problems of Regional economic planning*. Edinburg Edinburg university press.

Braudel, F. (1983) *Civilization and Capitalism 15th–18th Century: The Structures of Everyday Life*. London: William Collins Sons and Co. Ltd.

Braudel, F. (2017a) *II: Felipe Döneminde Akdeniz ve Akdeniz Dünyası Cilt I*. İstanbul: Doğu Batı Yayınları.

Braudel, F. (2017b) *II: Felipe Döneminde Akdeniz ve Akdeniz Dünyası Cilt II*. İstanbul: Doğu Batı Yayınları.

Brenner, N. and Keil, R. (ed.) (2006) *The Global Cities Reader*. New York: Routledge Press.

Brenner, N., Marcuse, P. and Mayer, M. (2012) *Cities for People, Not for Profit*. London: Routledge.

Broadbent, J. and Brockman, V. (2011) *East Asian Social Movements*. London: Springer.

Brook, D. (2013) *A History of Future Cities*. New York, W. W. Norton & Company, Inc.

Burckhardt, J. (2018) *İtalya'da Rönesans Kültürü*. İstanbul: Okyanus Yayıncılık.

Calhoun, C. (2008) Putting Emotions in Their Place, in Ruggiero, V. and Montagna, N. *Social Movements*. Oxon: Routledge (pp. 289–303).

Cartledge, P. (2009) *Ancient Greece: A History in Eleven Cities*. Oxford: Oxford University Press.

Carty, V. (2015) *Social Movements and New Technologies*. Oxon: Taylor&Francis.

Castells, M. (1983) *The City and the Grassroots*. London: Edward Arnold.

Castells, M. (1991) *The Informational City*. Oxford: Blackwell Publishers.

Castells, M. (2004) *The Power of Identity, The Information Age: Economy, Society and Culture*. Cambridge: Blackwell.

Castells, M. (2005) *The Network Society: A Cross-cultural Perspective*. Cheltenham: Edward Elgar Publishing.

Castells, M. (2010a) *The Rise of the Network Society*. West Sussex: Wiley-Blackwell Publication.

Castells, M. (2010b) *The Power of Identity*. West Sussex: Wiley-Blackwell Publication.

Castells, M. (2010c) *End of Millennium*. West Sussex: Wiley-Blackwell Publication.

Castells, M. (2015) *Networks of Outrage and Hope: Social Movements in The Internet Age*. Cambridge: Polity Press.

Castells, M. (2017) *Kent, Sınıf ve İktidar*. Ankara: Phoenix Yayınevi.

Chesters, G. and Welsh, I. (2011) *Social Movements: The Key Concepts*. New York: Routledge Publications.

Childe, V. G. (1948) Man Makes Himself, in Lond Clark, D. (2005) *Urban World/ Global City*. New York: Routledge Press.

Clark, D. (2005) *Urban World/ Global City*. New York: Routledge Press.

Clark, P. (2009) *European Cities and Towns 400–2000*. Oxford: Oxford University Press.

Collier, R. B. (1999) *Paths toward Democracy: The Working Class and Elites in Western Europe and South America*. New York: Cambridge University Press.

Cornwall, A. (2011) (ed.) *The Participation Reader*. New York: Zed Books.

Çelik, Z. (2015) *19. Yüzyılda Osmanlı Başkenti: Değişen İstanbul*. İstanbul: Türkiye İş Bankası Kültür Yayınları.

Davis, K. (2011) "The Urbanization of the Human Population", in Le Gates, R. T. and Stout, F. (ed.) *The City Reader, Trends, Theory, Policy*. 5th ed. New York: Routledge Press, pp. 20–31.

de Certeau, M. (2008) *Gündelik Hayatın Keşfi 1: Eylem, Uygulama, Üretim Sanatları*. Ankara: Dost Kitabevi.

della Porta, D. (1995) *Social Movements, Political Violence, and the State: A Comparative Analysis of Italy and Germany*. Cambridge: Cambridge University Press.

della Porta, D. (2015) Democracy in Social Movements, in della Porta, D. and Diani, M. *The Oxford Handbook of Social Movements*. Oxford: Oxford University Press (pp. 767–781).

della Porta, D. and Caiani, M. (2009) *Social Movements and Europeanization*. Oxford: Oxford University Press.

della Porta, D. and Diani, M. (2006) *Social Movements: An Introduction*. Oxford: Blackwell Publishing.

della Porta, D. and Tarrow, S. (2005) *Transnational Protest and Global Activism*. Lanham: Rowman and Littlefield Publishers.

della Porta, D. and Tarrow, S. (2008) Transnational Protest and Global Activism, in Ruggiero, V. and Montagna, N. *Social Movements*. Oxon: Routledge (pp. 339–349).

DHA (2020, July 10). İşte İstanbul'da günlük tüketilen su miktarı. Retrieved from https://www.haberturk.com/gundem/haber/1491660-iste-istanbulda-gunluk-tuketilen-su-miktari.

Durkheim, E. (2008) The Division of Labour in Society, in Ruggiero, V. and Montagna, N. *Social Movements*. Oxon: Routledge.

Eisinger, P. K. (2008) The Conditions of Protest Behaviour in American Cities, in Ruggiero, V. and Montagna, N. *Social Movements*. Oxon: Routledge (pp. 157–163).

Eldem, E., Goffmann, D. and Masters, B. (2012) *Doğu ile Batı Arasında Osmanlı Kenti*. İstanbul: Türkiye İş Bankası Kültür Yayınları.

Engels, F. (2013) *İngiltere'de Emekçi Sınıfların Durumu*. İstanbul: Ayrıntı Yayınları.

Engels, F. (2018) *Alman Köylü Savaşı*. İstanbul: Yordam Kitap.

Epstein, B. (1991) *Political Protest&Cultural Revolution: Nonviolent Direct Action in the 1970s and 1980s*. Berkeley: University of California Press.

Erdi-Lelandais, G. (2014) *Understanding the City: Henri Lefebvre and Urban Studies*. Newcastle: Cambridge Scholars Publishing.

Erdoğan, M. (2015) *Anayasal Demokrasi*. Ankara: Siyasal Kitabevi.

Ergün, N. (2004) Gentrification in Istanbul. *Cities*. 21(5), 391–405.

Erkut, G. (2014) *Dimensions of Urban Re-development: The Case of Beyoğlu, Istanbul*. Berlin: TU Berlin.

Ertep, H. (2009) *Chaos or homogenization? The role of shop signs in transforming urban fabric in Beyoğlu, İstanbul.* Visual Communication. 8(3), 263–272.

Escobar, A. and Alvarez, S. (2008) Theory and Protest in Latin America Today, in Ruggiero, V. and Montagna, N. *Social Movements.* Oxon: Routledge (pp. 235–247).

Eyerman, R. and Jamison, A. (2008) Social Movements: A Cognitive Approach, in Ruggiero, V. and Montagna, N. *Social Movements.* Oxon: Routledge (pp. 271–279).

Fainstein, S. S. (1995) *The City Builders: Property, Politics, and Planning in London and New York.* Oxford: Blackwell Press.

Farabi (2017) *İdeal Devlet.* İstanbul: İş Bankası Yayınları.

Faroqhi, S. (2010) *Osmanlı Şehirleri ve Kırsal Hayatı.* İstanbul: Doğu Batı Yayınları.

Faroqhi, S. (2014) *Osmanlı'da Kentler ve Kentliler.* İstanbul: Tarih Vakfı Yayınları.

Farrington, I. (2013) *Cusco.* Gainesville, Florida: The University Press of Florida.

Frankfort, H. (1970) *The Art and Architecture of the Ancient Orient.* Middlesex: Penguin Books.

Fraser, B. (2015) *Digital Cities: The Interdisciplinary Future of the Urban Geo-Humanities.* New York: Palgrave Macmillan.

Friedman, M. (1969) *The Optimum Quantity of Money.* Aldine publishing company.

Friedmann, J. (2002a) *The Prospect of Cities.* Minneapolis: The University of Minnesota Press.

Friedmann, J. (2002b) Intercity networks in a Globalizing Era, in Scott, A. J., (ed.) *Global City-Region: Trends, Theory, Policy.* Oxford: Oxford University Press, pp. 119–139.

Fuller, G. E. (2016) *Türkiye ve Arap Baharı.* İstanbul: Eksi Yayıncılık.

Gamson, W. A. (1995) Constructing Social Movement, in Johnston, H. and Klandermans, B. *Social Movements and Culture.* Minneapolis: University of Minnesota Press (pp. 85–107).

Gasset, J. O. (2017) *Kitlelerin Ayaklanması.* İstanbul: İş Bankası Kültür Yayınları.

Geddes, P. (1949) *Cities in Evolution.* London: Williams & Norgate ltd.

Geddes, P. (1968) *Cities in Evolution: an Introduction to the Town Planning Movement and to the Study of Civics.* London: Ernest Benn Limited.

Geniş, S (2007) Producing elite localities: the rise of gated communities in Istanbul. *Urban Studies.* 44(4), 771–98.

Giddens, A. (1990) *The Consequences of Modernity.* Cambridge: Polity Press.

Gökmen, G. P. and Özsoy, A. (2014) Urban transformation developments triggered by new legal regulations in Istanbul. *IAHS Journal.* 32(2), 139–148.

Goldstone, J. A. (2003) *States, Parties, and Social Movements.* Cambridge: Cambridge University Press.

Goldstone, J. A. (2016) *Revolution and Rebellion in the Early Modern World.* New York: Routledge.

Goodwin, J. and Jasper, J. M. (2015) *The Social Movements Reader: Cases and Concepts.* Chichester: Blackwell Publishing.

Gramsci, A. (2008) Notes on Italian History, in Ruggiero, V. and Montagna, N. *Social Movements*. Oxon: Routledge (pp. 55–59).

Gül, M. (2017) *Architecture and the Turkish City*. London: I.B. Tauris & Co. Ltd.

Habermas, J. (2008) New Social Movements, in Ruggiero, V. and Montagna, N. *Social Movements*. Oxon: Routledge (pp. 201–206).

Hall, P. (1977) *The World City*. 2nd ed. London: Weidenfeld and Nicolson Publication.

Hall, P. (2002) 'Global City-Regions in the Twenty-first Century', in Scott, A. J., (ed.) *Global City-Region: Trends, Theory, Policy*. Oxford: Oxford University Press, pp. 59–78.

Hall, S. (2012) *City, Street and Citizen*. New York: Routledge Press.

Hamel, P, Lustiger-Thaler, H. and Mayer, M. (2000) *Urban Movements in a Globalising World*. London: Routledge.

Hammond, M. (1972) *The City in the Ancient World*. Cambridge: Harvard University Press.

Harvey, D. (2012a) *Rebel Cities*. London: Verso Publication.

Harvey, D. (2012b) *Paris, Modernitenin Başkenti*. İstanbul: Sel Yayınları.

Harvey, D. (2015) *Sermayenin Mekânları*. İstanbul: Sel Yayıncılık.

Harvey, D. (2016) *Sosyal Adalet ve Şehir*. İstanbul: Metis Yayıncılık.

Hasson, S. (1987) *Urban Social Movements in Jerusalem: the protest of the second generation*. New York: State University of New York Press.

Haug, C. (2015) Meeting Arenas, in Goodwin, J. and Jasper, J. M. *The Social Movements Reader: Cases and Concepts*. Chichester: Blackwell Publishing (pp. 196–213).

Hénaff, M. and Strong, T. (2001) *Public Space and Democracy*. Minneapolis: University of Minnesota Press.

Henckel, D, Thomaier, S., and Zedda, R. (2013) *Space–Time Design of the Public City*. New York: Springer.

Herrschel, T. (2013) *Cities, State and Globalisation*. New York: Routledge Press.

Hirsch, E. L. (2015) Generating Commitment among Students, in Goodwin, J. and Jasper, J. M. (2015) *The Social Movements Reader: Cases and Concepts*. Chichester: Blackwell Publishing (pp. 105–114).

İbni Haldun (2013) *Mukaddime*. İstanbul: Kaynak Yayınları.

İnalcık, H. (2016) *Osmanlı'da Devlet, Hukuk ve Âdalet*. İstanbul: Kronik Yayıncılık.

Jacobs, J. (1964) *The Death and Life of Great American Cities: The Failure of Town Planning*. Harmondsworth: Penguin Books.

Jacobs, J. (1972) *The Economy of Cities*. Middlesex: Pelican Books.

Jacobsson, K. (2015) *Urban Grassroots Movements in Central and Eastern Europe*. Surrey: Ashgate Publishing Limited.

Jasper, J. (2007) Cultural Approaches in the Sociology of Social Movements, in Klandermans, B. and Roggeband, C. *Handbook of Social Movements Across Disciplines*. New York: Springer (pp. 59–111).

Jenkins, J. C. (2008) Resource Mobilization Theory and The Study of Social Movements, in Ruggiero, V. and Montagna, N. *Social Movements*. Oxon: Routledge (pp. 118–128).

Johnston, H. (1995) A Methodology for Frame Analysis: From Discourse to Cognitive Schemata, in Johnston, H. and Klandermans, B. *Social Movements and Culture*. Minneapolis: University of Minnesota Press (pp. 217–247).

Johnston, H. and Klandermans, B. (1995) The Cultural Analysis of Social Movements, in Johnston, H. and Klandermans, B. *Social Movements and Culture*. Minneapolis: University of Minnesota Press (pp. 3–25).

Kennedy, R. G. (1996) *Hidden Cities*. New York: Penguin Books.

Kienitz, F. K. (2014). *Sultanlarin Şehirleri*. İstanbul: Yeditepe Yayınları.

Klandermans, B. (2008) Mobilization and Participation: Social-Psychological Expansions of Resource Mobilization Theory, in Ruggiero, V. and Montagna, N. *Social Movements*. Oxon: Routledge (pp. 247–255).

Kornhauser, W. (2008) The Politics of Mass Society, *in* Ruggiero, V. and Montagna, N. *Social Movements*. Oxon: Routledge (pp. 73–79).

Kostof, S. (1994) His Majesty the Pick: The Aesthetics of Demolition, in Çelik, Z., Favro, D. and Ingersoll, R. *Streets: Critical Perspectives on Public Space*. Berkeley, California: University of California Press (pp. 9–23).

Kriesi, H. et al. (2002) *New Social Movements in Western Europe: A Comparative Analysis*. London: UCL Press.

Kriesi, H. and Wisler, D. (2008) Social Movements and Direct Democracy in Switzerland, in Ruggiero, V. and Montagna, N. *Social Movements*. Oxon: Routledge (pp. 163–170).

Kuyucu, T. and Ünsal, Ö. (2010) Urban transformation as state-led property transfer: an analysis of two cases of urban renewal in Istanbul. *Urban Studies*. 47(7), 1479–99

Larice, M. And Macdonald, E. (ed.) (2007) *The Urban Design Reader*. New York: Routledge Press.

Laxer, G. and Halperin, S. (2003) *Global Civil Society and Its Limits*. New York: Palgrave Macmillan Ltd.

Le Bon, G. (2001) *Kitleler Psikolojisi*. İstanbul: Hayat Yayınları.

Le Bon, G. (2008) The Crowd, in Ruggiero, V. and Montagna, N. *Social Movements*. Oxon: Routledge (pp. 34–47).

Le Bon, G. (2014) *Kitleler Psikolojisi*. Ankara: Tutku Yayınevi.

Lees, L., Slater, M. and Wyly, E. (2010) *The Gentrification Reader*. New York: Routledge Press.

Lefebvre, H. (2014) *Mekânın Üretimi*. İstanbul: Sel Yayıncılık.

Lefebvre, H. (2016) *Şehir Hakkı*. İstanbul: Sel Yayıncılık.

Lefebvre, H. (2017) *Kentsel Devrim*. İstanbul: Sel Yayıncılık.

Leitman, J. (1999) *Sustaining Cities: Environmental Planning and Management in Urban Design*. New York: McGraw Hill Publication.

Lloyd-Evans, S. and Potter, R. B. (1998) *The City in the Developing World*. Essex: Addison Wesley Longman Publication.

Lösch, A (1954) *The Economics of Location*. New Haven, Connecticut: UMI.

Mackenney, R. (2004) *Şehir Devletler 1500–1700*. İstanbul: Babil Yayınları.

Mardin, Ş. (1962) *The Genesis of Young Ottoman Thought.* Princeton, New Jersey: Princeton University Press.

Markoff, J. (1996) *Waves of Democracy: Social Movements and Political Change.* Los Angeles: Pine Grove Press.

Martin, L. and March, L. (2010) *Urban Space and Structures.* Cambridge: Cambridge University Press.

Martin, W. G. (2008) *Making Waves: Worldwide Social Movements 1750–2005.* Denver, Colorado: Paradigm Publishers.

Marwell, G. and Oliver, P. (2008) The Critical Mass in Collective Action, in Ruggiero, V. and Montagna, N. *Social Movements.* Oxon: Routledge (pp. 128–145).

Marx, K. (2008) The Eighteenth Brumaire of Louis Bonaparte, in Ruggiero, V. and Montagna, N. *Social Movements.* Oxon: Routledge (pp. 19–21).

Marx, K. (2018) *Kapital: Ekonomi Politiğin Eleştirisi Cilt I.* İstanbul: Yordam Kitap.

Marx, K. and Engels, F. (2008) A Contribution to the Critique of Political Economy, in Ruggiero, V. and Montagna, N. *Social Movements.* Oxon: Routledge (pp. 17–19).

Marx, K. and Engels, F. (2018a) *Alman İdeolojisi.* İstanbul: Kor Kitap.

Mayer, D. and Tarrow, S. (1998) *The Social Movement Society: Contentious Politics for a New Century.* New York: Rowman & Littlefield Publishers.

McAdam, D. (2008) Political Process and the Development of Black Insurgency 1930–1970, in Ruggiero, V. and Montagna, N. *Social Movements.* Oxon: Routledge (pp. 177–186).

McAdam, D., McCarthy, J. D. and Zald, N. (2008) Comparative Perspectives on Social Movements, in Ruggiero, V. and Montagna, N. *Social Movements.* Oxon: Routledge (pp. 279–289).

McCarthy, J. D. and Zald, N. (2008) Resource Mobilisation and Social Movements: A Party Theory, in Ruggiero, V. and Montagna, N. *Social Movements.* Oxon: Routledge (pp. 105–128).

McCarthy, J. D. and Zald, N. (2015) Social Movement Organizations, in Goodwin, J. and Jasper, J. M. *The Social Movements Reader: Cases and Concepts.* Chichester: Blackwell Publishing (pp. 159–175).

Melucci, A. (1996) *Challenging Codes: Collective Action in the Information Age.* Cambridge: Cambridge University Press.

Melucci, A. (2008) A Strange Kind of Newness: What's New in New Social Movements?, in Ruggiero, V. and Montagna, N. *Social Movements.* Oxon: Routledge (pp. 218–226).

Merrifield, A. (2014) *The New Urban Question.* New York: Pluto Press.

Meyer, D. S., Robnett, B., and Whittier, N. (2002) *Social Movements: Identity, Culture, and the State.* New York: Oxford University Press.

Milan, S. (2013) *Social Movements and their Technologies: Wiring Social Change.* New York: Palgrave Macmillan.

Milkman, R., Luce, S., and Lewis, P. (2015) Occupy Wall Street, in Goodwin, J. and Jasper, J. M. *The Social Movements Reader: Cases and Concepts*. Chichester: Blackwell Publishing (pp. 30–45).

Mill, J. S. (2014) *Özgürlük Üstüne ve Seçme Yazılar*. İstanbul: Belge Yayınları.

Moghadam, V. (2009) *Globalization and Social Movements: Islamism, Feminism, and the Global Justice Movement*. Lanham: Rowman & Littlefield Publishers.

Montagna, N. (2008) Social Movements and Global Mobilisations, in Ruggiero, V. and Montagna, N. *Social Movements*. Oxon: Routledge (pp. 349–357).

Moulaert, F., Rodriguez, A. and Swyngedouw, E. (ed.) (2003) *The Globalized City: Economic Restructuring and Social Polarization in European Cities*. Oxford: Oxford University Press.

Mudu, P. (2014) Ogni Sfratto Sara una Barricata: Squatting for Housing and Social Conflict in Rome. in SQOK, Cattaneo, C., and Martinez, M. *The Squatters' Movements in Europe. Commons and Autonomy as Alternative to Capitalism*. London: Pluto Press.

Mueller, C. (2008) Conflict Networks and the Origin of Women's Liberation, in Ruggiero, V. and Montagna, N. *Social Movements*. Oxon: Routledge (pp. 226–235).

Mumford, L. (1961) *The City in History: Its Origins, Its Transformations, and Its Prospects*. London, Harcourt, Brace & World, Inc.

Necipoğlu, G. (2016) *Osmanlı Mimarlık Kültürü*. İstanbul: Kubbealtı Yayınevi.

Nizam'l-mülk (2017) *Siyasetname*. İstanbul: İş Bankası Yayınları.

Oberschall, A. (2008) Social Conflict and Social Movments, in Ruggiero, V. and Montagna, N. *Social Movements*. Oxon: Routledge (pp. 95–105).

Offe, C. (2008) New Social Movements: Challenging the Boundaries of Institutional Politics, in Ruggiero, V. and Montagna, N. *Social Movements*. Oxon: Routledge (pp. 206–212).

Örs, İ. R. (2017) *Diaspora of the City*. New York: Springer.

Park, R. E. and Burgess, E. W. (2016) *Şehir: Kent Ortamındaki İnsan Davranışlarının Araştırılması Üzerine Öneriler*. Ankara: Heretik Yayınevi.

Piketty, T. (2014) *Capital in the Twenty-first Century*. Boston: Harvard University Press.

Pirenne, H. (2016) *Ortaçağ Avrupa'sının Ekonomik ve Sosyal Tarihi*. İstanbul: İletişim Yayınları.

Piven, F. and Cloward, R. (2008) Poor People's Movements, in Ruggiero, V. and Montagna, N. *Social Movements*. Oxon: Routledge (pp. 170–177).

Platon (2017) *Devlet*. İstanbul: İş Bankası Yayınları.

Poggi, G. (2014) *Modern Devletin Gelişimi*. İstanbul: Bilgi Üniversitesi Yayınları.

Purdue, Derrick (2007) *Civil Societies and Social Movements*. Oxon: Routledge.

Rivet, P. (1973) *Maya Cities*. London: Elek Books Limited.

Robertson, R. (1992) *Globalisation: Social Theory and Global Cultere*. London: Sage.

Rousseau, J. J. (2017) *Toplum Sözleşmesi*. İstanbul: İş Bankası Yayınları.

Sarı, Ö. and Esgin, A. (2016) *Toplumsal Analizler Ekseninde Kent Fragmanları.* Ankara: Phoenix Yayınevi.

Sassen, S. (2001) *The Global City: New York, London, Tokyo.* Princeton, New Jersey: Princeton University Press.

Sassen, S. (2002) *Global Networks: Linked Cities.* New York: Routledge Press.

Sassen, S. (2006) *Cities in World-Economy.* Los Angeles, California: Pine Forge Press.

Satterthwaite, D. (ed.) (1999) *The Earthscan Reader in Sustainable Cities.* London: Eartscan Publishing.

Savitch, H. V. (2008) *Cities in a Terror: Space, territory, and Local Resilience.* New York: Cleveland State University.

Schaeffer, R. K. (2014) *Social Movements and Global Social Change: The Rising Tide.* Lanham: Rowman&Littlefield.

Schmidt, K. (2012) *Göbekli Tepe: A Stone Age Sanctuary in South-Eastern Anatolia.* Heidelberg: ArchaeNova Publishing.

Schuurman, F. and van Naerssen, T. (1989) *Urban Social Movements in the Third World.* New York: Routledge.

Schwartz, G. M. and Nichols, J. J. (2010) *After Collapse; The Regeneration of Complex Societies.* Tucson: The University of Arizona Press.

Scott, A. J., (ed.) (2002) *Global City-Region: Trends, Theory, Policy.* Oxford: Oxford University Press.

Sennett, R. (2013) *Kamusal İnsanın Çöküşü.* İstanbul: Ayrıntı Yayınları.

Simmel, G. (2008) Conflict, in Ruggiero, V. and Montagna, N. *Social Movements.* Oxon: Routledge (pp. 29–34).

Simmel, G. (2017) *Gizliliğin ve Gizli Toplumların Sosyolojisi.* İstanbul: Pinhan Yayıncılık.

Sit, V. F. F. (2010) *Chinese City and Urbanism.* Singapore: World Scientific Publishing.

Smelser, N. J. (2008) Theory of Collective Behaviour, in Ruggiero, V. and Montagna, N. *Social Movements.* Oxon: Routledge (pp. 79–93).

Smith, J. (1999) Global Politics and Transnational Campaign against International Trade in Toxic Waste, in Porta, D. Kriesi, H. and Rucht, D. *Social Movements in a Globalising World.* New York: Macmillan.

Smith, J. (2015) The Transnational Network for Democratic Globalization, in Goodwin, J. and Jasper, J. M. *The Social Movements Reader: Cases and Concepts.* Chichester: Blackwell Publishing (pp. 184–196).

Smith, J. and Fetner, T. (2007) Structural Approaches in the Sociology of Social Movements, in Klandermans, B. and Roggeband, C. *Handbook of Social Movements Across Disciplines.* New York: Springer.

Smith, N. (2017) *Eşitsiz Gelişim: Doğa, Sermaye ve Mekânın Üretimi.* İstanbul: Sel Yayıncılık.

Snow, D. A. (2008) Frame Alignment Processes, Micromobilization, and Movement Participation, in Ruggiero, V. and Montagna, N. *Social Movements*. Oxon: Routledge (pp. 255–266).

Söylemez, M. (2011) *İslam Şehirleri*. İstanbul: Düşün Yayıncılık.

SQOK, Cattaneo, C., and Martinez, M. (2014) *The Squatters' Movement in Europe. Commons and Autonomy as Alternative Capitalism*. London: Pluto Press.

Stavrides, S. (2016) *Kentsel Heterotopya*. İstanbul: Sel Yayıncılık.

SUDER (2020, July 10) Kişi Başı Ambalajlı Su Tüketimi 138 Litreye Çıktı. Retrieved from https://suder.org.tr/kisi-basi-ambalajli-su-tuketimi-138-litreye-cikti/.

Swidler, A. (1995) Cultural Power and Social Movements, in Johnston, H. and Klandermans, B. *Social Movements and Culture*. Minneapolis: University of Minnesota Press (pp. 25–41).

Swyngedouw, E., Moulaert, F. and Rodriguez, A. (2003) 'The World in a Grain of Sand: Large-Scale Urban Development Projects and the Dynamics of 'Glocal' Transformations', in Moulaert, F., Rodriguez, A. and Swyngedouw, E. (ed.) *The Globalized City: Economic Restructuring and Social Polarization in European Cities*. Oxford: Oxford University Press, pp. 9–29.

Şenyurt, O. (2018) *Zamanın Mekânları Mekânın Zamanları: Osmanlı'da Mimari Mekân ve Yaşam*. İstanbul: Doğu Kitabevi.

Tainter, J. A. (1988) *The Collapse of Complex Societies*. Cambridge: Cambridge University Press.

Tallon, A. (2010) *Urban Regeneration in the UK*. Dawsonera [Online]. Available at: http://www.dawson-era.com (Accessed: 11 February 2012).

Tarrow, S. (2008) Power in Movement, in Ruggiero, V. and Montagna, N. *Social Movements*. Oxon: Routledge (pp. 145–152).

Tarrow, S. (2011) *Power in Movement: Social Movement and Contentious Politics*. New York: Cambridge University Press.

Tayfur, K. (2014) *Gezi Parkı'nın Geçmişi*. İstanbul: Atlas.

Tilly, C. (2008) Social Movements and National Politics, in Ruggiero, V. and Montagna, N. *Social Movements*. Oxon: Routledge (pp. 186–201).

Tilly, C. and Wood, L. J. (2013) *Social Movements 1768–2012*. Boulder: Paradigm Publishers.

Tonkiss, F. (2011) *Space, the City and Social Theory*. Cambridge: Polity Press.

Topçu, N. (2017) *İsyan Ahlâkı*. İstanbul: Dergâh Yayınları.

Touraine, A. (1988) *Return of the Actor: Social Theory in Post Industrial Society*. Minneapolis: Univ. Minn. Press.

Touraine, A. (2008) An Introduction to the Study of Social Movements, in Ruggiero, V. and Montagna, N. *Social Movements*. Oxon: Routledge (pp. 212–218).

Uysal, A. (2016) *Toplumsal Hareketler Sosyolojisi*. İstanbul: Tezkire Yayıncılık.

Van Gennep, A. (1960). *The Rites of Passage*. London: Routledge.

von Stein, L. (1959) *Geschichte der sozialen Bewegung in Frankreich von 1789 bis auf unsere Tage*. Hildesheim: Georg Olms.

Wallerstein, M. I. (2004) *World-systems Analysis: An Introduction*. Durham: Duke University Press.

Wapner, P. (2015) Transnational Environmental Activism, in Goodwin, J. and Jasper, J. M. *The Social Movements Reader: Cases and Concepts*. Chichester: Blackwell Publishing (pp. 175–184).

Weber, M (2012) *Modern Kentin Oluşumu: ŞEHİR*. İstanbul: Yarın Yayınevi.

Wheeler, S. M. and Beatley, T. (ed.) (2009) *The Sustainable Urban Development Reader*. 2nd ed. New York: Routledge Press.

White, S. (2011) *Osmanlı'da İsyan İklimi*. İstanbul: Alfa Yayınları.

Whyte, W. H. (2009) *Rediscovering the Center*. Philadelphia: University of Pennsylvania Press.

Wiarda, H. (2003) *Civil Society: The American Model and Third World Development*. UK: Hachette Publishing.

Wirth, L. (2002) *Bir Yaşam Biçimi Olarak Kentlileşme*. Ankara: İmge Kitabevi.

Zagorin, P. (1982) *Rebels and Rulers 1500–1660*. Cambridge: Cambridge University Press.

Zukin, S. (1991) *Landscape of Power: From Detroit to Disney World*. Los Angeles, California: University of California Press.

Zukin, S. (1993) *Landscape of Power: From Detroit to Disney World*. Los Angeles, California: University of California Press.

Index

Milton Keynes UK
Ingram Content Group UK Ltd.
UKHW050817240324
440028UK00005B/6